THEORIES AND APPROACHES
TO INTERNATIONAL POLITICS

THEORIES AND APPROACHES TO INTERNATIONAL POLITICS

What Are We to Think?

Fourth Edition

PATRICK M. MORGAN

Transaction Publishers
New Brunswick (U.S.A.) and London (U.K.)

Third Printing 1990
Fourth Edition
Copyright (c) 1987 by Transaction Publishers
New Brunswick, New Jersey 08903

Library of Congress Catalog Number: 86-19130
ISBN: 0-88738-093-X (cloth); 0-88738-630-X (paper)
Printed in the United States of America

Library of Congress Cataloging in Publication Data

Morgan, Patrick M., 1940-
    Theories and approaches to international politics.

    Includes bibliographies and index.
    1. International relations–Research. I. Title.
JX1291.M65   1986   327'.072   86-19130
ISBN 0-88738-093-X
ISBN 0-88738-630-X (pbk.)

To my Kellys

Contents

Acknowledgments

For permission to use copyrighted material in this book, grateful acknowledgment is made to the following sources:

(For Table 1-1) From *Political Order in Changing Societies* by Samuel P. Huntington. Copyright 1968 by Yale University Press.

(For Figure 4-2, and brief excerpt) From *International Politics Today* by Donald Puchala. Reprinted by permission of Dodd, Mead & Company, Inc. from *International Politics Today* by Donald Puchala. Copyright © 1971 by Dodd, Mead and Company, Inc.

(For Table 5-10) From *The Scientific Study of Foreign Policy* by James Rosenau. Reprinted with permission of The Macmillan Company from *The Scientific Study of Foreign Policy* by James Rosenau. Copyright © 1971 by The Free Press, a Division of The Macmillan Company.

(For Figure 5-5) From *Foreign Policy Decision-Making* by Richard C. Snyder, H.W. Bruck, and Burton Sapin. Reprinted with permission of The Macmillan Company from *Foreign Policy Decision-Making* by Richard C. Snyder, H.W. Bruck, and Burton Sapin. Copyright © 1962 by The Free Press of Glencoe, a Division of The Macmillan Company.

(For excerpts) From *The Korean Decision* by Glenn Paige. Reprinted with permission of The Macmillan Company from *The Korean Decision* by Glenn Paige. Copyright © 1968 by The Free Press, a Division of The Macmillan Company.

(For Table 5-2) From *Foreign Policy in Perspective: Strategy, Adaptation, Decision-Making* by John P. Lovell, The Dryden Press, publisher. Copyright © 1970 by Holt, Rinehart and Winston, Inc.

(For excerpts) From *International Behavior* by Herbert Kelman, The Dryden Press, publisher. Copyright © 1965 by Holt, Rinehart and Winston, Inc.

(For Figure 5-8) From *The Management of International Crisis: Affect and Action in American-Soviet Relations* by Holsti, Brody, and North in Dean G. Pruitt and Richard C. Snyder, eds., *Theory and Research on the Causes of War*. Copyright © 1969. By permission of Prentice-Hall, Inc., Englewood Cliffs, New Jersey.

Preface

People who go to the trouble of reading a preface deserve to be rewarded by finding that the author has come up with delightfully new and different things to say. On this score, what follows will be disappointing. Fortunately we have all learned to live with the fact that we seldom get what our good works deserve.

This is the fourth edition of this book. Though I have not thoroughly studied the matter, I have the impression that a normal "new edition" these days provides little value for the money. The used-book market has deflated sales of most texts beyond the first two years, with nasty effects on royalties as well. The response has been new editions so little changed that our books are rather too much like the "new" cars served up by the auto industry.

Transaction, I am pleased to say, insisted on more than cosmetic changes. In turn, I have refurbished and rearranged the book considerably. Chapters 1 and 2 are not much changed, but most of the rest are. There is one less chapter in this edition, material from prior editions has been reorganized to a considerable extent, and there is a fair amount of new material. Notes for most chapters have been pruned a bit (reversing their growth in earlier editions); instead, I have clumped additional bibliographic references under various headings at the end of each chapter.

I hope that this continues to be an unusual book that meets a need and therefore warrants a new edition. It is not as necessary as it once was; several texts now provide a summary chapter on theoretical perspectives and basic analytical problems. Still, the more extended treatment of these things here may remain useful. The book continues to be aimed at people new to the field who need a background against which to assess the explicit (but frequently implicit) theoretical notions in textbooks and lectures. Too often when the author or lecturer chooses one set of assumptions or explanations over another the student remains blithely ignorant that there was a choice. This is not willful distortion on the part of authors or lecturers; if we explained all such matters in detail, first chapters would run to scads more pages and courses would never get past part one of the syllabus. Perhaps this book can still help remedy that situation.

As I have said in the past, the book does not describe and critique approaches to the study of international politics in a fashion entirely satisfactory to the professional scholar. It is also not comprehensive. It does not discuss theories and approaches in international economics, international law, or international organization. It avoids arcane details on nuclear strategy and deterrence theory and says little about dependency theory and various approaches to imperialism. Within each chapter it does not do justice to all of the approaches considered, ignores some important studies, and discusses others so briefly as to distort them. All of this happens because I have tried to keep the book short, the disease of creeping verbosity (which afflicts academic authors) notwithstanding.

It is very gratifying that enough people have made use of the book to merit another edition. That one has been prepared is due to the contributions of various people. I am beholden to many colleagues for comments on how the book could be improved, and to my graduate students for stimulating seminars on the subject. Much of the work on this edition was carried on at Katholieke Universiteit in Belgium (during a Fulbright) in connection with the course I offered there on theories of international politics. I cannot say enough about the hospitality of the Belgians, the stimulating exchange with my Belgian colleagues and others in Europe, and the astringent effect of their skeptical responses to received American wisdom on international affairs. I must particularly thank Cynthia Avery, Bunny Hunt, Dolores Juve, and Marjie Roberts who typed and retyped, coping with my perverse scrawl when I was 6,000 miles away and thus unavailable for deciphering.

I have retained the original intention of providing a respectable introduction for beginning students to theoretical notions on the loose in the field, with the view that this is not something we should put off until the graduate level if we want to have a respectable discipline. I have also retained the idea of having the content weighty enough to assist graduate students and faculty, yet have it presented with enough clarity and humor to attract undergraduates. Keeping the contents up to date is steadily more onerous; the flood of new writings in the field is simply terrifying to one seeking to encapsulate it in a book like this. The proliferation of theoretical speculation has reached awful proportions, and Harry Eckstein in a valuable little book on theory in comparative politics helps explain why.[1] He says the reward structure in political science stresses conceptual originality, and as a result everybody wants to be a Newton! The Newton syndrome is wearing me out.

As for the writing style, I have continued trying to make the book readable, to carry on in an idiom that makes complicated matters somewhat comprehensible and interesting to people confronting the morass of international politics for the first time. I must confess I have not got it right, at least not to my satisfaction. But the objective is worthy and the spirit is willing—still.

Note

1. Harry Eckstein, *The Natural History of Congruence Theory* Monograph Series in World Affairs (University of Denver Graduate School of International Studies, 1980).

1

An Ointment with Many Flies

The purpose of this book is to encourage us to think intelligently about international politics, but this first chapter may well have the effect of discouraging us from trying. After reading this chapter we should be more aware of the intellectual and practical difficulties that lie at the heart of the subject. These problems are so central to the study and practice of international politics that they cannot be ignored, but no way has been found to solve them to everyone's satisfaction. So they fester like old wounds, disturbing the sleep and riling the digestion of student and practitioner alike. The subject is admirably designed to serve as punishment for one's sins. In fact, if we want to go into it deeply we may well develop a melancholy martyr's visage which will help convince others that what we are doing is worthwhile.

Does the Field Exist?

The first problem with the *field* of international politics is that no one can prove that it exists! Of course most of us think there is such a thing and people certainly advertise themselves as experts in it. The question is whether what these people study really constitutes a discipline, and whether it ought to. A great many of the government employees or academic specialists involved in this field were trained in political science, law, economics, history—not in something called international politics or international relations. The specialist knows that a field ought to have some fairly clear outer limits, plus its own basic assumptions, perspectives, and methods, and that this subject often does not seem to. It is not that no one has ever been bothered by this. Indeed, specifying the boundries and nature of the field was once a matter of grave debate among academic specialists, but the results proved so inconclusive and unprofitable that the attempt was largely abandoned. Books on international politics frequently supply a provisional or working definition of the field and let it go at that so the authors can get on to other things.

To some extent defining boundaries is a problem in all disciplines, for disciplines represent a scholarly division of labor imposed on the

1

seamless web of reality, and these days more and more subjects like biochemistry have grown up where the boundries of well-established fields intersect. This leads some analysts to consider defining the field of international politics a waste of time; to quote Marion Levy, "I start out with the bias that disciplines are the sorts of things people discuss when they do not have any very good ideas."[1] This is sometimes true, as anyone who has ever pored over such discussions can attest, but not always. The trouble is this. Our conception of what the field is subtly shapes what we study and where and how we look for relevant information and ideas. That is, a conception is a kind of map for directing our attention and distributing our efforts, and using the wrong map can lead us straight into a swamp instead of taking us to higher ground. Which is why giving this matter a quick once-over so we can get on to other things will not do. One of the good ideas Levy wants people in the field to have ought to concern what the field is about. Examples of what this should lead us to think about follow.

Consider the term *international politics*. The obvious implication is that politics among nations must somehow be different from other kinds of politics. But is this really true? What if international politics is really just a branch of politics in general? Then we would need no explicit or separate theory of international politics; instead we would simply study politics.

> No qualitative or "essential" difference in political processes can be found between lower political systems and the all-encompassing global system to warrant the study of the two different levels of politics by different methods.[2]

Presto! Our field just disappeared (and the reader can stop reading this book).

Unfortunately, no one knows for sure if this is true. We do not have a widely accepted general theory of politics into which we can plug the international variety, but some people think we will get one if we try hard enough. And until we have finished trying we cannot answer the question once and for all. International politics is a relatively young subject, and one of the reasons is that the search for a general theory of politics has been conducted for centuries within the context of *domestic* affairs. Humans live *in* communities, not *between* them, so their chief preoccupation has been politics within their societies. The rest of the world was full of outsiders, aliens, strangers dealt with only occasionally and at arms length. Indeed, many primitive peoples have as their tribal name the word in their language that stands for human beings—leaving all those "others" by implication as something less. International politics really became a subject of vigorous study and theory, with pretentions to being a field, only in this century as relations with outsiders became so much more costly and dangerous. As Raymond Aron once put it, "Trouble times encourage meditation."[3]

Are international affairs distinctive enough to warrant treating them separately? It has become commonplace to think so, and to write books accordingly. Hans Morgenthau, perhaps the single most influential scholar in the history of the subject, opened his classic analysis by observing that "international politics, like all politics, is a struggle for power," which seems like a straightforward assertion that there is nothing special about international politics. But it turned out to be special enough for him to be worth over 500 pages! What is the element that sets international politics apart? One traditional answer derives from a very influential way of thinking about politics in which it is seen as the authoritative allocation of values, which normally means that a government considered legitimate by its citizens makes the ultimate decisions as to who gets what there is to get. This makes international politics stick out like a sore thumb since, in the absence of a world government, there are only limited mechanisms for authoritative allocation. Therefore the struggle for and exercise of power must take different forms and dimensions in international politics than it does in domestic varieties—hence the length of Professor Morgenthau's book.

By way of illustration, one of the field's more weathered and leathery assertions is that in domestic politics the state has a monopoly on the legitimate use of force—part of its being authoritative—but in international politics there is no monopoly and each nation reserves the right to use force. As a result domestic politics produces and operates within something like law and order, while international politics borders on anarchy. This view has a number of implications. For instance, in international politics security, sheer physical safety, will be much more of a problem. Also the organizational elements will be less formal and well developed, and the same must be true of decision-making processes. Another implication would be that we had better not borrow concepts and models from a field like political science that start with the notion of an integrated society because that is precisely what is missing in international affairs.

This is a nice, neat formulation of the difference between domestic and international politics and at first glance it appears to be true. (Presto! Our field has reappeared.) Alas, it is not always or entirely true, as various scholars have pointed out. For one thing, a disturbingly large number of the world's governments do not look very authoritative or legitimate and fall more than a little short when it comes to having a monopoly on the use of force. Afghanistan, for example, or El Salvador or Angola. By the formulation outlined above Lebanese affairs really should be classified as a form of international politics! Needless to say, this is not very reassuring when it comes to defining the field.

Nor is the international scene quite as anarchical as that formulation suggests. There are enough elements of order around to permit observers to speak of an "international" or "global" community. Many interactions among states are governed by treaty, custom, or law. An elaborate complex of international organizations facilitates cooperation and world-community development, so that when people are starving from a famine in Africa, people and governments elsewhere try to do something to help. Analysts have detected various international regimes, patterns of interaction, cooperation, and decision making that manage important segments of international affairs. Alliances and other networks of agreement and commitment seek to regularize international society and moderate the behavior of nations. Granted the institutions and processes in the international arena are often less formal and well developed, but we are interested in the behavior of people and governments and if these less formal elements make much of that behavior rather predictable, then the effect is the same for purposes of study. All in all, the idea that nations are orderly within and anarchic between seem half true at best.

Let us push this view a bit further. Just how much law and order does a government supply? In some very well known areas of the United States many of the residents do not feel safe on the streets after dark, the streets being often described as a jungle. The American government obviously has lost any semblance of control over its border with Mexico, cannot get a handle on the flow of drugs into and through the society, is hardly about to put organized crime out of existence. Public buildings throughout the Western world have been turned into fortified redoubts from the threat of terrorism, and leading officials live with the constant risk of kidnapping and assassination. Or consider the facts in Table 1,[4] from just one small period. The number of cases in the first two categories is impressively large. Evidently having a central authority around to keep the peace does not guarantee that it will be kept.

On a more philosophical level, the idea expressed by some analysts that the international scene is anarchical clashes with their determination to subject it to serious study. To theorize about something involves starting with the assumption that the subject matter will turn out to

TABLE 1-1
Military Conflicts, 1958-1965

Type of Conflict	1958	1959	1960	1961	1962	1963	1964	1965
Prolonged, irregular or guerrilla insurgency	28	31	30	31	34	41	43	42
Brief revolts, coups, uprisings	4	4	11	6	9	15	9	10
Overt, militarily conventional wars	2	1	1	6	4	3	4	5
Total	34	36	42	43	47	59	56	57

have at least *some* regularities and consistencies. And clearly statesmen behave as if there were some; they act as if the world is tricky and dangerous, not that it is completely random or uncontrollable.

There! We've certainly demolished that way of distinguishing international from domestic politics. Or have we? Is there a big difference between a society where there is a government and it is agreed there ought to be, even if some people disagree violently about who should run it, and a system where the members do not want a true government established? Are the mafia, or street gangs, or terrorist groups vis-à-vis the larger society really pretty much the same as the leading members of the international realm sitting on well-developed capacities to destroy much of the planet? Somehow it seems intellectually awkward to equate the two kinds of situations, for the differences seem to be less a matter of details than of essentials, and the politics involved in international affairs seem at once more primitive and for bigger stakes.

Thus another possible distinction between international and domestic politics might rest on the relative importance, and attendant prestige, of the two. It is reported that President DeGaulle of France regarded statesmanship as cherishing and nourishing the nation's interests in the world, domestic affairs being prosaic and mundane. Harvard University's Stanley Hoffman once distinguished high from low politics, the former concerned with matters affecting the continued independent existence of the nation. Governments traditionally have different sets of officials to deal with foreign and domestic policies, and often those handling foreign affairs have greater prestige simply by virtue of the fact.

This presupposes a fairly clear dividing line, for we cannot find the field of international politics if we cannot say what is foreign and what is domestic. Yet

> Plato knew what recent analysts are discovering, that any distinction between foreign and domestic is no more than one of degree, that is, at most, a distinction of feeling and not of fact.[5]

The field is currently full of people who argue that as modernization progresses, the distinction between foreign and domestic policies simply breaks down, that interdependence has increased the interplay for foreign and domestic factors in shaping almost all major policies. Or one might go further and argue that what really moves a government to behave as it does in international politics is one or more aspects of its domestic politics, erasing much of the distinction between the two. For example, Lenin's theory of imperialism (a *foreign* policy) explains it as the highest stage of capitalism (a set of *domestic* conditions and policies).

Still another way to distinguish international from domestic politics that has been widely used is the concept of sovereignty. Nation-states are sovereign whereas you and I are not—therefore politics among them will be different than politics between us. There are at least three major problems with this. First, as one scholar puts it, the concept of sovereignty "defies brief analysis and its full meaning defies brief and noncontroversial statement,"[6] which is scholarese for saying that it does not mean anything precisely. The closest we can get is the idea that a sovereign state acknowledges no legitimate external restraints other than those it chooses to accept, and as such enjoys some degree of autonomy and constitutes something of a hard shell between its territory and citizens and the rest of the world.

Which takes us to the second problem with sovereignty, namely that the hard shell looks at time like a sieve. Foreign radio broadcasts, subversive ideas, ballistic missiles, and other insidious things can pass right through it. The Soviets have discovered this when it comes to rock music and blue jeans, the United States when it comes to drugs and illegal aliens—so much so that analysts once thought that we were about to observe the decline of the nation-state, due to interdependence and such. No doubt we have the feeling that this was a wee bit premature, that we still live together in a nation and this is not about the change. This is right, of course. Nations are not just chunks of territory and lines on a map; they are psychological entities as well. They exist as lines on the maps in our minds. People have continued to feel and act as if they were living in viable nation-states, so they are. Thus the nation, as somewhat sovereign somehow, will be with us for the forseeable future.

The final problem is that if we use sovereignty to define the field (as in: international politics concerns the political relationships among sovereign entities), it leaves out lots of other entities we might want to include which are not sovereign, such as colonies, international organizations, the World Council of Churches, Amnesty International, and the like. The most glaring omission would be the multinational corporation; many of these are larger economic entities than a majority of the world's nations. Some analysts think "non state actors" are of growing importance and to look just at states is to miss a big piece of the action. Also sovereignty is not permanent and unchanging. Massachusetts was once sovereign, Angola only recently became so. Pull all this together and clearly international relations includes relations between many entities of uncertain sovereignty. Nation-states continue to be the primary actors but there are many others as well.

Nor is this all there is to the matter of defining the field. Look again at the term *international politics*. Why *politics?* Put another way, can we—should we—single out politics for study? One of the most interesting developments in our subject in recent years has been a surge of interest in international political economy, the basic premise of which is that quite a lot of international politics is really about economic things and international economic activities are shot through with political features, so much so that politics and economics really flow together. And why stop there? Immanuel Wallerstein has called for

> rejection of the assertion that the various organizational rubrics of scholars . . . are in any sense to be thought of as "disciplines" or even as currently useful groupings of scholarly activity. . . . There is no such thing as sociology; there is no such thing as history; there is no such thing as economics, political science, anthropology, or geography.[7]

There goes our field again!

Pressing in this direction could quickly bring us to referring not to international *politics* but international *relations* instead. In fact at some schools one can specialize solely in international relations; almost nowhere is this true of international politics. The obvious question then becomes: Is politics all there is to international relations? Are these terms synonymous? If we caught the mood of this chapter you already know the answer: it is hard to say. On the one hand there are many interactions between nations that we would hesitate to call political. Is an international conference of geneticists or stamp collectors political? A world chess tournament? The world trade in girdles?

At one time a trip by American ping-pong players to China had political significance; the invitation was extended by Peking to signal a desire to thaw the frozen United States-Chinese relationship. As a form of political protest the United States and Soviet Union have sometimes suspended scientific and cultural exchange programs. Likewise, for each of the nonpolitical examples in the previous paragraph I can think of an actual or hypothetical situation where they would be very political indeed. The point is that the same phenomenon may be political at one time, in its aims and consequences, and quite nonpolitical at another; not only that, it may have short-or long-term political consequences that were completely unexpected and unintended. Thus if we are really only interested in international *politics* we need to figure out how to know when something in international relations is specifically political.

Hans Morgenthau tried to suggest a way. If international politics is a struggle for power, then those activities undertaken to enhance a nation's power and those which have this effect are political. But Morgenthau himself pointed out that power seems to be impossible to clearly define, locate, measure, or see. That being so, it seems unlikely that a reference to power will enable us to classify international interactions as being either political or nonpolitical. But if almost any interaction is likely to prove relevant to international politics at one time or another, then we may end up talking about international relations instead and use definitions of the field such as this one:

> Imagine all of the exchanges, transactions, contacts, flows of information, and actions of every kind going on at this moment of time between and among the separately constituted societies of the world. To this picture in the mind we should add the effects created within societies from all such interflowing events in earlier times, both of the immediate and the more remote past. Finally, the stream of these actions and responses should be conceived as moving on to the future of tomorrow and beyond, accompanied by the expectations, plans, and proposals of all observers of the phenomena.[8]

Such a definition takes us far beyond the boundries of any one subject and shows why international relations is often described as multidisciplinary in nature, since "if one tried to catalog the content of international relations, it would become apparent that its proper sphere is mankind."[9]

Why, then, talk about international *politics* in this book? My answer is that I think I can make a good case for the proposition that the political aspects of international affairs are by far the most significant, the most dangerous, the most in need of study. Politics is not everything but, in the matter at hand, it is the most significant. Defining the limits of such politics turns out to be impossible to do precisely, so that to the extent a separate field of international politics exists it does so only by custom or because it is useful and not because it is in the nature of things. In general, however, international politics concerns the relations among governments, and other contacts among peoples and organizations will be of interest only insofar as they affect, and are directly affected by, the relations among governments. Politics is the process of creating and managing human communities. Such communities differ a good deal in their size, complexity, purposes, and resources, and I have a strong suspicion that politics varies with the type of community. There is such a thing as an international community, primitive as communities go, and it is distinctive enough to require that we think in terms of a separate subject of international politics. It is through international politics that this community gets managed after a fashion, though there is little in the way of authoritative political direction of world affairs.

The term *international* literally means *among nations*. Yet humans have not always lived in nations; in fact, in the long reach of human existence they have almost never lived in nations. People have constituted tribes, villages, city-states, empires—lots of communities besides nations. Thus when we talk about *international* politics we are referring to a specific period in history that began for Europeans about 1500 A.D. and for most of the rest of the world only within this century. It is quite common for scholars to support conclusions about this or that aspect of international politics by referring to Thucydides' Greece or Machiavelli's Italian city-states, but is this proper? If it is then we should define our field as inter*state* not inter*national* politics. It is clear that there are significant parallels between the two. Much of the behavior Thucydides recorded sounds familiar. Thus the question to keep in mind is whether the parallels are crucial, or whether nations are different enough that relations among them call for a different theoretical perspective. It may be that nationalism, modernization, or the capacities for destruction or global operations associated with nation-states mean that activities such as war, or deterrence, or imperialism are not as they used to be. This is not a question to tackle here; I just want it to be a part of our thoughts as soon as we see someone referring to Chinese warlords or Pericles' Athens in the literature.

Not only is international politics a relatively recent period in human history, it may soon end! Nations are steadily less viable as autonomous, sovereign entities. Things that cut across national boundries keep proliferating—multinational corporations, problems in areas such as food or energy or population, terrorist groups, and so on. Have all of these so changed the nature of the world that old style international politics is already on its way out? Some analysts think so; others think such a transformation is not here yet but soon will be. There is another possibility we must also face. Maybe international politics is not changing, just the scale of the destruction governments can inflict, and that sooner or later the combination of the two will bring on a shattering thermonuclear war. That would put an end to international politics too. Thus you should keep in mind the possibility that international politics is a passing phase of human history and that, one way or the other, you may be in on its passing.

The Problem of What to Look At

The Level-of-Analysis Problem

Enough about the problem of delimiting the field. Since this book reviews theoretical approaches, it is best to spend time at the beginning on certain problems that affect the analyst no matter how he conceives of the field. In reviewing writings in the field you should always start by seeing how the author handles these perennial challenges. The first is the matter of what to look at. We cannot look at everything because that is physically impossible, but then we really do not want to look at everything, just at what is important. So we have to decide what is likely to be the most important, the most interesting, the most fruitful.

One aspect of this is what J. David Singer referred to as the "level-of-analysis" problem.[10] It can be illustrated by the following propositions:

1. The interactions of nations are ultimately the result of the decisions and behavior of individuals—such as presidents and foreign ministers—and so that is what we must study and try to explain.
2. The interactions of nations are ultimately the result of decisions and actions taken by small groups—cabinets, the Politburo—and by larger groups such as bureaucracies, interest groups, or elites, and therefore we must focus on behavior within and among groups.
3. International politics is dominated by the actions of nation-states, thus we must study the shaping of the foreign policy and behavior of the nation-state as a whole, as a complete unit.

4. Nations do not act alone. International interaction falls into clumps or clusters of nations; this is the thing to study—regional groupings, alliances, ideological blocs, and voting blocs in the U.N.
5. International politics as a whole constitutes a system. This system and its changes over time do more to determine nations behavior than anything else, so the best way to understand international politics is to study the system, not the members.

Which one would you choose? They all seem plausible and relevant, yet if we decide to work on all of them we will be back trying to look at everything. Picking from among them is what we might expect to be able to do *after* some serious study; it is a bit disconcerting to find that we must pick just to get started. In his article Singer concentrated on three and five, the nation-state level and the international system level, to make the important point that each level poses different handicaps and opportunities for the analyst. Focusing on the international system leads to minimizing the differences among nations and paying little attention to what goes on inside them, which may mean missing something important. Working at the nation-state level the differences among nations are apt to be more emphasized, cluttering our vision with so many details that we fail to see the larger reality.

I should point out that a sophisticated body of theory in any field normally operates at several levels simultaneously (as does Einstein's theories of relativity which yield insights applicable to levels ranging from subatomic particles to the shape and movement of the universe.) Given a body of validated and accepted theory, levels of analysis conveniently layer the pursuit of its implications—much as seams of ore can stratify the operations of a mine. But when no such theory exists, which is the case in international politics, levels of analysis complicate matters by competing for the attention of theorists while, like a prism with light, refracting their collective effort into many perspectives not readily united.

Various Information Difficulties

Determining the level of investigation is only one element in the problem of what to look at. Another is the type of evidence we want to accumulate within any level of analysis. Once again, it is a matter of what our preconceptions tell us will be important and useful. A geopolitical thinker looks at geographical data, a political economist may wish to focus on economic transactions, and so on.

Ideally, a person makes an educated guess as to what is important and how best to study it, and in the course of investigation determines by trial and error where the original guesses were wrong and adjusts accordingly. This turns out to be a lot more difficult than it sounds. Remember, we cannot look at everything, only what is relevant (and whatever irrelevant things that manage to sneak in). Why, then, should we see anything that we are not prepared to see? To a certain extent we perceive only what we expect to or want to—and theories, models, frameworks, and starting assumptions all have the effect of telling us what to expect and what we can safely ignore. Thus perception is always selective. Is it any wonder that we are in constant danger of looking at the world in such a way as to prove to ourselves what we already thought we knew, by looking only at information which conforms to our predilections? Even worse, analysts readily become attached to their particular ways of seeing, to their theories of starting assumptions or predilections. Thus not only do they tend to overlook information that tends to suggest they are wrong, but if confronted with it they tend to reject it and to hold on to their own views with some tenacity. That is why trial and error does not work like it should.

In an important study, Graham Allison attempted to demonstrate this point by applying three different conceptual models to the United States' decision making in the Cuban Missile Crisis, thereby coming up with three substantially different views of the events.[11] Now you can appreciate the importance of academic journals in the field, the media, and communications processes in general. Since we often see what we expect to see, it is important to hear regularly from others on what they saw when they used a different perspective, when they started out wearing different analytical lenses. However, this does not eliminate the problem. For instance, the greatest part of the study of international politics has been done in the Western world, particularly the United States; it can be argued that the field is therefore dominated by ways of looking at the world that reflect the culture and unique history of just one part of it, that the whole field is biased and the journals and media just reinforce that bias!

Next we should consider some of the deficiencies in the information the analyst has to work with. An obvious one is that a good deal of fairly important information is secret. In its scope at least, this problem is probably unique to international politics. In all areas of inquiry some information is hard to come by, but in few is there an organized effort by some people to keep the rest of us from learning what they know. Thus the problem has two sides. Not only is there information that is secret which we do not know but would like to (such as on Soviet decision making), but some people whose behavior we would like to explain know this information and may be acting on the basis of it.

Notice that the importance of a particular kind of information to your research varies with the level of analysis you are using. At the lowest level the health of the Soviet premier might be important; at the highest you would be dealing with macro events and the health of individual leaders would be irrelevant.

The problem of secrecy would not disappear if detente flourished and CIA or KGB personnel had to look for other work, because a certain amount of secrecy appears to be vital for decision making as well as for morale and effectiveness in governments. There are many facets to this, and we will touch on only a few here for purposes of illustration. Suppose we are advisors to the president and a decision arises on which we would propose action contrary to the views of his other advisors, public opinion, or the president himself. We know we could be wrong; we also know our advice will be unpopular if publicized. How candid will we be if we know that whatever we propose will become part of the unending Washington gossip or broadcast on the network news programs? And what if it turns out that our advice was wrong and to have followed it would have been silly or disasterous? Confidentiality promotes candor; and secrecy gives one a chance to pass through with minimum harm those inevitable periods when we are fools.

Now suppose the president is considering a sharp and imaginative departure in policy, but one that could potentially be very controversial at home and abroad. If word of this leaks out, domestic opponents and foreign governments will bring pressure to bear to eliminate this option, to prevent any further consideration being given to it. President Nixon was in exactly this situation in thinking about reversing United States policy toward China. Under such circumstances, secrecy preserves options and thus enhances flexibility, something decision makers can often use.

Next we come to information that is not officially secret but remains very difficult to get. In many new nations there is both the fear that research by Western scholars serves the nefarious purposes of intelligence agencies and an aversion to being studied as a guinea-pig society. Also, the truth may hurt newly nurtured national pride or the careers of the current crop of officials. The result for the researcher can be bureaucratic delays, interviews denied, questionnaires unanswered, access to documents and statistics curtailed.

Public officials often have little in the way of privacy, so they tend to protect fiercely what they can. It is not implausible that an official's relationships with his family, his sexual habits, his health, his repressed

fears and anxieties have some bearing on his decisions and actions, but
just try—in the name of scholarship—getting the information. (Leaders
in communist countries are particularly secretive on this score.) So we
often end up guessing instead, relying on fragments of evidence and
hints, reading the tea leaves in the cup of an individual's life.

Even readily available information often is less accurate or helpful
than the analyst would like. Most of the world's governments have
only a vague notion of just how many people they rule, how many are
unemployed, how many can read (even the United States government
is not at all sure how many illegal aliens are in the country). In some
countries a very large part of the economic activity, including that with
foreigners, is carried on illegally and is not accurately recorded. Hence
government estimates of gross national products are often simply
guesswork. Much of the information about important historical events
is incomplete or derives from sources of dubious reliability. Vast
amounts of widely disseminated information must be discounted because it was compiled and distributed by governments, agencies, and
officials for manipulation of public opinion or deliberately distorted to
enhance their images. This is what is meant by the old adage about the
existence of "lies, damn lies, and statistics," or why a British prime
minister once lamented that "if you believe the doctors nothing is
healthy; if you believe the clergy nothing is innocent; if you believe the
military nothing is safe."[12] Information is distorted because it is a
weapon; people consciously and unconsciously give out or withhold
facts in ways that reflect and enhance their points of view. Scholars
studying the Vietnam war wrestle with the stream of misinformation on
how the war was going, based on body counts or pilot reports of
bombing results that flowed through the government.

As we may have noticed, the kind of information we need and
therefore the degree to which the problems just outlined will apply
depends on the questions asked. Let us say we set out to test the
plausible hypothesis that the *more strongly* an official desires a foreign
affairs outcome, the more likely it will seem to him to come about (that
is, his wish influences his probability estimate). If this is so it would
help explain why officials sometimes cling to policies that other people
can see have little chance of success (Vietnam, for example?). Now
how do we measure that "more strongly"? Since the officials will have
various goals, we need to know how much more he yearns to fulfill this
one than the others—how much more important to him is A than B,
and C. In other words we need a preference schedule for this individual. Now we would have difficulty ranking and weighing our own
preferences, much less someone else's; and the difficulty will grow if

we seek the preference schedule not just of one official but of his colleagues, his department, or his government as a whole, to say nothing of doing this kind of analysis over a lengthy period in his career when his preference schedule may shift considerably.

There is also what we might call "Cheshire Cat information," which is information that never takes concrete form. Charles Frankel writes that an Assistant Secretary of State can develop delusions of godlike power because when he says he will order this or do that, while talking on the phone, some aide is listening in; he makes a note of what has been promised and starts the wheels turning to make it happen.[13] But such records are not kept at cocktail parties and other social encounters, in informal meetings among top officials (in fact that is why so much sensitive stuff is often discussed on such occasions). Who keeps records of bribes? Yet we know this can be an important ingredient in the behavior of officials, and it is one of the tools of the trade for intelligence agencies and multinational corporations. What about decisions to keep on doing what the government has been doing? There is unlikely to be detailed information on exactly when such a decision was reached, by whom, and on what basis. In all such circumstances something important may happen or not happen and for us to understand why may require information that does not exist other than in the memories of a few busy, distracted, forgetful, and hard-to-get-at officials—fading away like the Cheshire Cat in *Alice in Wonderland* with just enough traces left to mock our efforts.

Strangely enough, the final information problem I want to mention is the opposite of the others. It confronts officials as well as scholars and students. It is that there is entirely *too much information* about international politics, enormous masses of it pouring into government offices, piling up in intelligence agencies, and displayed in countless journal articles, books, documents, government reports and the mass media. Many of us working in this field have reached the point where we hate to see the mail—everyday it is just more articles that should be read, notices about what look like valuable books, more reason to feel one's not keeping up. Studies report the same problem in United States intelligence agencies—more information is gathered that can ever be successfully processed and used—and this is hardly just a problem for the United States. Much of the information we confront is false, irrelevant, repetitive, or useless but it takes time and effort to find that out, and what is left is still staggering—the world is too big and too complicated, and the efforts to understand it too numerous. Confronting it daily tends to deaden the mind, inducing a sense of futility, a feeling of drowning in a sea of data.

Further Problems of Perception

There are still other problems in acquiring information but let us turn our attention to what it is about—reality. For purposes of illustration let us assume there is *real* international politics out there somewhere. We can never perceive all of it, the best each of us can do is develop some version of it. We can study that reality and others' perceptions of it, using the latter to help us refine our image of the former. Now is that all there is to study? If we agreed we must have overlooked the perceptions held by those directly involved in international politics: like us, they have their own images and what they act upon is not reality but their versions of it. But how do we study their perceptions? To do so requires that we, in effect, slip into someone else's mind—an impossible task. So we find ourselves working with a second-order perception not only of reality but of someone else's second-order perception of reality.

Now you can see the importance of the problem of looking at the right things. Not only can we not comprehend all of reality, we would not wish to. Perception requires concentration, in which we cut ourselves off from some messages about reality in order to pay close attention to others. It is like studying a textbook—you have to keep the noise of the party down the hall from creeping in and distracting you. This is how we deal with reality, selecting only certain things for examination so that the world is simplified and made understandable, at least enough so that we can go on living in it. Now this is exactly the effect of theory in international politics. It helps us decide that arms sales are important and that we can forget the trade in tropical fish. It tells us the United States position on arms control is worthy of attention while that of Malta or Chad is not. It suggests whether we can safely ignore the personalities of decision makers in favor of a focus in the international system or whether, instead, there really is not any such thing as an international system.

We are already aware of one problem in all this, namely that it is entirely possible to look at the wrong things. Those who play chess or checkers will recall the shock one gets when the opponent makes a totally unexpected and devastating move. All the relevant information was right in front of you, you just did not see it. A related problem is that abstractions from reality are comfortable in that they are tidier and less complicated than reality itself; indeed, that is why we use them. But in doing so we may come to reside in the traditional ivory tower, living in a fabricated world where nations behave in regular and predictable ways which has few parallels with the ways real flesh-and-blood governments act. Any theorist sets out to simplify reality and he always runs the risk of overdoing it.

Too Many Uses of Theory

Why do we want to develop theory in the study of international politics? What is it good for? There is no easy answer for there are several possible functions of theory. One way to demonstrate this would be to lay out some sort of analytical framework and then see what theory might contribute to it. What follows is an attempt to do this.

Professor Morgenthau, you remember, asserted that all politics is a struggle for power. Let us try a different starting point and assume that international politics, like all politics, is concerned with the creation and management of human communities. Lots of things can contribute to sustaining a community: economic relations, education, culture, communications, etc. The distinctive contribution of politics is the ultimate management of that community. Sounds all right so far, but what does it mean? Well it would seem that management includes various things. One is rule; politics concerns who is ultimately in charge, and it does this via the distribution of power and authority. Another is decision making; a political system supplies the ultimate form of this in a community. Still another is order and security; no community can get by without this and providing for it seems to be an important contribution of a political system. Another is welfare; certainly members of a community often expect the political system to promote their welfare in various ways.

With this as our framework, how would we describe international politics? Probably the first thing that strikes us is that the community involved does not seem very highly developed. Among its most important members are the various national governments and they, with the support of many of their citizens, do not want or permit the emergence of governing institutions for the community with real power and authority—they prefer being autonomous. In addition these members do not broadly agree on values, expectations, goals, and perspectives; they frequently disagree with each other about these things, sometimes quite violently. This means the community is pretty decentralized and coordination or behavior can be quite difficult or even impossible. This being so, the coercive capacities of member states (and other members) are more important than in a more highly developed community—force is more important in determining what gets done. And since these capacities for coercion are decentralized, they are not necessarily used for the management of the community as a whole.

Elaborating on our description, it seems that international politics provides an uneasy and very limited form of *rule*—much of it comes from the strength of the member states, and since strength is unevenly distributed some states contribute a lot more to rule than others. But since the uneven distribution of that strength is often disliked, the rule that the most powerful provide is apt to be unpopular in some quarters, hard to make legitimate and authoritative. Next, it is clear international politics is able to provide only limited decision making, and what there is often seems difficult, slow, unavailable on some important matters, and insufficient to handle many issues and problems. International politics also looks weak in the area of order and security; members states do a lot to provide this on their own and worry quite a lot about it. Finally, international politics supplies welfare to only a limited degree; there are plenty of have-not nations, there is less welfare in much of the globe than available knowledge and resources would seem to permit. Having gotten this far, what can theory do for us?

1. Theory can be a statement as to what we think we have found out. Thus: "When well advanced, it is a spare and compact statement about what is known."[14] All we have set forth above is one way of describing international politics. We would know a lot more if we could explain it, and that's what a theory does. A theory notes the existence of relationships between things and explains why those relationships exist. For instance, we have a decentralized, not highly developed community and we have only limited provision for rule, decision making, order and security, and welfare: are those two things related, so that when we have the former we are bound to find the latter? If so, why? To take a second example, if the strongest member states have to supply a good deal of the rule available, and order and security too, is this directly related to the distribution of welfare (the strong take most of what there is to get)—or is it that the same things that make for national strength are also primarily responsible for national welfare (the strong do not take from the weak; what made them strong also made them well off). To answer questions like these we need a theory. In offering explanations theory gives us something to test. It also helps tell us, by omission, things we do not know and helps us decide what to look at or look for next. It also lends itself to prediction, since knowledge about what is can often be converted into assertions about what will be (checking predictions is one important way of testing a theory).

2. Theory can be a statement about what ought to be, in a normative

explaining what happens. It is also important to be clear about the distinction between individual idiosyncracies and *types* of individuals. Using the former, people make a difference because each one of us is different. People make a difference in the latter view because there are different types of people.

Still another reason for working at this level of analysis is both profound and commonplace in its origins and implications? What if we believe that the major aspects of international politics ultimately derive from the inner essence of man, from human nature? Early in Hans Morgenthau's textbook we find him saying that "the world, imperfect as it is from the rational point of view, is the result of forces inherent in human nature." And there is Montaigne's comment that "the souls of emperors and cobblers are cast in the same mold. . . . The same reason that makes us wrangle with a neighbor causes a war betwixt princes."

It may be rather disheartening to learn, however, that by itself a preoccupation with human nature does not take us very far. The initial problem is that one and the same nature is often used to explain entirely different kinds of behavior. How can it be human nature to like peace and to make war? If only one is the result of human nature, which one is it? Of course, we can always say that human nature is what people are—no more or no less. If people are both peaceful and murderous then that is human nature. The difficulty here is that by explaining everything, this really explains nothing. As Kenneth Waltz once said, referring everything back to human nature is like the runner who, when asked why he lost the race, replied "I ran too slowly." That may be a correct answer but it is not very helpful. We need other answers that tell us *why* he ran too slowly.[1] If people are sometimes kind and sometimes the reverse because it is human nature, we are still stuck for an explanation of why they were kind on this particular occasion but not on another.

There is an additional problem. Theorists discussing human nature do not always have the same conception of it. Here are some of the possibilities:

1. It could be that human nature is the product of our biological heritage. Being genetically derived, it would be pretty stable and thus could be manipulated or controlled only marginally. This may be what one scholar had in mind when he wrote that man's "strange mixture of cussedness and nobility has shown no signs of fundamental change since the stone age. . . ."[2] As this suggests, human nature may be not only innate but intrinsically flawed.
2. Perhaps human nature can change but it is stable over long periods.

This was Hegel's conception. However, Hegel thought that philosophers could understand the nature of man in a particular historical era only when that era was ending. A true understanding was possible only in retrospect and on the eve of its becoming irrelevant, a discouraging thought.

3. Another possibility is that standard human behavior not only changes, it develops. That is, the changes have a general direction and purpose. This is the fundamental assumption of the Marxists and thus has had a powerful impact. Grasp the direction and purpose of human development and you can predict the course of history—which is why Marx and Engels thought they were scientists.

4. Finally, maybe some elements in human nature are constant while others change. The brain is the source of behavior, and some parts of the brain have evolved rather rapidly while other parts appear to have remained relatively the same.

All of this says nothing about the characteristics we may wish to ascribe to to individuals as part of their nature. For example, how rational are they? If we think people are often quite rational, especially in dealing with foreign affairs, we will pursue a different way of devising explanations of what they do than if we believe that people are usually moved by the irrational or nonrational, by unconscious motives and feelings. Of course, deciding which description is more accurate requires that we come up with a definition of rationality and find some ways to detect its presence.

After this brief and inadequate introduction to the problems involved, let us turn to the kinds of studies frequently carried on at this level of analysis. To do justice to all of those that we might examine would take a book larger than this one so all I can do is try to whet your appetite with what I hope will be a tasty sample.

The Study of Specific Individuals

Harold Lasswell once suggested that "political science without biography is a form of taxidermy." If you think people make a difference and they do so because of qualities that make each of us different from anyone else, then studying the lives and careers of specific persons who are or were deeply involved in international affairs comes naturally to mind. We might be interested in Ayatolla Khomeini or Muamar Khadafi or the life of Gandhi. Henry Kissinger in office was reportedly more impressed by the role of personalities than was Henry Kissinger the scholar:

> I tended to think of history run by impersonal forces. . . . But when you
> see it in practice, you see the differences that the personalities make.
> The overtures to China would not have worked without Chou En-lai.
> There would have been no settlement in the Middle East without Sadat
> and Golda Meir and Dayan.[3]

In concentrating on key individuals our intention would be to outline
their particular contribution to events and explain why they acted as
they did. We might also wish to use them as case studies or illustrations
of the role of the individual in world affairs.

Various methods may be used. Perhaps the most familiar of these are
biography and its first cousin, the memoir. The main thrust of such
literature is that individuals in their glorious peculiarity alter the course
of events. Biographers of Lenin generally assert that his particular
genius was an essential ingredient for the success of the Bolshevik
Revolution. Many studies of the onset of the Cold War have concluded
that the shift in the personality and experience of the president, when
Roosevelt died and Truman took office, was an important ingredient.
As for memoirs, today there is an influx of "I was there and helped
make important things happen" literature. (One reason for this is that
public service is often not very remunerative but talking about it
afterward can be). Kissinger's memoirs make fascinating reading,
albeit with a pronounced tendency to provide rather too much of a
good thing. The urge to tell one's own version of events has triumphed
even in the formerly hush-hush profession of intelligence, and in fairly
closed societies like the Soviet Union—from which we have had the
elaborate accounts by the U.S.S.R.'s wartime generals and Khrushchev's memoirs.

In the broad sense, this kind of literature is *very uncongenial for the
development of theory.* There is an emphasis on explanation all right,
but usually not via reference to factors, singly and in combination, that
lend themselves to generalizations. In other words, the explanation
that emerges for some set of events, for example, the conclusion of the
SALT I agreements, is not likely to readily fit many other, somewhat
similar, sets of events which is the conclusion of all arms control
agreements or all major international treaties. It is also an uncongenial
literature in another sense. A theorist who wants to generalize about,
for example, the role of personality in shaping foreign policy decisions
has to obtain information about personalities from somewhere, and
often the most available source of it consists of writings like these. But
this means using information gathered and presented by persons
(biographers and autobiographers) who did not have the theorist's
perspective in mind; What they thought was important, worth men-

tioning, worth ignoring is not necessarily what he thinks. In addition, the authors of such works may well have had implicit (occasionally explicit) theories or theoretical inclinations that guided their writings. How reliable, then, is their information for the way he wishes to make use of it?

More attractive, therefore, for purposes of theory is a kind of biography (even autobiography—though this is very rare in international politics) designed not so much to stress idiosyncrasies as to lend itself to generalization. It may note peculiarities, but the main point is that the hero is representative of his time or embodies the interplay of larger forces. Barbara Tuchman's rewarding study of General Joseph Stilwell is a good example.[4] Stilwell was deeply involved in U.S. dealings with China during World War II. He had some distinctive qualities—as reflected in his nickname "Vinegar Joe"—but rather than his uniquiness, Tuchman highlights the clash between typically American attitudes and values he embodied and the dynamics of social revolution in Asia, a subject of more than passing interest in light of the American experience in Vietnam.

Another approach is the study of particular individuals, and thus a form of biography, via the application of a well developed theory or related body of knowledge. An excellent example is the retrospective application of psycho-analysis to the career of a major official or historical figure. This has stirred up controversy in political science and history, while producing some fascinating biographies. One is the study of Woodrow Wilson by Alexander and Juliette George.[5] They depict his personality as shaped by his relationship with a brilliant, devoted, yet excessively demanding and critical father. That relationship damaged Wilson's self-esteem, leading to a recurring compulsion to prove himself by great achievements. Critics or opponents threatened not only his policies but his precariously poised identity, and thus he condemned them and often rigidly rejected compromise. In the Senate debate on his plans for the League of Nations this personality made Wilson refuse to compromise, which cost him the support of so many otherwise favorably disposed senators that he suffered a crushing defeat.

Similar treatments of Stalin, Nixon, T.E. Lawrence (Lawrence of Arabia) and others have been produced with varying degrees of care and insight. Perhaps the most impressive is Robert Waite's study of Hitler. Waite's premise is that "Hitler was a pathological personality whose career cannot be understood without a careful examination of his personal life," particularly his childhood.[6] Drawing on clinical psychology Waite describes Hitler as a "borderline personality." Such a person has a strong tendency toward paranoia, a constant perception and fear of enemies, and an inability to trust others. He fantasizes himself as omnipotent, as a special, privileged person entitled to use or exploit others. He can be childish/selfish, narcissistic, and demanding of attention and adulation. He has phobias about dirt and feces, often linked to sexual perversions that involve these things. Ultimately he is driven by the lack of an integrated ego, a stable identity, which leads to a kind of dual personality displaying dramatically opposite traits: cruelty then kindness, sentimentality coupled with harshness, creativity alongside an urge to destroy. This divided self generates deep inner anxiety, fears about being inadequate or weak and profound feelings of guilt and self-loathing which include suicidal inclinations. He represses or copes with these terrifying feelings by identifying with the desireable self and projecting onto others the despised self. Thus, the world contains enemies to be destroyed, evil to be crushed, with the triumphs reaffirming his self-worth.

Tracing these patterns in Hitler's words and behavior, Waite then shows how they were reflected in his worldview and *his policies*. Germany became the embodiment of his noble self, of everything good (he spoke of being wedded to Germany), to be saved from monstrous enemies and especially from the infection and *pollution* of Jews. His preoccupation with appearing masculine, capable, and strong led to an emphasis on power, will, brutality, and obstinacy. By extension these became characteristic of German foreign policy, of the treatment of other states and conquered peoples and of Hitler's approach to military problems (use the offensive, never retreat, no surrender). Aggression and war were extensions of his psychological needs—of the urge to dominate, strike at enemies, display strength, and reaffirm his self-worth through enormous achievements. But the strain of self-doubt, self-loathing, and self-destruction also produced recurring mistakes that invited defeat (and punishment)—such as pressing beyond his spectacular early diplomatic triumphs into the war, letting the British escape at Dunkirk, the compulsion to attack the U.S.S.R., the reluctance to ever fully mobilize Germany during the war, and the grandiose declaration of war on the United States after Pearl Harbor. Ultimately only catastrophic defeat for Germany (himself) was suitable punishment for monumental weakness and failure.

Equally as interesting is Waite's effort to treat Hitler's personality in its context, to point out what elements in German culture, history, and society gave Hitler the broad appeal that would bring him to power. In other words, he tries to link personality factors with factors that operated at other levels of analysis. He also tries to carefully consider, and then reject, alternative explanations offered by others: that external factors forced Hitler into war and aggression, that he was really quite rational, that his behavior was due to Parkinson's disease or artereosclerosis or syphilis, that he suffered from brain disorders, or that the medicines prescribed by his quack personal physician were responsible.

We can see why such works are fascinating yet controversial. Psychoanalysis is interested in sexual and other personal matters we normally conceal or repress on grounds that public actions reflect deeply private needs and preoccupations. To study officials this way is to pry into "juicy" details—the results hold the same fascination as good gossip.

Critics take the view that gossip is about all this amounts to. They hold that from this perspective any great figure is apt to seem like a deviant personality, hardly an attractive notion, while his behavior is traced to childhood events at the cost of downplaying factors that shaped and confronted him as an adult. Psychoanalysis is itself suspect, for many regard it as philosophically and scientifically unsupported—a sort of twentieth century witchcraft. Also unacceptable to critics is that such studies are often done by political scientists or historians—the only thing worse than psychoanalysis being amateur psychoanalysis. Finally these studies attempt a clinical analysis as if the subjects were patients "on the couch." But they are not patients. They are usually dead and the analysis is done indirectly and at a distance, using fragments of a person's outer life to reconstruct his inner one. The writer's biases, or those of his time, dictate the evidence selected as important, with the results dressed up as science.

Of course, if officials gave their consent such investigations would not have to be retrospective. Harold Laswell once proposed that candidates for high office be required to undergo tests on mental fitness, an idea that is periodically reviewed. We have not tried this with politicians but it is exactly what the Pentagon does with people who handle its nuclear weapons. We assume the person elected to sit on one end of the red phone is stable, but we test those at the other end to make sure.

Waite's consideration of Hitler's possible medical ailments suggests another way of bringing a large body of theory and knowledge to bear on the study of individuals. For starters, I suggest Hugh L'Etang's *The Pathology of Leadership*,[7] which details the medical histories of many twentieth-century leaders. The premise of the book is that heart attacks, massive injections of drugs, failing eyesight, prolonged insomnia, fainting spells and other ailments which have afflicted the powerful cannot help but affect their decisions. Charles Frankel has something similar in mind in his "weariness theory of history." After detailing the physically exhausting level of work in the State Department, he writes:

> That men can be subjected to the pressures of the present method of doing business in the American government and still go on being flexible and responsive is a bad bet. But it is the bet on which we now run the American government.[8]

It should be emphasized that applying psychoanalysis or medicine to the analysis of the careers of specific individuals does not lead to a general *theory of international politics;* rather it is an attempt at explaining some segments of international politics by drawing upon *theory developed for other purposes.* What we need is a way to convert studies of this sort into generalizations pertaining not just to particular individuals or events but to larger categories of them. A good example is Ole Holsti's study of Secretary of State John Foster Dulles.[9] Earlier we noted that a person sees, in large part, only what he is prepared to see. Rather than use this to study Dulles, Holsti's sought to use Dulles as a case study in how any official's image of the world affects his perceptions. Holsti's used content analysis of Dulles' public statements on the U.S.S.R. from 1953 to 1959 in order to detect Dulles' image of the Soviet Union—which was that it was hostile and threatening. He then looked at what happened when the Soviets were conciliatory. Dulles interpreted this change in behavior attributed to Soviet failures and weakness in the face of United States determination. The Soviets were merely retreating to lick their wounds with no change in their basic hostility, and thus a continued tough line by the U.S. was called for. In other words, information that directly clashed with the image was interpreted in such a way as to preserve and reinforce that image. This invites the general conclusion that the prospects for reducing international tension by actions to change leaders' stereotypes of other nations are not good.

We could study great leaders not so much to understand them as to arrive at general conclusions about what makes a great leader. One account of eight great figures in twentieth century international politics finds the following typical elements in background or personality: incredible ego and motivation; a supportive, often religious, mother; a strong-willed father with whom there were intense conflicts or identification; a restrained, redirected, or unusual sex life; an aloofness or psychological distance from others; a coherent Weltanschauung or ideological worldview; and a tendency toward mental rigidity.[10]

Thus it is a step up, for theoretical purposes, to move from the study of an individual to study of some cluster of individuals, either because they are of the same type or faced the same circumstances, or because they were all involved in the same events together. The latter is attractive because politics is mostly a team sport; hardly anything in it is the result of a single person acting on his own. As we saw Waite's study of Hitler tries to take this into account. Most events in international politics involved many individuals, thereby multiplying the targets of our attention. To study a decision or series of actions, and to arrive at broader explanations, we are apt to want to look at more than one person.

One obvious way to do this is to interview the participants. Many social scientists studying international affairs use interviews to supplement their other sources. Many oral history projects have been established so people can record their recollections before they have passed away. Major events such as the Cuban Missile Crisis have been extensively investigated in this fashion. So have many other subjects, such as the perceptions and attitudes of diplomats.

As noted in chapter 1, there are drawbacks to interviewing. While still on the job, key officials may not be readily available, and when finally reached may not feel free to discuss their affairs with complete candor. Out of office they are subject to the inevitable tendency to justify their own roles and to repress, or simply forget, important details. One way around these difficulties is to probe official documents and personal papers to offset faulty memories or official biases and deliberate distortions. Much research at the individual level of analysis relies heavily on such scores, which lies behind the unrelenting academic (and journalistic) pressure to speed up the release of official materials by using such levers as the Freedom of Information Act. In this regard the American government is the most open in the world. Disclosures here often embarrass governments elsewhere. They embarrass current or past American officials too, as Richard Nixon and Henry Kissinger can testify! If officials are to be held accountable and good explanations of their behavior devised, access to such information may be vital. Yet if officials have no privacy can they ever be candid? One way they can retaliate is by putting less on paper, which would force us to rely more on their memories and personal accounts— putting us back where we started.

This helps make content analysis attractive. Documents, speeches, and the like can be closely scrutinized to better understand the perceptions and behavior of officials. This is analysis at a distance and need not raise issues of privacy and confidentiality. The assumption is that what officials say, and how, can yield clues even to unexpressed thoughts and perceptions. It is aptly illustrated by a series of studies on the onset of World War I conducted by Robert North and colleagues.[11] The public and private comments of the leading decision makers as they stumbled into that disastrous war were subjected to a systematic, often quantitative, analysis—word counts, measures of expressions of hostility, classification of themes, and even estimates of the intensity of the feelings expressed. (It is worth comparing these studies with Barbara Tuchman's *The Guns of August,* a completely different approach to exactly the same subject.) Among the many topics studied was the degree to which leaders on one side tended to see statements and actions by the opposing governments as more hostile than they actually were, and thus to overreact. Much evidence was found that this was the case.

Before finally leaving the study of particular individuals, we should take note of one other theoretically interesting approach. This consists of trying—on the basis of logic or empirical findings—to develop conclusions about when individual leaders are most likely to have a great impact on foreign policy, and when their personal qualities are of the greatest significance in determining what they do. Here are some examples of such propositions:[12]

> Individual leaders have the greatest impact:
>   The higher the level at which the decision is made;
>   The greater the personal interest of the leader in the decision;
>   The more nonroutine, crisis-like the situation;
>   The more authoritarian the political system.
>
> The personal qualities of individual leaders have the greatest impact:
>   The more limited the available knowledge about the problem;
>   The more ambiguous, unexpected the situation;
>   The less training in the subject the leader has had;
>   The less national security is involved.

Such assertions seem quite plausible but, needless to say, it is not easy to measure those "mores," "lesses" and "greaters" nor to gain sufficient access to a decision process to test them, particularly in countries less hospitable to nosy scholars than this one.

The Study of Individuals in General

This subheading may sound a bit foolish and we might question how one can have "individuals in general." What is meant by this is the attempt to understand how any individual or type of individual is likely to react in a particular situation. It involves such questions as: What are the effects of stress on a person's ability to think clearly or make decisions? Or, how do individuals generally go about making complex decisions? Sometimes answers are sought by turning to biology for assistance. At times the behavior of selected individuals in appropriately structured circumstances is examined. In other cases interviews and content analysis are the scholar's tools. Finally, in-depth psychological analyses are often used. Some examples follow.

Human Nature Revisited

Charles Darwin's theory of natural selection to explain evolution had a huge impact on the study of human beings in his own time and it continues to reverberate in the social sciences today. Darwin's theory stressed the interplay between the genetically derived characteristics of a species and its natural environment; those best suited to the environment survived, the others died out. But a corruption of his ideas came to see evolution and progress as the product of a constant struggle among species and, in Social Darwinism, this was translated into approval of struggles among individuals, people, and nations. In the latter part of the nineteenth century this was used to justify rampant capitalism, militarism, and imperialism—superior nations and cultures naturally dominate those that are inferior. Include God as lurking behind all this and some hair-raising rhetoric could result as in the excerpt from the Senate debate on whether the United States should rule the Phillipines:

> God has not been preparing the English-speaking and Teutonic peoples for a thousand years for nothing but vain and idle self-admiration. No! He has made us the master organizers of the world to establish system where chaos reigns. . . . He has made us adept in government that we may administer government among savages and senile peoples.[13]

There was a great deal of this, naturally enough, in Nazism and Fascism.

A more respectable effort to apply biology to the study of human social behavior, with particular reference to international politics, has been mounted in recent years by returning to the idea that there is an innate human nature. None of that stuff about superior races; instead the emphasis is on traits and behavior patterns found in all human beings. One of the more interesting lines of inquiry involves ethology and sociobiology, the central premises of which are that human behavior is biologically based, that it can be explained by understanding how it enhanced human survival in the process of natural selection, and that such an understanding can be attained by studies of the behavior of other animals. How does this work? Perhaps the most well known are studies by Konrad Lorenz and others on aggression—attacks by members of the *same species* on each other, up to and including killing.[14] It turns out that aggression is fairly common in nature and that it contributes in significant ways to the survival of species. It is used to divide up territory, spreading the species members around so that competition for available food supplies is limited. It plays an important role in the mating patterns of many species; the dominant male controls a harem and only he breeds offspring, or he controls other males too so he breeds more often. It also minimizes fighting in social animals, ones that live in packs or troops, by establishing a dominance heirarachy so that quarrels over food and mating are contained, and order is easier to uphold. But the aggression, while useful, must be restrained; if it led to constant killing the species would hardly survive. So many species have genetically developed inhibitions; at a certain point in a fight the loser concedes defeat in a way that inhibits the winner from further fighting and both survive. Turning to human beings, these studies see human aggression as biologically derived and as having been similarly useful in promoting human survival, but our earliest ancestors were so small that inhibitions on killing were not very necessary because they were not extensively developed. Alas, man the tool-maker steadily became a more efficient killer, so that human beings now have a unique capacity for homicide—such as in war.

This is reinforced by other innate human behaviors: intense group loyalty which includes a willingness to risk even death on the group's behalf, distrust of strangers and aliens, a preoccupation with territory and territorial defense, and strong inclinations to develop dominance heirarchies. All of these things, it is said, can be found widely displayed in international politics and contribute to the occurrence of war. Carrying the analysis to its logical conclusion, a creature which evolves behavior that might produce its extermination is flirting with extinction. In this sense man may well be an evolutionary mistake!

Without attempting to go into detail, some criticisms of this approach merit discussion because they raise interesting theoretical points. For instance, any evolution-based theory is open to the charge that by explaining everything it explains nothing, a point reviewed in chapter 1. If we believe all human behavior is genetically programmed, how could we test the theory: What would be evidence to the contrary? This is not an irrefutable argument but it bears thinking about. Next, if aggression is innate how often does it have to occur for us to declare it to be so? It certainly is not constantly on display because most people are peaceful most of the time and any one nation is only occasionally at war. Studies point out that even soldiers often display great reluctance to fight, women (half of the species) seem considerably less aggressive than men, etc.. It would seem at least as plausible that human nature is really a set of capacities and which ones are drawn upon depends on other factors and circumstances. Thus, people *can* be aggressive but are not *required* to be.

Other biologically based approaches have attempted to develop less far-ranging generalizations. For instance, there has been some interest in the biological effects of stress—shifts in the heart and respiration rates and even hormonal changes—on behavior. Stress narrows and intensifies attention, heightens the effects of basic personality traits and may reduce human tolerance for inaction and ambiguity. All this has been considered potentially relevant for understanding crisis decision making in international politics. Analysts have also been interested in possible generalizations about the effects of age, sex, jet lag (disruption of circadian rhythms) and, as L'Etang suggested, drugs and health problems.

The Impact of Personality

People are generous, stubborn, kind, tempermental and a host of other things that seem to bear on what they do and how they do it. It has occurred to scholars that the personalities of officials might shape their actions, as we saw earlier in studies of individuals. Now we examine attempts to identify *types of personalities* and explain how officials of each type tend to behave. To get a sense of how difficult this is, imagine that a list 10-15 of our acquaintences and try grouping them by personality. We will soon be wrestling with the question of which aspects of a friend are important (for this purpose) and which should be ignored, and how much alike people have to be before they belong in the same category. Our categories will begin to grow along with an uneasiness at placing someone in one category rather than another without more evidence. Then we should think about the evidence we would need to do the job right. As dismay mounts, imagine that our conclusions will be published for everyone to look at, criticize, and maybe laught at. Now we have a feel for the problem. Fortunately, it is a rare problem that will not yield to persistent effort, and we have some very persistent scholars.

Our first subject is the effect of "character,"—surely a fuzzy term if ever there was one. James Barber has been interested in the character of American presidents.[15] He defines character as a person's orientation toward life, and the interaction between a president's character and the temper of the times is what gives his term in office its tone and form. To get a handle on presidential character Barber suggests we examine it from two perspectives. First, does the president approach the job *actively* or *passively?* For example, does he take initiatives, involve himself in problems or does he wait on events and handle on those problems no one else can? Second, does he self-confidently enjoy political life or is he more impressed by its burdensome responsibilities and his own inadequacies? That is, is he *positive* or *negative* about it? Combining the two dimensions gives us four character types:

> *Active-positive*. An activist president who enjoys the job and is confident of his abilities (Franklin Delano Roosevelt, Harry Truman, John F. Kennedy)

> *Active-negative*. A compulsively active president because accomplishments and power help him compensate for low self-esteem, anxiety, and distaste for political life (Woodrow Wilson, Herbert Hoover, Lyndon B. Johnson, Richard Nixon)

> *Passive-positive*. An open, agreeable, but not very assertive president (William Taft, Warren Harding)

> *Passive-negative*. With low self-esteem and no desire to be active, the president is apt to retreat from nasty political realities behind principles and proper procedures (Calvin Coolidge, Dwight D. Eisenhower)

Barber sees character as the central element in a presidency, and the president as the hub of our political system. He urges us to be on the lookout for active-positives, as such men have generally been our most successful presidents. But beware of active-negatives because their compulsiveness and inner anxiety can develop into a deep emotional attachment to a particular policy, so that criticism becomes a personal threat and failure a terrible blow to self-esteem. Such presidents can pursue an incorrect policy rigidly, even when it is leading to disaster. As examples, Barber points to Wilson's mismanagement of the issue of United States membership in the League of Nations and Johnson's war in Vietnam.

The key is obviously how one decides what a president's character was. Barber applies ideas from psychology to a very careful look at each man's personal history. One of the virtues in his approach is *parsimony*—out of the many facets of character we could possibly consider Barber selects two as crucial. Another is *simplification* which is the endless details about each president's life are either pulled together under a few key concepts or ignored. These are precisely the things we want a theory to supply. Naturally, Barber's approach leaves him open to the criticisms of psychoanalytic studies mentioned earlier.

His theory can be, and has been, criticized for being too parsimonious and simplified because too many crucial details are left out or improperly lumped together.

Lloyd Etheredge is also interested in the effects of personality. He categorized 36 United States officials as either extroverts or introverts and as either domineering or not. (He defined extroverts as those who like being with people, even in their leisure time, and domineering officials as ones who constantly interfere with subordinates by checking up on them, giving elaborate orders, and supervising details.) He studied their views on two kinds of issues: 1.) whether to use force or the threat of force to deal with a problem, and 2.) whether to seek closer cooperation with the communist world. He hypothesized that high dominance types would be more favorable to military measures than low dominance officials, that extroverts would be more interested in bettering relations with communist governments than introverts, and thus officials would disagree with each other along these lines. He found that:

> In 78 percent of the cases involving issues of the use of force the difference along a personality dimension—everyday dominance of subordinates—is consistent with (and, interpersonal generalization theory would argue, explains) the observed direction of policy disagreemtnt. In 84.6 percent of the cases involving . . . initiatives toward the Soviet Union or Soviet bloc the differences along a second personality dimension, extroversion, is consistent with (explains) the observed direction of policy disagreement.[16]

Like Barber, Etheredge pulls his two dimensions of personality into a typology that links personality to behavior in office.

TABLE 3–1

	Introvert	Extrovert
High Dominance (Reshape)	Bloc (Excluding) Leaders	World (Integrating) Leaders
Low Dominance (Persevere)	Maintainers	Conciliators

Bloc leaders hold strong moral views and see the world as divided accordingly: They try to reshape the world (dominate it) by leading their side against the forces of evil. World leaders are more pragmatic; they would dominate by including everyone, drawing nations together. Maintainers are overwhelmingly oriented toward sustaining the status quo. Conciliators are open to change, stressing negotiation and accommodation—such as the Adlai Stevensons of history.

One interesting aspect of personality is *flexibility* which is Holsti's target in his study of John Foster Dulles. Lawrence Falkowski has devised another way to study the flexibility of foreign policy officials.[17] He began by defining flexibility as readiness to change goals and policies and by reasoning that a flexible leader would be most likely to change after passing through a severe crisis that produced a serious failure. By examining crises and measuring shifts in officials' goals and policies in the wake of disaster, he found modest confirmation of his view that officials can learn from mistakes but that some officials have more flexible minds than others. This raises an interesting question: How did he measure something as slippery as flexibility? Or crisis?

One problem was how to ascertain officials' goals and policies. Falkowski decided to examine their public statements, in documents, for the six month periods before and after a crisis. But what is a crisis and when is the result a failure? Here he used the *New York Times* index. He defined a crisis as something aroused from abroad that was a big surprise, left little time for decision, and involved a serious threat to the United States. A surprise then became something the *Times* printed no stories about until the week before the crisis broke. A serious threat became something about which the *Times* carried at least three articles per day for a number of days. And a failure was when the editorials in the *Times* and four other leading papers said so. If 75 percent or more of those editorials said United States officials failed, then they failed.

To make "flexibility" more specific, i.e., to "operationalize" it, Falkowski broke down officials' public statements into *referents, goal themes,* and *policy themes.* A referent is an object cited. For example, if a president said: "As in Korea and Vietnam, we will fight to uphold our commitments," this contains two referents to foreign events. A goal theme is a statement of an objective ("peace in the Middle East"), and a policy theme is an expression of how to achieve the objective ("We support Arab-Israeli negotiations"). This enables Falkowski to measure changes in all three areas before and after a crisis. He tallied each, weighing changes in goals as most important, then changes in policies, with changes in referents as showing the least flexibility. This made it possible to weigh each official's flexibility, to give each a score compared to the others.

There were other hurdles to be cleared and we should be able to think of drawbacks to some of Falkowski's solutions to his problems, but these things need not concern us. The point here was to give us a sense of how the research was conducted. As we can see, this sort of content analysis reveals interesting avenues of inquiry, but it is not something we should casually study. It is difficult work when properly done. On the other hand, many of the steps involved are not exotic and the reasoning behind those steps is not esoteric.

Decision Making

Holding high office means having to decide, often when the matter at hand is quite complex and the right thing to do is not at all clear. It would be nice to know how people make such decisions. Of course, studies of personality are designed in part to tell us this. Here we will look at attempts to characterize the nature of the *decision making process* itself, not things like character, flexibility, or the tendency to dominate.

In chapter 1 we considered the possibility that there was nothing special about international politics, that broader theories of behavior might well apply. Irving Janis suspects this is the case when it comes to decision making. For years Janis and Leon Mann, a fellow psychologist, have been studying decision processes, and they believe their conclusions pertain to decisions on everything from marriage to foreign policy.

Figure 3-1 displays the decision process as they see it.[18] Notice there are five stages, the first being when an important opportunity arises or information appears that a person's present course is wrong or harmful (i.e., smoking is bad for you). In stage 1 the risks of not changing are evaluated. Only if it is worthwhile to consider doing something new does the person move to stage 2. This is a crucial stage, because it is where decisions often go wrong. If the answer to question 2-2 is no, the person simply adopts that alternative and does not bother to consider others ("I'll just smoke less"). If he pushes on to question 2-3 and the answer is no, then defensive avoidance sets in ("lung cancer won't happen to me" or "what does the Surgeon General know") or other kinds of wishful thinking appear. If he gets to question 2-4 and the answer is no then the problem is hypervigilence (panic); the person grasps at straws, seizes anything ("I'll quit next month, for sure"). In all these cases the result is that stages 3 and 4 are very brief, and not many alternatives are seriously considered. Often unexpected costs and consequences emerge, making it hard to live with the decision (trying to smoke less is a constant struggle and soon you give in). Avoiding those traps is not easy but success leads to vigilence—their word for trying to learn as much as possible and thoughtfully weighing alternatives, which moves the person into stages 3 and 4. The result is a decision to which the person is strongly committed, and since it has been carefully considered it is more likely to turn out well.

To illustrate part of this theory Janis and Mann describe the behavior of Admiral Kimmel, commander-in-chief of the Pacific Fleet at Pearl Harbor in 1941. The admiral and his staff got caught in stage 2. In the fall of 1941 warnings of war and possible threats to the fleet steadily increased, becoming very ominous in early December. To have fully prepared for a possible attack would have been expensive and disruptive by halting training exercises, cancelling shore leaves, and increased patrolling. Nevertheless, Kimmel was worried and discussed his concerns with his aides. They all reassured each other via wishful thinking and downplaying the chances of an attack, rationalizing away information that conflicted with their expectations. They never really got past answering question 2-2, so even some simple steps to increase vigilence, such as more aerial surveillance, were not taken. On 7 December the Japanese caught the base by surprise, killing over 2000 servicemen, and the admiral's career sank with his fleet.

Alexander George has also tried to characterize the decision making process of foreign policy officials, in terms that often closely resemble those of Janis and Mann.[19] George emphasizes that foreign policy decisions often pose problems of value complexity, where several important goals are in conflict, and uncertainty. Officials can respond by either carefully analyzing their problems or defensively coping with them. Under the latter he points out that officials often ignore or downgrade value conflicts, preferring to believe they can have their cake and eat it too. They may procrastinate and by not knowing what to do, they do nothing. Sometimes they panic. They are also given to bolstering, wherein they consider various options but they inflate the probable results of the one they most agree upon and similarly exaggerate the risks and costs of the ones they do not like.

George sees decision makers as often trapped by routine intellectual and perceptual errors in working through their problems. One is an overemphasis on situational variables to explain/justify their actions ("We really do not have any choice under the circumstances"), but on dispositional variables to analyze other governments' actions ("They had lots of choices; the one they picked therefore indicates their hostile intent" or "We did what we had to do, it is up to them to choose whether there is trouble or not"). The same thing happens in evaluating outcomes. If a previous decision turned out well then it is because *we* did the right thing, if it turns out badly it's because of forces beyond *our* control. Then there is the tendency for officials to think facts are more important than theory, ignoring their tendency to use simple rules of thumb and failing to be aware that they are operating with theoretical premises which they are barely aware of and which should be carefully examined.

FIGURE 3-1
Janis-Mann Decision-Making

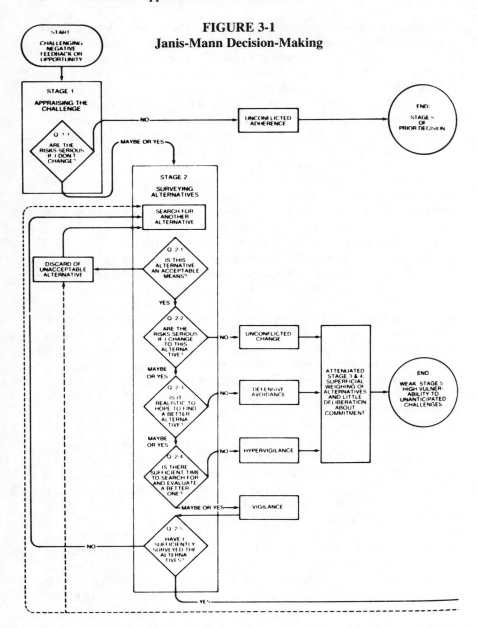

FIGURE 3-1 (Continued)

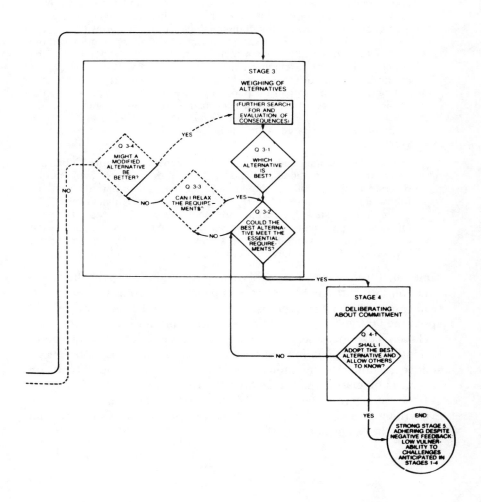

Like George, Janis and Mann point out that individuals are usually reluctant to make difficult decisions. Having to do so arouses anxiety and stress, and decision-makers face other sources of stress as well. How does stress affect decision making? One of the more interesting ways of trying to grapple with this question is to apply laboratory observations about human behavior to analysis of the actions of officials, drawing on the finding of experimental psychology.

Here is a description of one experiment where the subject was the effect of stress on problem-solving. The participants had to be carefully selected, and you will see why if you imagine your own reactions to the test situation.

> A solitary soldier was stationed in a remote bunker. While his comrades were wiring in some explosives in a nearby canyon, he was instructed to complete the wiring of a remote control circuit and then to throw a switch to put the circuit into the line. The instructions were slightly ambiguous. When the soldier completed the wiring and threw the switch, an explosion rocked the bunker. In a moment, an intercom informed the soldier that someone had been badly hurt. The only way aid could be summoned was by a telephone in the control cabin. When the soldier attempted to call for aid he found that the phone was dead! Instructions telling what to do to repair the phone were available on the phone. As the soldier completed each step in the instructions, an automatic device timed his problem-solving. . . . The behavior of the soldier in this stress situation was compared with the behavior of soldiers in two control groups. . . .
>
> In the experimental condition, the soldiers repeatedly ignored a placard on the front of the phone that specified that if the operator could not be reached a circuit failure should be assumed, and repair instructions followed. They continued to try to get the operator, usually until the intercom suggested that perhaps the phone was out of order. The time taken to begin repairs was significantly longer than for soldiers in the control groups. Evidently, in the stress condition, the men could not bring themselves to believe a fact with such dire implications.

Time taken to make the repairs was consistently longer in the stress situation. Soldiers tried to get screws out without using a screw driver readily available. They kept losing their concentration as they thought about the injuries or their possible responsibility for the accident.

Having described this experiment, Joseph de Rivera then turned to real international situations where great stress seems to have produced similar results. He mentions the effects of stress and fatigue on American officials in the Cuban Missile Crisis, and notes that in August 1914 as tension mounted Kaiser Wilhelm began to misread cables, see everything as a sign of others' hidden hostility toward Germany, and display other signs of panic.[20]

Here we see one of the greatest attractions of this approach. We think stress must affect decision makers but we cannot very well experiment on them to find out how: "How can we give a Taylor Manifest–Anxiety Scale to Khrushchev during the Hungarian revolt, a Semantic-Differential to Chiang Kai-shek while Quemoy is being shelled, or simply interview Kennedy during the Cuban missile crisis?"[21] What we can do is substitute experiments with non-officials in what we think are sufficiently comparable situations?

Perception

In various ways many of the preceding approaches are concerned with perception. Studies of personality seek an appreciation of how someone "saw" the world. One way stress can affect behavior is by skewing perceptions. Many traps in stage 2 of the Janis-Mann diagram involve distorted perceptions. But perception is so personal that to study it almost means getting inside another's mind, which is a lot easier in science fiction than in social science.

Once again we may turn to experimental findings in psychology for help. Here is Joseph de Rivera's discussion of how one's beliefs can distort perceptions. He first reviews an experiment by a colleague:

> He took a detective story, cut out every couple of sentences, pasted them on cardboard, then mixed up the sentences in a box with sentences from the other stories. Persons participating in the experiment were told that a crime had been committed and that they should use the box of information to find out about the crime and who was responsible. Each person was given five assistants . . . almost every person began by having his assistants go through the sentences to find clues. As soon as information of interest was reported, the leader began to form a hypothesis that controlled the next step of the search process. . . .After half an hour of search . . . an objective test was given to all the participants to determine how much information they knew.
>
> Two important results were obtained. First, it was established that the average assistant knew more facts than the average person directing a search operation. Second, it was discovered that the only way to have the leader correctly determine the crime was to prevent him from forming hypotheses until many pieces of information were in his possession.
>
> What was happening is evident. A person would form an idea of the state of affairs on the basis of a little information. Once he had this idea, it was almost impossible to change it because it governed his perception of future information.

We have returned to the idea that people see what they expect to see. De Rivera's next step was applying the results in an analysis of a real international situation. During the early stages of the Korean War there were fears of Chinese intervention, and as United Nations troops pushed toward the border between China and North Korea there were warnings from Peking and even preliminary clashes with Chinese troops. Yet prior to the massive Chinese attacks, United States intelligence in Korea concluded that Chinese intervention was most unlikely!

> As in Bavelas' demonstration, the Far Eastern Commander's chief intelligence officer interpreted all information in the light of his belief that it was a bad time for the Chinese to intervene. When aerial reconnaisance failed to find masses of Chinese troops, he took this as evidence supporting his hypothesis and did not worry about the possibility that the masses of troops were well hidden in small groups. As in Bavelas' demonstrations, men in the field had a much better idea of the actual situation. For example, the Commander of the Marines in the field was so worried at this ignoring of Chinese strength that he wrote the Marine Commandant in Washington, constructed an airfield in case emergency evacuation was necessary, and delayed carrying out orders to move forward. He thereby avoided a trap and managed to evacuate the bulk of his troops.[22]

I have used de Rivera's own account so you can see the exact procedure. Note that it involves extrapolating from the behavior of individuals in an experiment to explain the behavior of decision-makers in a real situation. Obviously to do this on a large scale the scholar must become intimately familiar with both international politics and psychology, an onerous task. Robert Jervis has mounted just such an effort, which has resulted in an exceedingly important book.[23] Jervis identifies a number of standard cognitive processes and practices based on the findings in psychology. One is striving for consistency, the strong tendency for our beliefs and perceptions to become (or be made to seem) consistent. We are uncomfortable if some of the things we believe appear contradictory, or if we receive some information that clashes with our view of reality. This discomfort can be a good thing, leading us to develop new beliefs and theories. But a much easier way to deal with it is to ignore or downplay information we do not like, to assert that our views are perfectly consistent no matter what, to seek out only information that tells us we are right. Like Dulles, we twist information so it conforms to what we believe. Another common practice is one that Alexander George also mentions, which is the avoidance of value trade offs—again by manipulating arguments and information. Still another is seeing the behavior of others as consistent, planned, and rational. We are far more ready to understand that we make mistakes, and might be emotionally upset and act irrationally at times, than to assume this of others. Still another standard mistake is failing to see that the evidence which fits one's own view might be equally or more consistent with alternative views.

When Jervis turns to international politics he finds plenty of examples of similar patterns of (mis)perception at work. For instance, people who favor a policy frequently cite an abundance of logically independent reasons as if they were all connected. People who favored the test ban treaty in 1963 saw nuclear testing as dangerous to health, a source of international tension, and militarily useless. There was no need for all three to be true because they were not logically connected, but test ban supporters were sure of all three, while their opponents took the contrary view on each. Doing this allows us to ignore value trade offs and minimize the perceived costs of our policies. If we think testing is military useful, it is also nice to tell ourselves it is not a health hazard. Such mental maneuvers can convince us that the costs we will have to bear will not be much of a sacrifice after all. When the British discovered after World War I that they could not afford to keep a fleet in Singapore, which would leave the Empire in the Far East virtually defenseless, they rationalized that in case of trouble a fleet could always be sent out there. In the midst of World War II trouble did indeed arise from Japan, and when Britain had no ships to send the Empire was easily overrun.

Jervis finds that officials quite often overestimate the hostility of other governments and underestimate the degree to which their own statements and actions appear threatening to others. They are apt to be too confident that they understand what is going on, that they can influence or control situations that arise. They are too often preoccupied with their own plans, perspectives, and difficulties to develop any real understanding of how the world looks to others. Their settled perceptions are maintained by powerful cognitive mechanisms that resist discrepant information and discount alternative interpretations, and are most likely to change only when information that they are wrong arrives in an overwhelming way—such as when a disaster or near disaster occurs.

Jervis draws his examples from both ancient and modern history and from the behavior of officials all over the globe. His objective is a set of insights about perceptions and misperceptions by foreign policy officials *irrespective of their culture or political system,* because they are drawn from our growing knowledge about how the human mind itself works.

There are numerous other aspects of perceptions that have received a good deal of attention. While it is not necessary to review them here,

I do wish to mention one of interest. The United States sponsor and take part in numerous foreign exchange programs in the hope that increased international understanding will result, a hope shared by other governments and societies. However, interviews with participants and with those who come to the United States on their own to study or visit has uncovered the fact that the outcome is not always so sanguine. It seems that personal characteristics of the visitor, such as his relationship to his own country or his goals for the trip, as well as beliefs held before the trip on, say, the status Americans accord his country can affect the results. They can cause him to avoid contact with Americans, be defensive about his society and take home some rather nasty impressions of ours. In much the same way, it appears that foreign travel by American businessmen does not make them more cosmopolitan and less nationalistic, merely less parochially concerned about their business interests and more interested in American relations with the world as a whole.[24]

We should be alert to a final group of studies that at first glance appears to fall at this level of analysis but which are really extensions of theoretical analysis at a higher level. As a hypothetical example, we conclude from a survey of crises over the past 25 years that while the Defense Department regularly espouses a direct and forceful course of action the State Department usually urges caution and raises second thoughts. Suppose we want to know why this is so. Of the possible studies that might be carried out we decide to examine the personal qualities of recent secretaries of state and defense and, sure enough, we find the former have been people inclined to notice intangibles, to be cautious and hesitant and impressed by uncertainty and risks, while the latter have all been decisive managerial types who look for hard data, stress taking action, and confidently press for getting the job done. We have now developed an analysis at the individual level. But suppose, on further investigation, we find that presidents, their advisors, and congress always approach appointments to these two positions by seeking out just these kinds of people because the state calls for a diplomatic sort of person while defense is a tough managerial job. We have just shifted away from the individual level of analysis; what was first explained in terms of the nature of the individuals involved is now handled by reference to the way the larger political system makes appointments.

The example illustrates a number of points. First, the analyst often moves to the individual level of analysis to achieve a more complete understanding, in the sense of getting a better feel for more details. Second, if we do not watch it the fascinating details may obscure the existence of a simpler, neater explanation at a higher level of analysis. Finally, the line between analyses at different levels can be exceedingly thin, such as the one between the level discussed in this chapter and the one to follow. We have been interested here in studies that focus on individuals, but it is compelling to want to examine persons within a particular organizational or societal context. We want to know how stress affects people, but we are also likely to want to know how it influences a state department official or a Pentagon officer, a United States president or a Japanese prime minister, that is, someone with a particular role in a specific institution or society. After all, people do not act in a vacuum.

Further Comments on These Approaches

We will return to the list of questions set out at the end of chapter 2 and understand how asking such questions helps clarify the nature of the various approaches. We may skip the first two, on the level of analysis and the purpose of the theory. The third had to do with the general conception of man that is employed. Clearly at this level there are a number of alternatives. The standard biographer is quite likely to combine many of them, to believe that men are complex and imperfect, that human nature is but a modest guide to explaining our behavior in any given situation. This is what so often annoys the scientist about biographies: At one point the hero is depicted as moved by his personality, at another by his family and upbringing, at still another by his culture or his personal experiences as an adult, and so on.

The analyst drawing on cognitive psychology will most likely assume, with de Rivera, that the individual is "mercilessly affected by objective forces" such as the basic nature of perceptual processes. This is a more deterministic view of man. However, it lends itself both to the view that there is a distinctive human nature and to the belief that there is not. If people are completely the product of their social upbringing, then they are obviously determined by outside forces rather than inborn qualities. On the other hand, if we all respond to stress or other stimuli in some rather predictable ways and this is true cross-culturally, then that would satisfy most definitions of human nature.

The same duality can be found in biologically based approaches and those which draw upon clinical psychology. As we noted, it is possible to assert that the main lines of individuals' behavior are genetic in origin, a product of natural selection, so that human nature explains nearly everything. Or we can assume that our genetic endowment merely equips us with a range of capacities, but that how and when we draw on them, singly and in combination, is not predetermined. Similarly in clinical psychology some schools of thought have stressed innate or instinctual drives and predispositions which, when the child interacts with the world around it, molds its personality and shapes adult behavior. Yet the whole thrust of clinical psychology has been to enable individuals to understand and thereby gain more conscious control over themselves, so that a Hitler does not have to work out his inner conflicts through fantasies and urges that endanger us.

De Rivera himself did not subscribe to a completely deterministic model of man. He hoped studies of the psychological dimensions of foreign policy behavior would improve it because "it is obvious that a person can gain an additional degree of freedom by controlling the pertinent circumstances." Jervis and Alexander George express similar sentiments. Janis and Mann conclude their book with a discussion of how the information they present can be used to improve human decision making. Robert North suggests that all such studies can free us from "the limits and determinisms of the past." He uses flying as an analogy. Man was earthbound by the laws of the universe until knowledge revealed ways to use those laws to attain the freedom to fly. In this sense, freedom becomes a function of knowledge; the more we know the freer we are or can be.[25]

As to the question about the motivations of international actors, clearly analysts working at this level think that, to an important degree, states and other actors are extensions of the individuals who compose them. As to what motivates individuals there is little agreement. The number of possible factors that have somewhere been suggested and investigated as relevant is simply staggering. We have looked at only some of them in this chapter.

The fifth question referred to the degree to which international politics is considered unique. By and large, analysts at this level do not operate as if they are dealing with a very queer bird, and they cheerfully draw freely on other disciplines for theoretical ideas and methods of research. If one assumes that personal peculiarities are crucial, then international politics would be unique only in the sense that everything else is, and it depends on the individuals involved. Otherwise the biographer and historian relies pretty much on the same methods and techniques whether his subject is someone involved in international or domestic affairs. Ethologists see similarities in human aggression and group loyalty at all levels. Psychiatric analysis stresses very early childhood experiences and personality development, no matter if the child grows up to play a role in world politics or not.

Those who draw on clinical psychology readily extrapolate from experimental settings to international ones, though there is less of this than there used to be. Psychologists are now inclined to put more stress on the *context* within which psychological factors work, and this can mean that international politics has its unique elements that must be taken into account.

As to the types of information required by the approaches described in this chapter, we can say that they seek very detailed knowledge about the behavior, perceptions, and thought processes of individuals—either in order to develop a theory or in order to fully test the one that is being applied. This is an ambitious requirement and the quantities of information needed are simply enormous. Nor have theorists at this level had much success in limiting the relevant variables to make analysis more manageable, though people like Barber can be commended for making the effort.

This means that the methods employed, the subject of the last question in chapter 2, vary considerably, in keeping with the diversity of the information sought. We touched on some of these methods—interviewing, content analysis, animal studies, experiments, and retrospective psychoanalysis. Others include the working methods of the historian: oral history, scrutiny of documents, examinations of personal papers and even junk which are the things people and governments throw away.

Difficulties and Drawbacks

This chapter closes on a somewhat pessimistic note with a look at some of the drawbacks to analysis at this level. Some we have briefly reviewed, some will have occurred to you already, and others may be new. First, we tend to find people awfully complicated. Theorists at this level do too, which is a pity because theory is supposed to be parsimonious. We have plenty of factors that seem like they might be relevant, such as age, sex, health, personality, genetics, cognitive processes, and so on. If we could arrange it that a few factors explain most of what we want explained, that would be much better. But such factors often are turned up only at a higher level of analysis. It is difficult to generalize at this level because we are so sensitive to the myriads of factors involved. Consider the following argument as to personality variables:

> I suspect that they often will account for very little of the variance in any given outcome. My theoretical view—and there is little evidence for or

> against it—is that there will be considerable uniformity in the politically relevant attitudes of those involved in foreign policy roles . . . for policy-relevant predictions (but not for explanatory purposes), we can afford to "black box" the cognitive and effective elements.[26]

By "black boxing" it is meant treating people as interchangeable atoms, as cogs in a larger system. For a complete explanation we need to know what goes on in officials' minds. But if, in given positions and situations, they behave pretty much the same way this may be all we need to find out. An official's mind can be a black box we cannot see into; we cannot explain exactly why he does what he does, but do we really need to? The same argument can be applied to the idea that there is a human nature. If it is constant enough, if it is universal, we can black box it. In summary, investigation at this level can lead us to highlight the dissimilarities and complexities of individuals behavior, and starting where differences are most obvious can make it very difficult to see which ones are important and which ones we can safely ignore.

There are other difficulties. For example, whom do we study? Ordinary citizens? Civil servants and professional officers or diplomats? Politicians and elected officials? Are some people better placed to have an impact and, if so, can we confine our studies to them? The problem would be solved if we could assume all people are basically the same, but are they? Suppose someone is a politician precisely because he is different from the rest of us? Harold Lasswell suggested they *are* different in their psychological makeup from ordinary citizens. Many psychology experiments are performed on college freshmen but that may not tell us much about politicians.

The problem in applying the results of psychology experiments (or studies of animal behavior) to the behavior of decision makers is that we can end up assuming precisely what we should be trying to test. You can see what is missing if you look at what would be the ideal procedure:

1. Do the experiments
2. Do the same experiments with decision makers
3. Draw conclusions as to how good a guide the results of step 1 are for the findings in step 2
4. Use this as the basis for extrapolating from experimental results in the future

What is often missing is step 2. In fact we experiment and extrapolate precisely because we cannot easily conduct step 2. (We study animals as a way to get around some of the difficulties of studying people.) This ought to make us cautious in our conclusions but things do not always result in this manner. Also, selecting the real-life events to which experimental results apply, or the events which findings from biological studies are used to explain, is not always done with care. That the two are parallel is often simply assumed. It is all too easy to poke around in the history of international politics to find examples that fit the assumption.

Thus we must not dismiss too lightly the often-voiced argument that there is something distinctive about politics or about international politics. Kenneth Waltz finds that psychologists and arthropologists in the 1940s and 1950s came up with suggestions on how to end war that were so simple-minded, more so worse than useless, i.e. positively harmful, because they knew a good deal about their own subjects but next to nothing about politics.[27] It could be that only certain types of people go into politics, or that politics has its unique imperatives, dynamics, and limitations. A third possibility would be that the milieu of the politician acts as a screen which sifts out all but a few kinds of people. For example, most people consciously or unconsciously would like to avoid stress. What are we to make of people who deliberately seek positions where they will face important decisions under great stress? Does this mean they have a greater tolerance for stress? Are they attracted to it whereas we are inclined to turn away, or more rational under stress than average? If so, then the pressures of politics and the promotion ladder may act to eliminate those who cannot bear the heat before they ever get to the kitchen. The same may be true of health, both mental and physical. We all have health problems. What if high officials are people who differ from the rest of us because they more readily surmount or ignore such problems by force of concentration or will or desire and ambition? Would the same qualities also affect their decision making and behavior in office?

Next there is the problem of generalizing cross-culturally. As in the field as a whole, the bulk of the studies reviewed here have been done in the Western world, particularly in the United States. The individuals studied have been overwhelmingly the product of Western culture. Nor can we readily remedy this. Content analysis, interviews, and biography all require of the researcher an intimate familiarity with the language and culture of the subject. (I am not certain how one does psychobiographical analysis cross-culturally.) Communist countries are inaccessible for most such research. We think we know a great deal about the American side of the Cuban Missile Crisis but next to nothing about the Russian and Cuban experience.

It often seems that studies at this level require a certain amount and various types of information seldom available until long after the events, or careers, in question. The kind of study attempted by Waite or a definitive historical biography of someone currently holding, or recently departed from, high office is truly impossible. Some of the relevant information may be exceedingly difficult to pin down even years later, sometimes *because* it is years later.

The methods used at this level of analysis can also be challenged in various ways. We noted some of the complaints about biological approaches or about psychohistorical studies. Evaluating personalities is still a crude business at times. With content analysis, the vast amounts of information required and the tedious work involved often result in single-case analyses. The same is true elsewhere—we get a study of one leader, analysis of the outbreak of one war, or individual reactions to one crisis. Now the problems here are not insuperable, and often we have no choice but to proceed one case at a time. Still, there are obvious dangers: The one case may be unrepresentative, the conclusions reached may bias the way we look at future cases, or it can be difficult to ensure that cases are properly defined to facilitate comparison.

There are significant attempts to follow up, to test results from one study in other circumstances and to seek generalizations. But even then some difficult problems remain. Content analysis assumes our verbal behavior reflects with fair accuracy our inner thoughts and feelings. The same is true with interviewing (and of psychohistory). Yet each of us has experienced situations in which words failed us. And official speeches, testimony, letters, and other documents are most often a collective product. For example, aides submit ideas in draft language, other aides write successive versions, several people add last minute corrections, and the "author" may toss in impromptu alterations as the spirit moves him. Historians and others who work with such sources admit that they pose difficulties, particularly when it is impossible to fully recreate the content in which the communications took place.

The final argument to raise here leads into the next chapter. It can be asserted that politics, including international politics, is basically a group activity, dominated by the dynamics of the groups involved. From this perspective the individual is caught in a flow of powerful collective forces and does not have much of an impact on the way things are or are going to be. Frankel's reflections on his first day in office made the point admirably:

> The taste of power, or whatever it was I tasted that first day, went to my
> head too, but not quite as I had been warned it would. I had come into

the office with projects and plans. And I was caught in an irresistible movement of paper, meetings, ceremonies, crises, trivialities. There were uncleared paragraphs and cleared ones, and people waiting for me to tell them what my plans were, and people doing things that had nothing to do with my plans. I had moved into the middle of a flow of business that I hadn't started and wouldn't be able to stop. There were people in place to handle this flow, and established machinery in operation to help me deal with it. The entire system was at my disposal. In a word, I had power and power had me.[28]

Notes

1. Kenneth Waltz, *Man, The State and War* (Columbia University Press, 1959) p. 29.
2. Ernest LeFever, "The Limits of 'Hard" and 'Soft' Research in Foreign Policy," in Norman Palmer, ed., *A Design for International Relations Research: Scope, Theory, Methods, and Relevance,* Monograph 10 (American Academy of Political and Social Science, October 1970), p. 203.
3. Quoted in Hugh Sidey, "An International Natural Resource," *Time* (February 4, 1974), p. 24.
4. Barbara Tuchman, *Stillwell and the American Experience in China* (New York: Macmillan, 1970).
5. Alexander and Juliette George, *Woodrow Wilson and Colonel House, A Personality Study* (Day, 1956). A critique of their approach that offers an alternative interpretation of Wilson's psychohistory is Robert C. Tucker, "The George Wilson Reexamined: An Essay on Psychobiography," *American Political Science Review* (June 1977), pp. 606-18.
6. Robert G. L. Waite, *The Psychopathic God, Adolph Hitler* (Basic Books, 1977), p. xvii.
7. Hugh L'Etang, *The Pathology of Leadership* (Hawthorne Books, 1970).
8. Charles Frankel, *High on Foggy Bottom* (New York: Harper and Row, 1968), p. 218.
9. Ole Holsti, "The Belief System and National Images: A Case Study," *The Journal of Conflict Resolution* vol. 6, no. 3, pp. 244-52.
10. Robert Isaak, *Individuals and World Politics* (Duxbury Press, 1975), pp. 3-19.
11. For examples of this work see Dina Zinnes, "The Expression and Perception of Hostility in Prewar Crisis: 1914," and Ole Holsti et al., "Perception and Action in the 1914 Crisis," in J. David Singer, ed., *Quantitative International Politics: Insights and Evidence* (Free Press, 1968), pp. 85-158. Further studies are listed and nicely summarized in Michael Sullivan, *International Relations: Theories and Evidence* (Englewood Cliffs, N.J.: Prentice-Hall, 1976), pp. 53-58.
12. For a list of such propositions see Charles Kegley, Jr. and Eugene Wittkopf, *American Foreign Policy: Pattern and Process,* 2d ed. (New York: St. Martin's Press, 1982), pp. 513-14. Also relevant is the discussion on pp. 540-43. For another list see Margaret Hermann, "When Leader Personality Will Affect Foreign Policy: Some Propositions" in James Rosenau, ed., *In Search of Global Patterns* (New York: Free Press, 1976), pp. 326-60.

13. Quoted in Richard Morris, *Evolution and Human Nature* (New York: Avon Books, 1983), pp. 77-78.
14. Konrad Lorenz, *An Aggression* (New York: Harcourt Brace Jovanovich, 1966).
15. James Barber, *The Presidential Character* (Englewood Cliffs, N.J.: Prentice-Hall, 1972). The best critical evaluation of the book is the lengthy review essay by Alexander George, "Assessing Presidential Character," *World Politics* (January 1974), pp. 234-82.
16. Lloyd Etheredge, "Personality Effects on American Foreign Policy, 1898-1968: A Test of Interpersonal Generalization Theory," *American Political Science Review* (June 1978), pp. 434-51. The long quotation is on pp. 446-47, and the typology in Table 3-1 is modified from his version on p. 449.
17. Lawrence Falkowski, *Presidents, Secretaries of State, and Crises in U.S. Foreign Relations: A Model and Predictive Analysis* (Boulder, Colo.: Westview Press, 1978).
18. Irving Janis and Leon Mann, *Decision Making* (New York: Free Press, 1977) pp. 190-91.
19. Alexander George, *Presidential Decision Making in Foreign Policy: The Effective Use of Information and Advice* (Boulder, Colo.: Westview, 1980).
20. Joseph de Rivera, *The Psychological Dimension of Foreign Policy* (Charles E. Merrill, 1968), pp. 151-54.
21. Richard Brody, "The Study of International Politics Qua Science," in Klaus Knorr and James Rosenau, eds., *Contending Approaches to International Politics* (Princeton University Press, 1969), p. 116.
22. de Rivera, pp. 54-56.
23. Robert Jervis, *Perception and Misperception in International Politics* (Princeton University Press, 1976).
24. Studies on these matters: Peter Grothe, "Swedish and Norwegian Attitudes Towards the United States," *Cooperation and Conflict*, no. 3, 1976, pp. 183-200; Ithiel de Sola Pool, "Effects of Cross-National Contact on National and International Images," and Anita Mishler, "Personal Contact in International Exchanges," in Herbert Kelman, ed., *International Behavior* (Holt, Rinehart and Winston, 1965), pp. 106-29, 550-61; Margaret Cormack, "American Students in India: Ambassadors or Cultural Polluters?" *International Studies Quarterly* (September 1973), pp. 337-57.
25. See de Rivera, p. 5; and Robert North's discussion in Palmer, pp. 118-20. The same view is ascribed to Kenneth Boulding in Cynthia Kerman, *Creative Tension: The Life and Thought of Kennth Boulding* (University of Michigan Press, 1974), p. 17
26. J. David Singer comment in Palmer, p. 181.
27. Waltz, pp. 42-79.
28. Frankel, pp. 5-6.

Bibliographical Remarks

There are numerous works bearing on the application of psychology to the study of international politics. Donald Sylvan and Steve Chan, *Foreign Policy Decision Making: Perception, Cognition, and Artificial Intelligence* (New York: Praeger, 1984) contains articles that are significant studies and which also cite much of the significant work that has been done on perception, personality, cognitive processes, and related factors as they affect officials' foreign policy behavior. Christer Jönsson, "Introduction: Cognitive Approaches to International Politics," in Jönsson, ed., *Cognitive Dynamics and International Politics* (New York: St. Martin's Press, 1982) also reviews numerous cognition-oriented approaches as they can be applied at several levels of analysis. The book contains articles that cover both individual and higher level-of-analysis research.

Other relevant works include Lawrence Falkowski, ed., *Psychological Models in International Politics* (Boulder, Colo.: Westview, 1979); Ralph Pettman, *Human Behavior and World Politics* (New York: St. Martin's Press, 1975); and Miriam Steiner, "The Search For Order in a Disorderly World: Worldviews and Prescriptive Decision Paradigms," *International Organization* (Summer 1983), pp. 373-413, which uses brief case studies of individual leaders to outline a psychology-based alternative to conceptions of rational decision-making.

An older approach which has been receiving renewed attention is the idea that officials have an "operational code" which affects their behavior and which can be detected. It is discussed in the Jönsson book cited above in Gunnar Sjöblom, "Some Problems of the Operational Code Approach," pp. 37-74, and Ole Holsti, "The Operational Code Approach: Problems and Some Solutions," pp. 75-90. An interesting attempt to construct the cognitive world, and thus the operational code, of Chinese decision-makers, and which contains a good review of alternative approaches is Davis Bobrow et al., *Understanding Foreign Policy Decisions: The Chinese Case* (New York: Free Press, 1979). A final example is Stephen Walker, "The Motivational Foundations of Political Belief Systems: A Re-analysis of the Operational Code Construct," *International Studies Quarterly* (June 1983), pp. 179-201.

An example of how psychology can be used as a basis for offering analysis and advice on a major issue is the work of Ralph White over the years on U.S.-Soviet relations. See for instance, Ralph White, *Fearful Warriors: A Psychological Profile of U.S.-Soviet Relations* (New York: Free Press, 1984).

The book by Ralph Pettman cited above is one of several which lump psychological and biological approaches together for purposes of discussion. Another place where the two are taken up together is Gerald Hopple, ed., *Biopolitics, Political Psychology and International Politics* (New York: St. Martin's Press, 1982). A recent effort to lay the basis for research into the effects of drugs on the behavior of officials is Roy Lubit and Bruce Russett, "The Effects of Drugs on Decision-Making," *Journal of Conflict Resolution* (March 1984), pp. 85-102.

4

What Can Just One Person Do?

In this chapter we move up a rung on the level-of-analysis ladder. This takes us to studies interested less in individuals than in groups, less in the peculiarities of persons than in their patterned behavior in social interaction. From here on, the emphasis is on forces larger than the individual and his particular gifts and limitations. Some analysts even assert that nearly all human activity can be explained by reference to group behavior. However, most believe the influence of these factors is just important enough to be worthy of study, not that it ought to be the only subject of investigation.

In the last chapter we broached the idea that in the end everything comes down to individuals. If this idea seemed familiar and attractive, it may be surprising to recall how often we entertain an entirely different assumption. When people commit crimes, particularly those trapped in ghettos and poverty, is the society at least partly to blame? If someone answers yes, he must feel he knows something about the individuals involved even though he is not personally acquainted with them; he assumes that they are partly a product of their social environment. Is voting the result of the individual's conscious choice? Well, we can make reasonably good predictions about how a person will vote if we know his income, race, level of education, religion, and how his parents voted. We are all to some extent what someone or something else has made us.

Now consider these examples. Suppose the president appointed a panel to report on the dangers of smoking, a group composed of one vice-president from each of the tobacco companies. An observer would probably mumble (or shout) something about a "whitewash." Would the conclusions of university researchers be more reliable on smoking than those of researchers who work for the tobacco industry? The problem here is not that the people involved are manipulated by social forces beyond their awareness and control. Rather it is that belonging to a particular group or organization brings with it certain commitments, interests, and perspectives, and we expect a member will act in accordance with them. If State Department officials think and act in a distinctive fashion, their doing so doesn't surprise us, for we expect the State Department's ways of seeing and doing things to be reflected in the behavior of its members. Whether the officials conform deliberately or involuntarily, the focal point of our analysis can then be the department rather than the particular individuals involved.

This approach gives us the following reasons for studying groups. One is that, as mentioned at the end of chapter 3, politics and government look awfully collective in nature—to get anything decided and done takes organization (parties, bureaucracies, interest groups) and coalition building (to win elections, pass legislation), collective decision making (in a cabinet, the Politburo, a committee) and organized implementation. Next, groups often appear to be the agents of interests and demands—what people want out of foreign policy depends on the groups (elites, classes, interest groups, bureaucracies) to which they belong. Finally, groups seem to be powerful agents in shaping learning, perception, and communication—who we talk to, what we read, how we see things, what we think.

At this point, I hope, the reader's eyebrows are up a bit, and he or she is ready to pounce and cry "gotcha!" If alert, the reader will have noticed that a good many of the approaches covered in chapter 3 study individuals precisely by sorting them into groups. After all, what was Barber doing if not classifying presidents in terms of personality? Waite analyzed Hitler's career by applying insights developed in studying the group (labeled "borderline personality") with Hitler's type of personality disorder. Using cognitive psychology or evolution to discuss perceptions of officials or their reaction to stress means saying we know something about them because they belong to the group called "human beings." This being the case, where is the difference between what is discussed here and what was discussed there (and why is it necessary to put up with reading this chapter too)?

I will admit I have been "got," at least up to a point. There is some overlap between many individual-level approaches and work at the group level. The difference between analyses at these two levels may have little to do with whether, for purposes of study, people are classified into groups. However, there is a difference and it is this: the group-level analyses discussed here are almost always concerned with groups that are self-conscious; the group is aware of its existence, and so are most or all of its members, and normally it has an organized expression of that existence. The same is not true of psychopaths nor of Barber's "active-negative" presidents; sadly, it is seldom true of the group called "human beings." But it is quite true of the Politburo or an interest group or the State Department of the West German Christian

Democrats. This is not to say that the impact of the group occurs entirely on the conscious level, just that the group and its members know it exists and that, at least on some matters, they act collectively. Self-conscious groups do not have to be created in the mind of the analyst; they already exist, and the object is to use that fact in devising explanations.

The key steps in a group level of analysis are as follows: (1) identify a self-conscious group and describe its characteristics; (2) show that the group displays one or more standard patterns of behavior with respect to some aspect of foreign affairs; (3) show that these patterns of behavior have a significant impact on foreign affairs; and (4) explain (2) and (3) by means of a theory. The first two steps are easier than the last two. As might be suspected, investigation of groups and internal group processes as they bear on foreign affairs is a complicated business. Once again I should emphasize that my readers are getting a sample of various approaches; I am leaving it to them to follow up on whatever they find interesting.

Groups inside a Government
Small Groups

Ignoring traditional wisdom, we will start by thinking small. Much of the business of any government, even the largest ones, is conducted in small, often intimate, groups. These are rarely more than fifteen to twenty members in size. The Soviet Politburo varies from ten to fifteen members; the U.S. Supreme Court has nine; the National Security Council has four statutory members (and two statutory advisers); many interdepartmental committees are three to five in size. Ad hoc groups formed to deal with emergencies tend to number no more than fifteen and are often smaller than that. A very large cabinet or board will usually have a formal or informal "executive committee" that really runs things. Conspiracies to overthrow governments are also organized by small groups, and it is not uncommon to find a handful of people (hidden communists, outside agitators) blamed for disasters or failures.

Thus, it is only natural that someone would decide to examine small-group behavior in order to gain insights into international politics. Consider for a moment the matter of group size. As to maximize size, there is an inevitable limit if each member is to have a reasonable opportunity to participate in the discussion. The more complex the matter at hand, the more impractical to have any sizable numbers of people involved. In a harried government, size is also limited by the simple matter of schedules: the more people invited, the more difficult it will be to find a date open on everyone's calendar. Finally, the purpose of a meeting can influence its size. To let enough people in on a decision and the reasons for it so that a sufficient consensus can be generated to carry it through may call for a fair-sized gathering. But if the purpose is to allow individuals to develop a certain rapport and intimacy, nothing much will be achieved by meeting in a group of a hundred. During wartime summit conferences Churchill, Stalin, and Roosevelt would often take each other aside or meet apart from their aides so as to get the size of the group down to the proper level for exchanging confidences. In the negotiations on intermediate-range nuclear weapons in 1982-83, at one point the American and Soviet chief negotiators went for a "walk in the woods" so the two of them could draw up a very sensitive draft agreement out of earshot of their negotiating teams (and even their own governments!).

Other elements in small-group dynamics hold potential interest for students of international politics. Joseph de Rivera notes that one important official was not invited to several crucial meetings on the U.S. decision to intervene in Korea in 1950. To explain why, he cites studies on the way a group rejects a deviant. In one case the experimenter introduced into groups discussing juvenile deliquency a person instructed in advance to disagree with the majority's conclusions, and then asked each member afterward to list those who should be included for the next meeting. Normally the deviant was excluded. Early in the Reagan administration, the secretary of state strongly disagreed with the secretary of defense at a National Security Council session on an arms-control issue. Asked by a White House aide after the meeting to spell out the Pentagon's position in a memo, the secretary of defense added the suggestion that he and the aide meet with the president to go over it (just a helpful review, of course—no need to invite the Secretary of State).

De Rivera concludes that excluding a deviant can homogenize discussion and that therefore a good group leader is one with the ability to tolerate and use a deviant member creatively. Others hold the same view: pressures for consensus must not be allowed to corrupt the decision process by excluding uncomfortable, but possibly correct, views. But there is another side to this issue. The pressure for consensus in a small group can also be used by a skillful dissenter to force a group to accept much of his position if agreement is to be reached, even though the agreement would not reflect the views of most members. Richard Perle, an assistant secretary of defense, used this tactic repeatedly in struggles inside the Reagan administration over the stance to adopt in arms-control negotiations. So at one point when a high-level working group was set up by the White House, Perle was carefully excluded in favor of his superior, who was even asked not to tell Perle the meetings were taking place. And at another point, Perle's counterpart in the State Department carefully arranged to meet with the Joint Chiefs of Staff—who are, after all, very much a part of the Defense Department—without any word to the assistant secretary of defense.[1]

Analysts have frequently drawn on evidence from experiments or historical examples to analyze other facets of group discussions. For instance, communication and decision in a group can be heavily influenced by the relative "status" of its members—lieutenants are unlikely to challenge the opinions of generals, no matter how ill-advised these opinions may be. Presidents have sometimes deliberately not attended meetings of the National Security Council or other high-level bodies because, as various analysts have noted, just a whiff of the way the president is leaning on an issue can paralyze further expression of the opposite view. President Nixon sometimes sat through meetings where a firm consensus was reached and then called each of the participants separately to hear their exact, and often different, views. Findings about these matters have been used not only to explain how foreign policy decisions are made, but how they might be improved.

This is a major concern in the literature on intelligence. How are high-level officials to be kept from forcing intelligence analysts to write assessments of what is going on that reflect the officials' views? Israeli investigations into how that government was caught by the surprise Arab attack in October 1973 concluded that high officials were so certain the Arabs could not and would not attack that lower-level military and intelligence people could not get a fair hearing of their evidence that an attack was quite likely. At one point in the Nixon administration Secretary of Defense Laird was publicly charging the Soviet SS-9 missile was designed to be a first-strike weapon. Confronted with an intelligence report indicating that it was not, Laird insisted that the report be rewritten. In other words, inside a government what is taken as true for purposes of decision making is often determined by the power and status of who said it.

The preceding chapter referred to the behavior of individuals under stress. Studies of small groups under stress have also been conducted. Whereas stress in isolated individuals may lead to heightened aggression, neurotic behavior, and the like, in groups it often results in the members' becoming "less argumentative and aggressive, and more cooperative and friendly."[2] Numerous commentators have pointed out that American foreign policy often seems creative only in a crisis. Some have suggested that presidents, realizing this, sometimes deliberately let certain matters reach crisis proportions before attempting to deal with them. Only in this way can they get the necessary group cohesiveness and solidarity so that when they venture into uncharted waters with the ship of state everyone is pulling in the same direction on the oars.

Another example of using psychology research to illuminate the behavior of small groups under stress concludes that many heads are not always better than one. Irving Janis insists, "Groups can bring out the worst as well as the best in man."[3] Janis feels he has put his analytical finger on certain processes that can arise within a small group facing major policy decisions, particularly in a crisis. He calls these processes "groupthink." Its central element is a strong cohesiveness, a team spirit that helps the group convince itself it is doing the right thing and allows members to live with a decision that calls for doing terrible things—for example, resorting to force in connection with which others will be killed or maimed. To sustain and benefit from this group cohesion, each member submerges doubts and second thoughts, and a member who does not is subject to strong disapproval for not "getting on board" and may even be excluded from future sessions. Thus emerges a false but very comforting unanimity based on the feeling that the group is undoubtedly correct, is inherently moral in its decisions, is clearly better informed than outsiders, has all the relevant information, and has picked the best possible course of action. Information that clashes with this perspective is discounted or ignored; a member may even arrange that the others do not have to be bothered with it by screening it out.

Janis uses groupthink to explain why otherwise able, intelligent, and responsible officials soberly authorized the Bay of Pigs invasion in 1961, a fiasco so complete it would be laughable if lives had not been lost. He feels the same processes were probably at work in the repeated American escalations of the Vietnam War and other foreign policy disasters, and he also has used groupthink to analyze the Watergate affair that led to President Nixon's downfall. As possible candidates in other nations' foreign policy decision making, one might suggest the invasion of the Falkland Islands by Argentina or the Israeli invasion of Lebanon.

Groupthink is a variant of an intriguing phenomenon known as the "risky shift." For years studies found that under certain circumstances groups were more likely than individuals to adopt a risky course of action—that in fact a group might well adopt a course riskier than almost any of its members would choose on his or her own. This finding suggested governments might well be inclined to take too many chances—not a pleasant thought in the nuclear age. But further research, across many governments and cultures, has suggested that on very important decisions the reverse is usually true.

This finding is much more in keeping with common knowledge about one sort of small group, the committee. A major difficulty in making foreign policy is coordination. It is not just a matter of the government's letting its right hand know what its left hand is up to, because the government always has at least ten or twenty hands (and a few feet) going at once. It is a matter of getting all the various agencies involved in any particular problem to agree on just what to do and how to do it. Consensus is critical if there is to be much in the way of effective action.

Coordination also bears on the problems of timing and time. Harassed officials who spend their days putting out fires must somehow get to where they can look ahead, spotting problems before they mushroom into crises and considering solutions while there are still options, before the government is committed and there is no time to try something else. Late in the fourth quarter and ten points down is not the best place to work out a brand-new play.

A possible solution is the use of committees. The trouble is that committees tend to coordinate by compromise, which leads to government at the lowest common denominator. Not much room for creative thinking, new ideas, or taking risks can then exist. Foreign policy becomes whatever the government can agree upon. President Kennedy once responded to a visitor's proposal by saying, "That's a first-rate idea. Now we must see whether we can get the government to accept it." Henry Kissinger's solution was to set the regular agencies and committees to spinning their wheels in one direction, while President Nixon and he (plus a few trusted aides) took the country in another. Of course, once a policy is accepted it inevitably involves several agencies in its implementation—a fact that means, of course, more committees!

This can be a particularly serious problem in the business of intelligence analysis. Suppose the U.S. intelligence agencies disagree about how to interpret a potentially serious situation, as they often do, and a committee is used to arrive at the final estimate. One or another of the agencies probably has an accurate view, but it is most unlikely that a compromise of all their views is correct. The reader can appreciate the drawbacks in doing things this way if he imagines himself as a patient talking with the chief surgeon, who tells him that the surgical team members do not agree on what is wrong and how to fix it and so they are going to do the operation they were most able to agree on.

Organizational Dynamics

Many analysts are leery of accepting the idea that anyone is really in charge and running modern governments. Instead they favor an assumption that the elaborate machinery takes on a life of its own. To ask who was responsible for U.S. actions in Vietnam or who directs Soviet actions in Afghanistan is in this view to miss the point, because in many respects the making of foreign policy is mindless. Policy and action emerge from the dynamics of particular organizations (the Pentagon or State Department, for example), or are shaped by the processes involved when bureaucratic agencies grapple for power, position, and influence. The bureaucracies control the perceptions and perspectives of their members, thus limiting flexibility and originality to such an extent that we readily equate bureaucracy with inertia. (Remember that in physics "inertia" refers not to the tendency of an object to be still, but to its tendency to keep on doing whatever it is doing). This outlook depicts bureaucracy as having more influence on events than individual officials do, and thus claims that

> the effect of top policy-makers' personalities . . . should not be dismissed, but at the same time one must recognize how little variance in diplomatic outcomes can be accounted for by these variables in the bureaucratized decision-making of the mid-twentieth century.[4]

Broadly speaking, we can identify two options at this point. The object of investigation can be bureaucracy in general or one bureaucracy in particular. That is, we may study the operations and interactions of large, complex organizations and apply the findings to, say, the State Department, or we can study the State Department. The former is by far the most attractive for purposes of theory. In line with this we will take up each option but give more attention to the first one.

It will not surprise anyone that when asked the central question— how do bureaucracies shape a government's foreign policy decisions and actions?—our scholars do not agree. Some adhere to an "organizational process" model, others to a "bureaucratic politics" model, and some to a combination of the two. You should keep in mind, as we move through this thicket, the following problems. First, in almost any decision and action, elements of both models can probably help to explain it, but whereas the two models are analytically distinct the evidence is often fuzzy: it can fit either model. The second problem is the very fact that the models are analytically distinct; they should not be used interchangeably or just lumped together, because they suggest quite different explanations of why governments do what they do.

The organizational process approach may be quickly summarized. A government consists of a set of organizations, which exist to perform various elaborate functions. The government's decisions and actions can be thought of as the outputs of these organizations. The bulk of an organization's work is routine, and by its very nature the organization develops and then follows standard operating procedures for doing almost everything, routines from which it very rarely departs. Among the consequences of this state of affairs are, first, that most actions of the government result from the set procedures and precedents of its organizations, the ideas and preferences of the highest officials notwithstanding. Cabinet secretaries, presidents, and prime ministers come and go, but business goes on as usual. Second, organizational routines are the major resource the decision makers have for taking action. If the organizations do not have a particular action in their repertoires, then it is unlikely to be taken: the problem will be twisted so that it fits what can be done, and not the other way around. Third, because of these governmental facts of life, organizations structure the situation within which decisions are made—including when and how it is perceived.

A variant of the organizational process model has been developed by John Steinbruner.[5] Usually called the "cybernetic paradigm," it uses analogies like the thermostat to explain how organizations and governments work. A thermostat has only a few things to do (order a heating system to turn on or off), and it does so by paying attention to just one piece of information from the environment, the room's temperature. Organizations (and each of their components) have a list of things to do, and in taking action they pay attention to only a few key kinds of information; that is, they monitor a small number of critical variables. Complex multifaceted problems are converted into routine repetitive responses by the process of parceling out pieces of each problem to different organizations and by the way each organization behaves. Steinbruner also links this process to the way people's minds work. Recall the discussion in the last chapter about cognitive consistency: we like our beliefs and perceptions neat and tidy, we screen out dissonant information and explanations, and so on. Steinbruner says this process leads individuals to develop simple conceptions of complex problems, to ignore a great deal of information and the careful weighing of options, to select standard answers, and to check on only a few indicators of how they are doing. Thus, people and the organizations they compose deal with the world in parallel fashion.

Obviously this conception of how governments act in world affairs leaves a pretty small role for individuals. Even the president or a cabinet member is best thought of as a powerful pest. He can disrupt the routines somewhat, shuffle people around a bit, or inject a few new ideas, but cannot fundamentally change the way in which things get done. Government looks not like a scalpel but like a blunt instrument, one often wielded in an essentially inertial fashion. This conception also leaves a rather small role for other governments. If governments are largely set in their ways and monitor the outside world in only a limited, routine fashion, no wonder they bump into and misunderstand each other so often!

Graham Allison used an organizational process model to offer one perspective on the Cuban Missile Crisis, such as why the Soviets built the missile sites exactly as they had in the Soviet Union—a modus operandi that made them much easier for Americans to spot. The Steinbruner model has been applied to the 1960s struggle over whether to develop a NATO Multilateral Nuclear Force and to study the development of the controversial F-111. James Fallows has described the development of the M-16 by organizational routines. People outside the government developed a light automatic rifle with a small bullet, because of studies showing that a large bullet to be used to hit a target at great distance was not necessary—that in modern war, rifles just are not used that way. The rifle worked well until the Army got hold of it, for the Army's standard operating procedures for designing rifles called for a heavy bullet for accuracy and stopping power at long range (information clashing with this view was ignored). By the time the Army was done, the M-16 had heavier bullets that made the recoil often jam the rifle—not a good situation in a firefight; men in Vietnam were killed as a result. Soldiers often threw their rifles away in disgust (the Viet Cong would not take them, either!), even sold the original rifles on the black market. The same sort of analysis has been used to explain how fighter aircraft have been developed, the inordinate scale of the Soviet defenses against bombers, or why the Soviet Union cannot mount a true blitzkrieg. Claire Sterling once wrote a blistering account of foreign aid in Nepal, stressing that all sorts of national (U.S., Soviet, Chinese, etc.) and international aid agencies were applying routine solutions to underdevelopment (building roads, clearing forests, developing lumber exports) that had dreadful ecological, and ultimately economic, consequences high in the Himalayas.[6]

We can also find this perspective in Charles Frankel's literate and sensitive depiction of life at the top of the State Department. Frankel points out that policy is one of a bureaucracy's established routines; it specifies what is to be done and the means to be used. As such it becomes the bureaucratic equivalent of property; to change policy is to take someone's property away. To expect marked initiative in this regard from the property holder is to ask the impossible. Frankel identifies this state of affairs as the source of the inertia—the "steady, unwitting resistance" to any new idea, which so often typifies government. In a ludicrous yet revealing example he depicts his encounter with the only frog in one of the State Department's backwater ponds:

> I recall an officer in the Department who was the government's specialist on an international agreement affecting tariffs on educational materials. The United States had signed the agreement, but, for sixteen years, had neglected to implement it by passing the legislation necessary. . . . The officer of which I speak had spent these years nourishing and guarding the agreement, answering people's questions about it and keeping the prospects for it alive. When I told him in my office one day that I had made a decision . . . to push hard to get the agreement finally implemented, I had a nervous moment or two. The ends of his mouth twitched; he tried to form words but couldn't. And then he poured out all the reasons why people would oppose the agreement and all the difficulties we would encounter in trying to get it implemented. As success in what he had for so long been trying to do loomed over the horizon, this gentleman began to look increasingly like a man about to see his ancestral home torn down to make way for a new turnpike . . . he understood the necessity but resented it; he was plainly worried about where he was going to live afterward. He had become accustomed to his place, alone with his agreement, suspended indefinitely between signature and final implementation.[7]

One of the implications of organizational process models is that even very costly errors may be difficult to correct. Men dying in Vietnam because of poorly designed M-16s did not move the Army ordnance people. On the western front in World War I generals persisted in frontal assaults that squandered men for minimal gain long after the futility of such operations should have been clear, while at sea it was next to impossible to break through routine thinking to develop the convoy system that sharply reduced losses to submarines.

The other model mentioned above is bureaucratic politics, and it too can be summarized briefly for our purposes. Once again governments are said to consist of a set of organizations. But the central idea is that government decisions are the outcome of elaborate political games. Each game exists because officials heading the various agencies disagree—they value different things, they have the competing interests of their agencies to represent, and they have varying perspectives because of their different positions. Each agency wants things: money, people, space to carry out their functions; a degree of autonomy to do what they exist to do; the ability to prevent other agencies from horning in on their functions; the opportunity to provide rewarding work, career mobility, and other things good for employee morale. And so officials try to shape government decisions accordingly. The pulling and hauling that results is the game. Each player brings his temperament, his skills, and his agency's resources, applying these to problems and issues as they arise. He judges which ones to fight hard and which to let pass, but some are unavoidable (such as the annual budget). Included in the game are time pressures, a lack of complete information, often limited options.

This model leaves more room for the qualities of participating individuals, but the emphasis is usually on the dynamics of groups and their interactions. Professor Allison has also applied this model to the Cuban Missile Crisis, and elements of it are central to the analysis offered in many recent works. We might briefly touch on one study of the early years of the U.S. missile program.[8] The United States had a good start on missile development after World War II, yet progress was so desultory that it was the Soviets who developed the first workable intercontinental missile, setting off the "missile gap" fears of the later 1950s. Why? The Air Force had a vested interest in flying bombers— that is what pilots wanted to do, how officers could best get ahead, how the Air Force saw itself. Missiles would have no pilots. In fact, they could replace planes, eliminating lots of pilots. They could even be treated as artillery fired from land or sea, largely eliminating the Air Force! Hence the Air Force strategy was to fight to control all missile development programs—keeping the Army and Navy out—but bring those programs along at a leisurely pace while continuing to push bombers as the nation's primary strategic force. The Air Force was eventually dislodged to make room for a crash program in missile development, by the ploy of setting up the program outside regular Air Force channels so that it had its own budget and reported directly to the Secretary of Defense. The Air Force was not converted, it was circumvented.

This example gives us an image of government as constantly torn from within as agencies vigorously compete, forming temporary alliances across departmental lines, leaking news items to win support or embarass rivals, hoarding and manipulating information within the government. It is the power each group can bring to bear in such activities that largely determines policy. Strobe Talbott has much of this in-fighting in his account of Reagan administration decision making on arms control; it has been regularly applied to interpret Soviet policymaking as well. It shows up in many descriptions of U.S. policymaking during the Vietnam War. For an earlier example, the first effort to create a peacetime intelligence agency was crushed when J. Edgar Hoover, who wanted no such rival to the FBI, leaked the whole idea to the press. There are as well bureaucratic politics analyses of foreign economic policy decision making.

Consider some of the implications. In the bureaucratic politics games, the president is just one player among many, and his chief opponents are, in fact, the leading officials he appointed to his administration. This view changes our sense of what the presidency is all about:

> Underneath our images of Presidents-in-boots, astride decisions, are the half-observed realities of Presidents-in-sneakers, stirrups in hand, trying to induce particular department heads, or congressmen, or senators to climb aboard.[9]

In addition, government decisions and actions will often emerge out of internal preoccupations and concerns, and will not be very well designed to cope with external situations; that is, governments are usually self-centered. Decisions and actions will reflect political compromise; they thus will often not be very rational and indeed may well be inconsistent with each other. This prevalence of compromise is also why the process of making foreign policy so often seems chaotic and leads to a government's giving off multiple, conflicting signals. The process is a noisy, hurly-burly scramble and cannot be orchestrated so as to appear neat and tidy. International politics then becomes, for purposes of analysis, interaction of the outcomes of bureaucratic politics within the various nations.

Now that we have laid out the two models, we must recall the earlier point that it can be difficult to decide which is relevant. The Air Force still pushes for manned bombers, and the B-1 debate has run on into the Reagan administration. Is this organizational inertia, or is it the self-interest of the Air Force in having planes to fly? That is hard to say. The answer is probably both, but it is difficult to know which is the more important and when.

On another point, in the United States several waves of attempted reform in the making of foreign policy have rested on hopes that tinkering with the organizational structure would clear up many problems, making planning effective, decision makers rational, and action smooth. The willingness of a president to pursue reform is perfectly understandable. How nice it would be if he could really control his own branch of the government! But these models suggest this is bound to be a somewhat futile exercise. Every president sooner or later declares war on leaks (Reagan included), but since leaks are part and parcel of bureaucratic politics, every president loses this battle. In recent years, analysts have argued for reforms with such bureaucratic facts of life in mind.

Turning from organizational dynamics in general, we now move to explorations of the inner workings of particular institutions. The starting point is the idea that a bureaucracy develops its own way of life, over and above that of the government it serves. Its members collectively take to looking at the world in a particular way; the institution begins to influence the duties and viewpoints of its members more strongly than their own personalities and preferences do.

Thus, it has long been asserted that the White House always has a distinctive atmosphere and a unique view of the world. Watergate opened this inner life to searing public exposure, and the consensus was that the institution can be so ingrown as to corrupt its occupants' hold on reality. The refusal of the White House to acknowledge bad news or accept well-founded criticism figures prominently in accounts of various presidencies—of Vietnam in the Johnson White House, of Iran in the Carter years, of how Europeans would react to Reagan efforts to force them out of assisting the building of a Soviet pipeline. Similar fears have been expressed about the Kremlin, especially since many high Soviet leaders have very little personal experience of the outside world.

What about other institutions? Allow me to ask how often one hears the phrase "military mind." It can only mean that people in the armed forces do not think like the rest of us. The reason could be that only certain kinds of people choose a military career, but it is commonly thought that the services themselves shape their members and align their thinking. In Washington this phenomenon is almost unanimously held to be true of the State Department; its image is perfectly reflected in the nickname "Foggy Bottom." Usually we disparage others who lack the good sense to think as we do, and so uncomplimentary phrases like "military mind" and "Foggy Bottom" are often used uncharitably. However, we need not dislike such institutions to take the underlying premise about the effects of bureaucracy seriously.

Such effects in State are a frequent subject of scorn. The scathing remarks of John Kenneth Galbraith while he served as ambassador to India are somewhat typical. He once wrote in a letter to the president:

If the State Department drives you crazy you might calm yourself by contemplating its effect on me. The other night I woke with a blissful feeling and discovered I had been dreaming that the whole Goddam place had burned down. I dozed off again hoping for a headline saying no survivors.[10]

Members of the Pentagon in the Reagan era soon became disenchanted with the State Department's effect on retired General Alexander Haig, who was serving as secretary of state. Said one: "Al's been taken over by the striped-pants types; he's been co-opted by the softies."[11] State has often been faulted for never coming up with new ideas, for not being able to complete its tasks quickly, for being resistant to change in policy or practices and unwilling to follow presidential orders. It has been described as so cautious, so determined to clear everything with anyone in the department who might remotely have an interest, that its "operating procedures [are] among the most complex of all federal agencies."[12] A favorite target is the language used by the department, the "public passive voice," in which nothing is ever definitely asserted by anyone in a fully authoritative way.

What causes all this? Organization theorists know that within every formal organization lives an informal one, an inner network of norms, ties, and relations that has much to do with how the organization functions. In State, studies have found that the informal norms severely curb interpersonal conflict; everyone is expected to keep his or her cool. Competitive, aggressive behavior is ruled out, conformity in (low profile) dress and conduct is imposed—a policy that makes State Department people appear bland to White House aides or cabinet and congressional people, for whom being competitive and abrasive can be a way of life. The Foreign Service officer must find a way to practice "tactful aggressiveness" to get ahead. This form of bureaucratic self-protection means avoiding initiatives that might provoke controversy. It is coupled with elitism, an attitude that the department's tasks are complex and its understanding unique, something not appreciated by outside critics. The "don't make waves" syndrome and disdain for outsiders' views make the department unresponsive to accusations of weakness and to new ideas.

But there is a "chicken and egg" question here. Which come first: department norms that iron out creativity and flexibility, or inflexible and cautious people who create and then reinforce those norms? Support for the former view can be found in assertions that the department became this way after the frightful intrusion of McCarthyism, which humiliated the Foreign Service, and in a study that interviewed over 250 Foreign Service officers and found they were extremely high in "flexibility and adaptability" in thinking and social behavior. This finding supports the view that these "professional diplomats work within a social milieu which induces conformist behavior." On the other hand, a study comparing attitudes and beliefs of Foreign Service and Pentagon officers concluded that differences seemed due to self-selection more than anything else; military offices were more conservative not because of the services but because more conservatives chose military careers.[13]

Work on the State Department has been duplicated by studies that tackle other institutions, incuding those in other societies, that are concerned with foreign affairs. We lack the space to consider them here and must turn from organizational dynamics to the effects of crisis on group behavior.

Crisis

There has long been speculation that decision making in a crisis is somehow different from decision making under normal circumstances. In the last chapter we noted kinds of studies interested in the effects of a crisis—or of conditions usually associated with a crisis, such as stress—on individuals. In turn, analysts have been intrigued by the possible effects of crisis on the behavior of groups, or the behavior inside groups, in making foreign policy. Groupthink is one example, although it is not intended to apply only to crisis situations. Although space will not permit any lengthy discussion, a few remarks might be in order.

Since a crisis is believed to affect other things, that is, group behavior, studies must proceed by defining "crisis." Doing so poses more difficulties than one might expect. The most widely used definition holds that a crisis is a situation that has emerged unexpectedly, poses a threat to important values, and appears to leave little time for decision (a high-threat, short-time surprise). However, the term "crisis" is often applied to events or situations in which only a high threat, or a high threat combined with one of the other two, is present; a "world food crisis" or trouble once again in the Middle East will not come as much of a surprise. By the same token, sometimes officials feel all the symptoms of a crisis when surprise and pressure for quick action exist but no very great threat is involved. For example, British officials had to face surprise and pressure as a result of the Argentine invasion of the Falklands, which was surely a crisis but certainly posed no grave threat to the nation.

This idea is important, because to study the impact of a crisis it is necessary to separate crisis from noncrisis decision making, if possible so as to compare the two. However, most research on crisis has involved careful study of single or multiple cases of crisis, and only occasionally have the findings been systematically lined up alongside what we think we know about "ordinary" decision making and action. This failure to compare findings and common knowledge limits our confidence in the findings. Also a problem is the fact that the findings about crisis are not entirely consistent. However, here are some examples of tentative conclusions or not fully tested hypotheses that can be found in various studies:

- In a crisis stress tends to improve group cohesiveness up to a point, beyond which it can produce panic, heighten acrimony, and even lead toward group disintegration.
- Crisis lead to small, ad hoc, group decision making.
- In a crisis the relevance of individual variables—personality, personal preferences, etc.—in affecting decisions is reduced.
- A crisis results in increased searches for information and a reduction/compression of the channels through which it passes to high officials.
- A crisis reduces (enhances) the degree to which rational decision making processes are employed by a group of decision makers.

As these examples are meant to suggest, the state of our knowledge about the effects of crisis on groups falls short of ideal. Perhaps this situation exists because there is no compelling theoretical reason why we should expect crisis to have a uniform impact; it seems at least plausible that the effects of crisis vary with the nature of a group of decision makers, the normal style of the group leader and of the group as a whole, the nature of the government, and so on.

Groups outside the Government

To this point we have been reviewing studies and findings on the kinds of groups, small or large, of which a government is composed. But there are other groups of interest that exist entirely, or mostly, outside a government; in this sense their impact on what a government does comes from beyond it. Investigation here must grapple with two nettlesome questions: How and to what extent does the group affect the government, and, in turn, to what extent does that effect determine the government's policies and actions in foreign affairs? Neither is so readily handled as to bring ease into the life of the scholar.

Elites

An old subject of interest and investigation is the role of elites in foreign policy. I mentioned earlier that we are interested in groups that self-consciously exist and that there we are looking at groups outside of a government. On both one can raise some questions about elites. For one thing, it is obvious that members of elites readily penetrate governments; it is wrong to treat an elite as entirely outside. My only defense is that as the term is normally used the greater part of the membership is not to be found inside; there is an overlap, but the elite is "larger" than the government, whereas some elements in a government are not at all members of the elite. We might also quarrel about whether elites are always self-consciously so. I will grant that elites can be a bit fuzzy-minded on this and that an elite lacks the precise organizational expression possessed by other groups. However, the way most people use the term, the members of an elite share so many things—values and interests, perspectives, social characteristics, wealth, status, or whatever—that they can usually tell who belongs and who does not, who fits and who does not fit.

The Vietnam War helped revive interest in the idea that an elite has a crucial influence in shaping foreign policy decisions (as in David Halberstam's "best and brightest," who led the United States into the war)[14] and that interest has been enhanced by the rising attention being paid to political economy, which is the interplay of political and economic factors in foreign affairs. Critics of the Vietnam War often focused attention on "cold warriors" or "security managers," a small elite charged with having created the U.S. cold war perspective in the 1940s, then having shaped public opinion within this perspective, then filling key posts in the foreign policy apparatus, and finally driving the ship of state onto the shoals of Vietnam. Richard Barnett writes that these people have been of a "predictable type":

> Even when not employed by the government they transact business with one another, give each other awards, belong to the same clubs, and review one another's memoirs. Almost all of the 400 crucial bureaucratic appointments since 1945 (in the White House and the Department of State and Defense) have involved men whose civilian offices can be placed within ten blocks in the cities of New York, Washington, Detroit, Boston, and Chicago.[15]

It is argued that such interrelationships inevitably constitute a rather cloistered community of shared views. Since they reinforce each other, the argument goes, these people constitute an alliance of powerful (and profoundly mistaken) perspectives and interests in foreign policy— perspectives and interests they have imposed whether in office or not.

Others have asserted that this elite was more conscious and calculating, not simply deluded by self-reinforced misperceptions. "Cold War revisionist" historians have argued that a small elite—driven by a desire to dominate world affairs so as to enhance (their version of) U.S. economic and political interests—challenged and threatened the Soviet Union through U.S. policies, misrepresented that country to the American people, and thereby provoked the Cold War. The Vietnam War, in this view, was just the latest product of this imperious establishment. On the other side of the political spectrum one finds the longstanding refrain that foreign policy has been too long in the grip of a liberal eastern establishment, centered on the Council on Foreign Relations or the Trilateral Commission.

The growing interest in international political economy has sustained interest in elite analysis even as the controversies over the Vietnam War have died down. There has been a resurgence of Marxist, or Marxist-like, perceptions and analyses. In its most notable form, this approach asserts that the state is always (or nearly always) an instrument of the dominant elite (the "ruling class," in Marx's own terms). The classic Leninist theory of imperialism, as well as those of Hobson and Schumpeter, ascribed it to certain elite interests and behavior patterns—those of a capitalist elite for Lenin and Hobson, of a fading feudal aristocracy for Schumpeter. It is fair to say that this remains the touchstone of all foreign policy analysis in the Soviet Union down to the present day: foreign policies reflect class structures, more particularly the dominant class's interests. But even non-Marxists are sometimes deeply influenced by this view.

A variant of elite analysis is what I like to call the "old-school-tie" approach. Up to this point we have been dealing with the impact of groups upon, or through, their members. Now we turn to the residual influence of groups on their former members. The old-school-tie approach goes something like this: if officials were all formerly businessmen (or military officers or regular Communist party members) or attended the same elite schools (Ivy League, OxBridge in England, the University of Tokyo) they would share a distinctive way of seeing and doing things. The Foreign Service in this country has often been characterized this way. British intelligence was roundly criticized for operating on an "old boy" network wherein someone was above suspicion if he came from an elite preparatory school and university and had the proper family connections. Kim Philby had the right old school tie and rose to be head of British counterintelligence, but unfortunately he had all the wrong ties with the Soviets and ended up residing comfortably in Moscow. (John LeCarré's *Tinker, Tailor, Soldier, Spy* is a novelistic treatment of that scandal.)

This is the approach employed by Henry Kissinger in an often reprinted article. He argues that American leaders inevitably apply a pragmatic, short-term approach to problems because of the nature of the legal and business professions from which they are predominantly drawn. The legal profession is preoccupied more with actual, here-and-now cases than with hypothetical situations, and it values quick reactions to unforseen problems at some expense to careful planning. Business also rewards those who manipulate real situations and hard facts, who get to the "bottom line." Both encourage coordination and conciliation among conflicting interests as the way to solve problems. This background is why, says Kissinger, U.S. decisions on foreign policy emerge out of compromises, in which personal persuasiveness and advocacy skills are very important. Issues get stated in stark, black-and-white terms because spokesmen for various interests maneuver in this way for attention and establish extreme positions in order to get the most out of the final compromise. Often issues are not seriously examined until they reach crisis proportions, and there is a bias toward legalistic solutions to the neglect of historical factors. "In short, the American leadership groups show high competence in dealing with technical issues, and much less virtuosity in mastering a historical process."[16] Kissinger applies a similar kind of analysis to the Soviet Union, drawing conclusions about how rising to power through the Communist party affects the Soviet leaders' entire approach to the outside world.

A variant on the old-school-tie approach is the concept of generation cohorts, which has frequently been applied in Soviet studies. The idea is that an older generation of Soviet leaders, a self-conscious group that experienced World War II, the last years of Stalin, and rising to great power together, is now passing from the scene. Surrounding the emergence of Mikhail Gorbachev has been an aura of expectation that this event would mean new policies reflecting a new generation's perspective. This concept is not only a staple in journalistic analysis but can frequently be found in academic studies as well.

Finally, we might simply define an elite as the small group of people with unusual power and influence at any particular time. This definition waters down emphasis on an elite as well as self-perpetuating or as constituting a self-contained subculture. In a later chapter we will look at Robert Gilpin's analysis of the international system, but here we might note that it includes the view that "the objective and foreign policies of states are determined primarily by the interests of their dominant members or ruling coalitions."[17] Gilpin says nothing about these "ruling elites" other than that they exist and that they determine their states' objectives. Given such a view, we would like to know something about the members' attitudes and perceptions, and this approach is widely used. It must be said that it is rather dull in comparison with some classic elite analyses—the element of conspiracy of the "haves" against the rest of us is missing. If there is a staid side to things, trust scholars to find it.

An excellent example of elite attitude analysis is offered by Bruce Russett and Elizabeth Hanson. They review the many theories, often very influential, that hold that economic interests of business leaders directly shape their perceptions and policy preferences, that is, theories of capitalist imperialsim, the military-industrial complex, or the peaceful effects of international trade and investment. From these theories they derive numerous hypotheses about how businessmen ought to feel about such matters as defense spending or dealing with communist countries. Then they supply evidence on businessmen's attitudes derived from a survey of corporate vice-presidents, from content analysis of business publications, and from the behavior of the stock market during major international events. They also compare business attitudes with those of military officers, politicians, and other elites. They find little support for the hypotheses or the theories behind them:

> Such economic theories seem to make only a small contribution to our understanding of elite perspectives on American foreign policy. At the least, future research on the role of economic interests must invoke a much more complex theory—for example, one that considers the interaction of such interests with personality, life experience, and communication patterns.[18]

Interest Groups

This is one of the favorite subjects of political commentators. The interest group and its handmaiden, the lobby, are ubiquitous in Western political systems, and to some analysts they are just about all there is to politics. As with elites, it is often suggested that they not only exist outside the government but overlap with it, such as by "capturing" some important sector in the government that then comes to reflect their views. It is easy to show that interest groups exist, are active, and have at least some effect on the foreign policy of some states. The difficulty is in trying to show that they are a more important factor than others, that they dominate some aspect of foreign policy.

By and large interest groups have not been considered as influential or active in foreign as domestic affairs. Still, at times they have been granted an important role. Discussions of U.S. policy in the Far East after World War II refer to the importance of the "China lobby," and many journalists and scholars assign great influence on U.S. policy in the Middle East to a network of pro-Israeli groups. The influence of farm interests in shaping the European Community's Common Agricultural Policy has long been a source of unhappiness in the United States (because the CAP reduces U.S. farm product sales in Europe), and it is evident that interest groups in Japan have curtailed that government's ability to foster greater imports despite heavy pressure from Japan's trade patterns.

A favorite example has been the "military-industrial complex," depicted as an interest group octopus with tentacles that reach into universities, corporations, Congress, foreign governments, and the national security complex in the executive branch. Such an analysis can also be projected abroad, for the Soviets have been discerned to have a military-industrial complex of their own. As an example of how studies of interest groups proceed, the literature on the complex stresses the network of personal and corporate ties that has grown up. Hundreds of retired military officers hold executive positions with companies doing business with the Pentagon; there is also traffic the other way, many top civilians in the Defense Department having formerly served as defense contractors or with law firms that represented such companies. Also considered significant is the fact that many congressmen maintain active status, and in some cases high rank, in the military services, and that defense contractors have been known to drop a coin or two into elected officials campaign funds or to supply gifts and favors to officials.

Interest group analyses tend to turn on the perceived relationship between a group and the state. The underlying question is: Should the state be seen as an extension of the group, an instrument at the group's disposal, or is the group only one of many competitors for influence with the state or even, at times, an instrument the state manipulates. Both can be found in, for instance, the literature on the military-industrial complex. The former tends to be characteristic of studies which stress elitism in foreign policy—certain interest groups become key elite elements whose interests that state reflects. The latter view is most typical of pluralist-oriented studies. Here interest group influence is seen as greatest on narrow, technical matters of little general interest, especially when a crisis or major national security matter is not involved; otherwise interest groups are depicted as largely offsetting each other or as often beset by conflicting pressures from their members (such as when export oriented firms in an industry differ over protectionist trade proposals with firms that have mainly a domestic market). As the clash between elitist and pluralist conceptions runs throughout American political science, it is unlikely to be resolved any time soon on just foreign affairs matters.

One final point worth noting is that we are handicapped in studies of interest groups (and also elites) by inadequate *access* to assess the impact of *corruption*. We know that it is a widespread phenomenon in politics, that it can be found in nearly all types of states and is simply enormous in some. But it is, by its very nature, hidden. It is often subtle (doing favors), it is readily disguised, and it can take deferred forms (such as promises of later employment for current officials). We may suspect that it has a good deal to do with foreign policymaking, but it is seldom easy to prove that conclusively. And corruption is practiced by governments (through intelligence agencies) and multinational corporations, not just domestic interest groups—so knowing corruption exists must be supplemented by sorting out the responsibilities of interest groups from those of other actors.

Public Opinion and National Images

The largest, reasonably self-conscious, group in any society is the citizenry. It is not unreasonable to suppose that the citizens may have some effect on their government's behavior in international affairs, and this has led scholars to try to figure out just what that effect amounts to. Their investigations can be lumped into two broad categories, those concerned with public opinion and attitudes and those which focus on national culture. Here we will look at public opinion, and then take up national culture in the next section.

Public opinion on foreign affairs is a slippery subject. We could get a firm grip on it if we could answer the following, quite different, questions: 1. What is it? What is the content of public opinion on foreign affairs? 2. How is it formed? What (or who) determines public opinion? 3. How relevant is it? How does it influence a government's decisions and actions?

In order to define what public opinion is, it is now easy to detect at least some *aspects* of public opinion in certain countries but very difficult to do this in many others. Scholars must make do with limited access to many of the publics that might be of interest. This is the problem of access once again. Governments are the source of the headache, as usual. Some would rather not have anyone know what their citizens are thinking, anyone, that is, except the government. All too many run their societies in such a way that it is wise for the citizens to be chary of expressing views different from what the government wishes them to be. Still, when we open this cupboard we find it is not completely bare.

We know that in general the public is not terribly interested in foreign affairs. Only a small proportion of the population in any country could be considered well informed, certainly far less than is comforting in the democracies. We also know that citizens oversimplify foreign issues and problems, and lean heavily on stereotypes of other peoples and governments as well as of their own. We know that at the level of opinions on current matters public opinion can be volatile, that it can shift rather substantially in a short period of time on the same issue (although shifts of over 10 percent in a short time appear to be rare).

Lying beneath opinions or attitudes are more fundamental beliefs or images or even moods. These, it turns out, appear to be quite stable, very slow to change once formed unless confronted with highly dramatic, almost overwhelming events. For Americans World War II was such a breaking point, turning basic public belief away from isolationism toward the internationalism that has characterized it ever since. For Russians it is apparent that the war inculcated a deep desire for peace, a profound concern about security, and a fixed suspicion toward Germans. Various analyses have detected long term mood swings or cycles in American public opinion, suggesting that deeper beliefs do eventually change and in perceptible directions.

How do we learn such things? One way is by conducting public opinion polls and interpreting the results, a method now so familiar that we need not consider it in detail here. Content analysis can also be useful when applied to newspaper editorials, letters to the editor, the amount of media time or space devoted to foreign affairs, and other topics of a similar nature. Congressmen and the White House practice a crude form of this when they tabulate opinions expressed in their mail. It is also possible to treat electoral results as saying something about public attitudes on foreign affairs. However, this has to be done with care because elections are almost never decided primarily on foreign affairs issues. The recent development of exit polling (used by the United States media even in such unlikely places as El Salvador) can refine our clues about just what was on the voters' mind when they went to the polls.

As an illustration of how public opinion shifts we can study John Mueller's work.[19] He and Leila Cain used public opinion poll data from Britain and the United States during World War II to demonstrate that war fever, (support for and approval of a war) rises very sharply just before and after a war begins, then tails off slowly but steadily. In further research Mueller compared poll data on the United States' opinion during the Korean and Vietnam wars. Once again support dropped from initially high levels, and he uncovered a reasonably close relationship between the rate of decline and the increase in American casualties. He also found the decline leveled off eventually, leaving "hard-core" supporters who were not very ready to change their opinion.

One way of studying the formation of deeper images—in this case the images of outsiders—is to outline the qualities and characteristics people assign to them. Some years ago one particular study used interviews to determine the stereotypes the people of five nations held of themselves and each other. The results are summarized in Table 4-1. One conclusion:

> In light of the stereotypes of Russians and Americans respectively harbored by the various populations . . . it is not surprising that most American international moves during the period in question (the early years of the cold war) were welcomed with favor by many of the peoples of the world, while Russian mores were viewed with suspicion and apprehension.[20]

Still another way to obtain national images or moods is to bear the methods of judgments traditionally most associated with historians, where one surveys many different, often subtle, indicators and tries to pull them together with a penetrating interpretation. John Stoessinger's *Nations in Darkness* uses such a method to trace the relationship between the United States, the Soviet Union, and China since 1945 in terms of their images of each other.[21] No attempt is made to define just where such images were located—in mass opinion, in the ideas of elites, or in the minds of decision makers. Instead he attempts an impressionistic judgment, and his sobering conclusion is that each nation has been burdened by totally inadequate conceptions of the other two, and that these images have been strongly resistant to change. Similarly, Robert Dallek has tried to probe the "undercurrents, of mood, tone, or milieu, or a climate of feeling" that shaped his book *The American Style of Foreign Policy*.[22] The crux of his interpretation is that United States foreign policy in this century has consistently been a reflection of profound *domestic* conflicts and anxieties, often unconscious but deeply unsettling. What we have done abroad has been driven by tensions arising out of what we were becoming as a people here at home. He thinks this may be true of other nations as well.

If we switch from what public opinion *is* to the question of *how it is formed,* the whole subject becomes ominously more complicated. At least four kinds of relevant factors are identified in the literature: personal traits and characteristics, social position, external events, and governments. The first includes such things as sex, personality, or level of education. Often the impact of some of these factors can be

TABLE 4-1
International Stereotypes Among Five Populations (1948)

I. Adjectives most frequently used to describe *Russians* by:

British	French	Germans	Norwegians	Americans
Hardworking	Backward	Cruel	Hardworking	Cruel
Domineering	Hardworking	Backward	Domineering	Hardworking
Cruel	Domineering	Hardworking	Backward	Domineering
Brave	Brave	Domineering	Brave	Backward
Practical	Cruel	Brave	Cruel	Conceited
Progressive	Progressive	Practical	Practical	Brave

II. Adjectives most frequently used to describe *Americans* by:

British	French	Germans	Norwegians
Progressive	Practical	Progressive	Hardworking
Conceited	Progressive	Generous	Practical
Generous	Domineering	Practical	Progressive
Peace-loving	Hardworking	Intelligent	Generous
Intelligent	Intelligent	Peace-loving	Peace-loving
Practical	Generous	Hardworking	Intelligent

III. Adjectives most frequently used to describe *fellow countrymen* by:

British	French	Germans	Norwegians	Americans
Peace-loving	Intelligent	Hardworking	Peace-loving	Peace-loving
Brave	Peace-loving	Intelligent	Hardworking	Generous
Hardworking	Generous	Brave	Brave	Intelligent
Intelligent	Brave	Practical	Intelligent	Progressive
Generous	Hardworking	Progressive	Generous	Hardworking
Practical	Progressive	Peace-loving	Progressive	Brave

investigated by simply adding more questions to public opinion surveys. Thus, it turns out that men tend to advocate more forceful and aggressive approaches to foreign problems than women. However, to trace the effects of personality requires the techniques of social psychology. The most notable of such findings is that a degree of personal aggressiveness and authoritarianism correlates well with harsh attitudes in foreign affairs such as superpatriotism and intense mistrust of foreigners.

As to the effects of knowledge, it is generally believed that this has important and beneficial effects, such as leading to more sophisticated and consistent views based on a higher level of attention and knowledge. However, two scholars who explored aspects of this came up with somewhat disturbing results.[23] They interviewed 558 residents in the Detroit area, asking questions not only about policies people endorsed on a number of issues, but also questions to determine each person's knowledge about foreign affairs in general and his or her beliefs. First, they found that the more knowledge a person has about foreign affairs the less likely he is to advocate belligerent policies—which confirmed others' findings. Second, they found that more knowledge means increased support for current government policy and in turn more knowledge includes more familiarity with what that policy is and thus greater susceptibility to its influence. Finally, greater knowledge did not mean more concensus. The more sophisticated the citizen the less likely he is to advocate policies that contradict his basic beliefs. But increased knowledge does not alter those beliefs; it makes people with different beliefs advocate different policies—that is, it polarizes them.

The second category of factors listed above was social position. The bulk of the population is uninformed about foreign affairs but a small segment does keep reasonably well in touch. The latter has been called the attentative public. Even smaller is that segment that takes an active part in international affairs. A classic version of these publics in foreign affairs appears in Figure 4-1,[24] and some version of this way of characterizing public opinion has influenced most analysts. The intriguing element is that moving from left to right in this figure generally means moving up the social class structure. Those in the attentive segment and beyond tend to have above average incomes and education, to hold mainly professional and managerial occupations, to live in urban areas, and to be between 30 and 60 years of age. Some findings suggest that in moving to the right side one finds opinions to be less absolutist and moralist in nature, more gradualist and pragmatic.

The third category contains the actions of other governments and

FIGURE 4-1
The Public and Foreign Policy

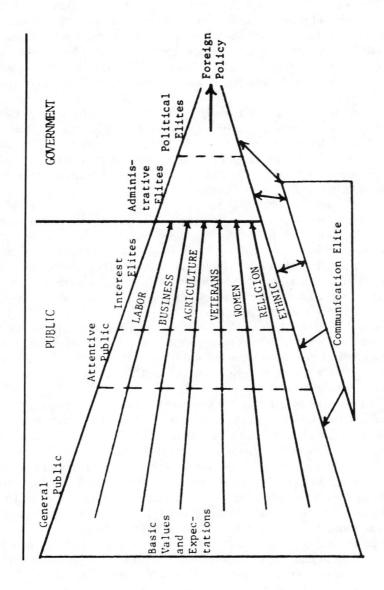

societies. How do external events affect people's thinking. One re-search effort tackled this by reviewing eighteen cases of shifts in popular images in connection with important external events. Such events could be a) government induced, b) spectacular, or c) cumulative and less spectacular; it was hypothesized that a combination of any two aspects would induce more change than just one, while a combination of all three would produce the largest shift. The study was more complex than this summary indicates because it was necessary to list types of shifts (a total of six) and six different aspects of any image that might be affected. The findings confirmed earlier conclusions that national images and beliefs are not readily changed by events. "Almost nothing in the world seems to be able to shift the images of 40 percent of the population in most countries, even within one or two decades. Combinations of events that shift the images and attitudes even of the remaining 50 or 60 percent of the population are extremely rare. . . ."[25]

When we turn to the impact of the government' on its citizens' views we complicate the discussion still further. We know that a government can do a great deal to shape public opinion and that governments work extremely hard at this. They are assisted in doing so by a good many things. In most societies the government controls, or substantially influences, the media and the education system. The government's leverage is also sustained by its position as the focal point of national feelings and loyalty, its stature as authoritative, and its collection of expert resources on foreign affairs.

What, then, can we say? We know that governments can readily gain public support in crisis and confrontations. Time and again in this country, studies have shown, such situations bring with them an increase in the public approval ratings of presidents in the polls, and the same appears to be true abroad (as with Prime Minister Thatcher and the Falkland Islands War). But this support can, and does, erode—as President Carter found out when the hostage crisis with Iran dragged on. Thus, it appears that there are limits on the success governments can achieve in creating and manipulating public opinion, in a crisis or on everyday matters, that public opinion leads an existence partially independent of the government. Finally, we know that societies are increasingly penetrated by information from outside, whether the government likes it or not—there are too many short-wave radios around to pick up foreign broadcasts, too many instances where people in one country (Cuba, East Germany, even the Soviet Union) can pick up television signals from another, too many flows of people (businessmen, foreign students, tourists) who carry information with them across national boundaries.

So what? How does public opinion affect foreign policy? This was, you recall, the last of the three questions analysts seek to answer about public opinion. We may start by assuming—as analysts always do—that *all* governments, no matter how authoritarian, require at least public acquiescence (as the Shah of Iran abruptly discovered) so public opinion is never completely irrelevant. If the public withdraws its support over a foreign policy matter, the government is in trouble. The Tsarist government experienced this during and after its war with Japan in 1904-1905 (and fatally so during World War I) as did the Galtieri government of Argentina which was forced out by its defeat in the Falkland Islands war.

A good illustration of how public opinion, while not necessarily the dominant factor, cannot be ignored is the way in which public uneasiness about national security and nuclear weapons has stimulated a good deal of concern among security specialists and officials in the United States and Europe in recent years. Demonstrations and other protests in Europe against the deployment of new American missiles, the public interest in a nuclear freeze and protests about the immorality of nuclear deterrence in the United States, and heightened doubts on both sides of the Atlantic about the viability and value of NATO (North Atlantic Treaty Organization) have led to speculation that the public consensus which has sustained NATO and deterrence policies for years is now eroding.[26]

However, it is clearly not the case that the public's impact is always and everywhere the same. First, we must take into account the way governments often shape public opinion about foreign affairs. Second, governments vary a good deal in their responsiveness to public opinion. They are not equally democratic, and a democratic government may be guided by public opinion on one issue and unmoved by it on another. (Various European governments in 1984-1985 began accepting American intermediate range missiles even though polls showed a majority of their citizens opposed to deployments.) Finally, there is mass opinion and then there is the attentive public and elites, and the impact of the latter may be an entirely different matter. How shall we take all these things into account at the same time?

Donald Puchala has designed three preliminary models (see figure 4-2)[27] with this in mind. Each depicts an alternate way public opinion could be linked to foreign policy. In pattern A the masses influences elite opinion which in turn influences the government. In pattern B the reverse takes place. In pattern C it is the elite which induces a shift in both government policy and mass opinion. Puchala believes historical examples exist for each pattern, and moreover that we can use the

FIGURE 4-2
Model Influence Patterns Linking Public Opinion and
Governmental Policy

PATTERN A — MASS-INDUCED POLICY CHANGE

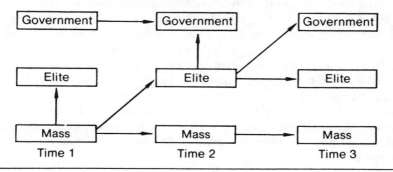

PATTERN B — GOVERNMENT-PRODUCED OPINION CHANGE

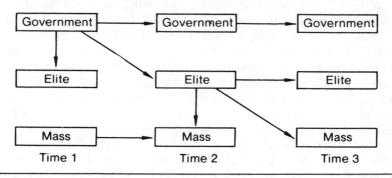

PATTERN C — ELITE-INITIATED POLICY CHANGE

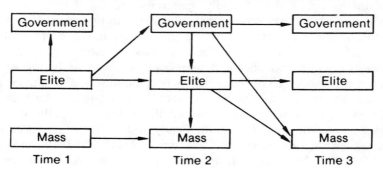

models to see which pattern prevails in various societies and on what kinds of issues.

The difficulty of figuring out the effects of public opinion, according to a very nice analysis by Barry Hughes, is that they vary with the nature of the issue, the speed with which the government has to act, and the focal point in the government for a decision.[28] He constructs a typology of issues (listing eight in all) and reviews historical examples of each. He finds that public opinion can have quite an impact on an economic issue (which hits us where it hurts—in the pocketbook) that has a major security component and allows a fair amount of time for a decision—good examples would be the overall size of the defense budget or whether to get out of the war in Vietnam. Where the issue is highly technical, made in mainly small congressional committees or lower level executive branch offices (on tariff regulations, for instance) interest groups are likely to wield major influence while the general public does not.

National Culture

We should not ignore one final way of thinking about the effect of groups because it bears directly on a subject to which we gave same attention in the preceding chapter. There we considered the possibility that many patterns of social behavior which bear on international politics—on war, or territoriality, or creation of dominance heirarchies—are ultimately derived from the genetic makeup of human beings. The chief rival to this view stresses culture and socialization because human behavior is not innate, it is learned. This would mean that societies (and ultimately their governments) basically do what they teach themselves to do.

One way to look more closely at this is to consider a society's general approach to outsiders. Presumably it makes some difference to foreign policy if we view outsiders as hostile, untrustworthy, or inferior as opposed to friendly, generous and equal or superior to ourselves. One study used anthropological data to suggest that when people inside a society are forced into strong multiple crosscutting loyalties and affiliations this leads to positive social relations and reduces domestic hostility and aggression. Unfortunately, those who do not share this web of relationships become totally alien thus people outside the society are readily suspected and despised. An example offered was the Mundurucu' of the Brazilian rain forest. In this location a husband would move in with the family of the bride which frequently was a home in another village. This divided his loyalty between family and friends in his old village and his hunting companions and new in-laws in another, making violent altercations between villages unattractive. This internal peace, however, contrasted starkly with attitudes toward other tribes. Outsiders were so alien they were defined essentially as game animals, and so:

> An enemy was not merely a person to be guarded against but was a proper object of attack, and the Mundurucu' pursued this with extraordinary vigor and stamina. . . . The men and women of enemy groups were killed and decapitated; the heads were later ceremonially shrunk. Any warrior who took a trophy head was specially honored. . . . They enjoyed warfare and looked upon the mere existence of other groups as inviting attack.[29]

Margaret Mead found that some societies in New Guinea created reservoirs of aggressiveness in adults, that erupted in war, instigated by the manner in which they reared children. In one society, babies were almost never coddled or caressed, and children were taught to compete and fight with each other constantly. The older ones were allowed to bully and tease smaller children, and permitted to insult and humiliate old people. To get a wife a young man had to trade another woman for her, usually one of his sisters, but that would diminish the women his father had to trade for more wives for himself, inviting a fierce struggle between the two. Mead found that other societies did not teach or inculcate aggressive behavior at all, and were more peaceful with their neighbors as a result.

Thus anthropologists have discovered societies with little or no conception of war (eskimos, King Bushmen), or ones which sharply limited the deadlines of warfare. Tribes were discovered which made war only with unfeathered arrows (limiting accuracy) or deliberately blunted spears, or only by aiming at the enemy's legs—or even by exchanging insults and volleys while always standing just out of range. Some American Indian tribes honored "counting coups" above all else—the point was not so much to kill an enemy as to get close enough to touch him and escape unscathed.

Along the same lines is the emphasis in behavior psychology on behavior as learned. An early school stressed conditioned reflexes (as with Pavlov's dogs salivating when hearing bells that meant food), but attention soon shifted to operant conditioning in which all creatures, humans included, interact with their environment and are shaped by the responses. This led B. F. Skinner to reject concepts such as consciousness, freedom, and dignity as meaningless—one could explain all behavior without them—and to design a behaviorist utopia where there was no aggression because it was not taught.

Problems and Difficulties

Up to this point we have considered only briefly some of the difficulties these approaches pose, but we cannot close this chapter without discussing this further. To begin, we may notice that the potentially relevant groups continued to build. There were committees and other small groups, interest groups, bureaucracies, professions, elites, the public, and others I purposely neglected to mention. It is not obvious, once we settle on a group level approach, just which group to study. Some are a great deal more accessible than others, and there is always the temptation to conclude that the accessible must be what is important because that would make life so much easier. Bureaucratic elements lure attention because they are there over the long haul; on the other hand, the dynamics of a Politburo or presidential staff seems important too. It is true that the bulk of national actions is routine and handled as such, but it is the master problems and great crisis that light our lives and beckon the analyst. We could agree that all these groups merit study in various kinds of situations, but the matter of proper emphasis would still remain.

Next there are lots of information and measurement problem. In chapter 3 we noted how difficult it can be to peek inside someone's mind. Approaches at the group level do not have to go to such lengths, but the relevant information is still in mountainous proportions and often very hard to obtain. Organizations strive mightily to preserve the confidentiality of their internal processes. Even congress has a rough time digging out reliable information on just how the Pentagon does business, and officials willing to testify about cost overruns and weapons malfunctions soon find themselves looking for work. Communist parties usually carry this to the point where a secret internal communications network exists inside the regular one. This passion for secrecy may force the analyst to rely on the memories of officials, which is disturbingly selective, and on information "leaks." In fact, a major ally of the analyst is the irate or embattled official who leaks valuable information. The Pentagon Papers represented a massive leak but analysts seldom get such a golden opportunity to probe the inner workings of foreign policy.

Even the Pentagon Papers uncovered no smooth path to insight. Daniel Ellsberg helped write and edit one volume, he was one of the first to read them completely, and he was personally involved with some of the decisions on Vietnam. Yet he describes his conclusions about why and how decisions were made on Vietnam as "tentative and transitional" for the following reasons:

1. The Papers "remain opaque" as to the policymakers' motives.
2. Presidents and White House staff "leave only a closely guarded and insubstantial trail of documents."
3. Bureaucrats (says Morton Halperin) "rarely write what they sign, and rarely sign what they write." And they often say and write things they do not entirely believe.
4. A major function of a special assistant (such as Ellsburg) is "to deal with what cannot be written down" and thus does not appear in the documents.[30]

If the Papers are such a flawed guide to inside processes, despite releasing materials usually available only years later, then we can properly suspect that we shall never know enough through leaks to explain foreign policy decision making.

As for measurement problems, a good illustration is the measuring of public opinion. Polling has standardized our perceptions of public views in Western societies, but in most of the world gauging public opinion is more like a guessing game. Almost all the successful work has dealt with what public opinion is and how it is formed but the measurement problems are difficult although manageable. However, in tracing its impact the difficulties become much more formidable. How do we know when an official acts in response to public opinion? Asking him will not necessarily help since few officials will admit to authoritarian or elitist tendencies these days. We may assume that, at best, public opinion is only one of the things he takes into account, but how to measure its relative importance? What if its chief effect is to shape, ever so subtly and unconsciously, the official's entire world view, his way of perceiving reality? This would make the impact both crucial and impossible to precisely assess. For these reasons, it may be fair to say that we know little of consequence about how public opinion actually affects foreign policy, other than that in most cases its effects appear marginal. We have a general feeling that public opinion carries some weight even in totally undemocratic societies, but the measurement problems there are truly insurmountable.

Nor are such difficulties confined to the study of public opinion. Turn back to the account of Henry Kissinger's study and reflect for a moment on how you would design a study to try to confirm his observations. Most literature on the military-industrial complex simply infers the existence of a pattern of influence rather than demonstrates it. Trying to pin down national images or a national style to something really precise gives uneven results—the subject always seems composed of two parts shiftiness and one part smoke. The Stoessinger study is noticeably vague on just where one finds our national image of

China or the Soviet Union, and Dallek's discourse on the American style is not always convincing about some inherently intangible linkages.

Bureaucratic politics and organizational process approaches are very influential. Unfortunately, the light they shed is a subject of much debate. Remember that they have frequently been lumped together because the evidence often fits either one. The trouble is that they are not the same kinds of explanations at all. One describes decision makers as consciously crafty, the other sees them as stuck in cognitive and organizational ruts. When two quite different approaches can use the same evidence then either the approaches or the data are disturbingly fuzzy. Thus most critics find these approaches to be too crude in their concepts and explanations. Another common criticism is that they underestimate the importance of political leaders, and President Reagan's term in office will give critics plenty of ammunition. The president's announcement of his "star wars" initiative was not driven by the bureaucracy (that same day a pentagon official was up on Capital Hill expressing little optimism about the prospects for the research!) but it sure sent shock waves through the government. It is worth noting that studies using these approaches often introduce other variables to explain key events. In the Beard study, a turning point comes when a civilian secretary of the Air Force becomes convinced of the need for a crash missile program. He maneuvers to turn things around, and we cannot explain his decision and the resulting policy without more or less abandoning bureaucratic politics, and even at that level of analysis, something critics have detected in other such studies.

Other comments we might make are reruns of those in the previous chapter. In extrapolating from studies of groups outside national politics to describe groups within, we must always ask if the two are sufficiently comparable. This would apply to the studies discussed by de Rivera. We could also react to examples of primitive societies in the same way: Are they really sufficiently like modern nation-states? And after all, how many societies are there that do not make war? Irving Janis' studies are at least about actual government decisions but the cases are selected in a nonsystematic way, so the findings are more suggestive than rigorous.

Another old friend is the problem of cross-national generalization. Once again the bulk of the studies that fall within the confines of this chapter have been conducted by westerners within Western culture— on public opinion for instance. One exception is the study of bureaucracy, which has been explored in non-Western societies and even communist ones. However, even here there can be difficulties. I was once associated with a seminar where the impact of bureaucracy on foreign affairs was assessed in the usual terms—inertia, self-interests and infighting, resistance to new ideas. One member of the seminar came from a third-world country where he had served as a foreign affairs official under a government that had been in power for years. He startled us by reporting that in his nation the bureaucracy was a refuge for young men with new ideas. The inertia came from above, outside the bureaucracy.

Once again I have left for last a comment that points toward the next chapter. It is one that applies to approaches in both chapters 3 and 4. It may appear that many of the approaches reviewed were valid yet incomplete. We are likely to think that personal and individual factors are of some importance along with the influences of groups and institutions. Also we are apt to consider still other factors as relevant also. This leads us to think in terms of combining a number of approaches, explaining international politics by reference to a range of factors at several levels of analysis. To do this we need a suitable vehicle or resting place, where all the various factors come together and interact, and where a theory might be designed that cut through to a simplified picture encompassing them all. It is this that makes the nation-state an attractive level of analysis, so attractive that in fact that the next two chapters are devoted to it.

Notes

1. The first example is from Joseph de Rivera, *The Psychological Dimension of Foreign Policy* (Merrill, 1968), p. 211; the ones on the Reagan administration are from Strobe Talbott, *Deadly Gambits* (New York: Knopf, 1984) pp. 70-71, 154-55, and 260.
2. J. David Singer, *Human Behavior and International Politics* (Skokie, Ill.: Rand McNally, 1965), pp. 217-18.
3. Irving Janis. *Groupthink,* 2d ed. (Houghton, Mifflin, 1983), p. 3.
4. Singer, p. 153.
5. John Steinbruner, *The Cybernetic Theory of Decision* (Princeton University Press, 1974).
6. Works referred to include: Graham Allison, *Essence of Decision (Little, Brown, 1971); Steinbruner; James Fallows, National Defence* (Vintage Books, 1982), pp. 76-106; Claire Sterling, "Nepal," *Atlantic Monthly,* pp. 14-25.
7. Charles Frankel, *High On Foggy Bottom* (New York: Harper and Row, 1968), pp. 59-60.
8. Edmund Beard, *Developing the ICBM, A Study in Bureaucratic Politics* (Columbia University Press, 1976).
9. Richard Neustadt, as cited in Roger Hilsman, *The Politics of Policy Making in Defense and Foreign Affairs* (New York: Harper and Row, 1971), p. 2.

10. John Kenneth Galbraith, *Ambassador's Journal* (Boston: Houghton Mifflin, 1969), p. 187.
11. Talbott, p. 49.
12. Charles Kegley, Jr. and Eugene Wittkopf, *American Foreign Policy, Pattern and Process*, 2d ed. (St. Martin's, 1982), p. 359.
13. The first study is David Garnham, "State Department Rigidity: Testing a Psychological Hypothesis," *International Studies Quarterly* (March 1974), pp. 31-39. The second is Bernard Mennis, *American Foreign Policy Officials, Who They Are and What They Believe Regarding International Politics* (Ohio State University Press, 1971).
14. David Halberstam, *The Best and the Brightest* (New York: Random House, 1972).
15. Richard Barnet, "The Game of Nations," *Harpers* (November 1971), p. 55.
16. Henry Kissinger, "Domestic Structure and Foreign Policy," *American Foreign Policy* (Norton, 1974), pp. 9–50.
17. Robert Gilpin, *War and Change in World Politics* (Cambridge University Press, 1981), p. 19.
18. Bruce Russett and Elizabeth Hanson, *Interest and Ideology, The Foreign Policy Beliefs of American Businessmen* (New York: W. H. Freeman, 1975) p. 250.
19. Joel Campbell and Leila Cain, "Public Opinion and the Outbreak of War," *Journal of Conflict Resolution* (September 1965), pp. 318-29; John Mueller, "Trends in Popular Support for the Wars in Korea and Vietnam," *American Political Science Review* (June 1971), pp. 358-75.
20. Donald Puchala, *International Politics Today* (New York: Dodd, Mead, 1971), pp. 54-55. The original study on which Table 4-1 was based was William Buchanan and Hadley Cantril, *How Nations See Each Other* (University of Illinois Press, 1953).
21. John Stoessinger, *Nations in Darkness*, 3d ed. (New York: Random House, 1978).
22. Robert Dallek, *The American Style of Foreign Policy* (New York: New American Library, 1983).
23. William Gamson and Andre Modigliani, "Knowledge and Foreign Policy Opinions: Some Models For Consideration," in Naomi Rosenbaum, ed., *Readings on the International Political System* (Englewood Cliffs, N.J.: Prentice-Hall, 1970), pp. 53-64.
24. Chadwick Alger, "Foreign Policies of U.S. Publics," *International Studies Quarterly* (June 1977), p. 283. The figure is derived from work by Gabriel Almond.
25. Karl Deutsch and Richard Merritt, "Effects of Events on National and International Images," in Richard Kelman, ed., *International Behavior* (New York: Holt, Rinehart and Winston, 1965), pp. 54-55.
26. See many of the articles in *Defence and Consensus: The Domestic Aspects of Western Security Part I, Part II, and Part III,* Adelphi Papers No. 182,,183, 184 (International Institute For Strategic Studies, 1983).
27. Puchala, p. 67.
28. Barry Hughes, *The Domestic Contest of American Foreign Policy* (New York: W. H. Freeman and Co., 1978), pp. 197-220.

29. Robert LeVine, "Socialization, Social Structure, and Intersocietal Images," in Kelman (note 25),,pp. 54-55.
30. Daniel Ellsberg, *Papers on the War* (New York: Simon and Schuster, 1972), pp. 74-77.

Bibliographical Remarks

The following list contains a sample of the works that apply organizational process and bureaucratic politics models to the analysis of aspects of American foreign policy: Bruce Blair, *Strategic Command and Control: Redefining the Nuclear Threat* (Washington, D.C.: Brookings Institution, 1985); Paul Bracken, *The Command and Control of Nuclear Forces* (New Haven: Yale University Press, 1983); Stephen Cohen, *The Making of United States International Economic Policy*, 2d ed. (New York: Praeger, 1981), pp. 30-41, 110-45; *Report of the Commission on the Organization of the Government for the Conduct of Foreign Policy, Volume 4, Appendix K* (Washington, D.C.: Government Printing Office, 1975); I. M. Destler, "National Security Advice to U.S. Presidents: Some Lessons From Thirty Years," *World Politics* (January 1977), pp. 143-76; Robert Coulam, *Illusions of Choice: The F-11 and the Problem of Weapons Acquisition* (Princeton University Press, 1977); Morton Halperin and Arnold Kanter, *Readings in American Foreign Policy: A Bureaucratic Perspective* (Boston: Little, Brown, 1973); Graham Allison and Morton Halperin, "Bureaucratic Politics: A Paradigm and Some Policy Implications," *World Politics* (Spring 1972 Supplement), pp. 40-79; Morton Halperin, *Bureaucratic Politics and Foreign Policy* (Washington, D.C.: Brookings Institution, 1974); John Steinbruner and Barry Carter, "Organizational and Political Dimensions of the Strategic Posture: The Problems of Reform," *Daedalus* (Summer 1975), pp. 131-54; Graham Allison and Peter Szanton, *Remaking Foreign Policy: The Organizational Connection* (New York: Basic Books, 1976); Graham Allison and Frederic Morris, "Armaments and Arms Control: Exploring the Determinants of Military Weapons," *Daedalus* (Summer 1975), pp. 99-129.

Examples of critiques of the bureaucratic politics model include Robert Art, "Bureaucratic Politics and American Foreign Policy: A Critique," *Policy Sciences* (December 1973), pp. 467-90; and Jerel Rosati, "Developing A Systematic Decision-Making Framework: Bureaucratic Politics in Perspective," *World Politics* (January 1981), pp. 234-52.

Mention is made in the chapter of treating particular organizations as having their own organizational personalities. Any number of works could be cited on this; if the State Department is used as an example the following are relevant: I. M. Destler, *Presidents, Bureaucrats and Foreign Policy: The Politics of Organizational Reform* (Princeton University Press, 1972), pp. 154-67; Chris Argyris, "Some Causes of Organizational Ineffectiveness within the Department of State," Occasional Paper No. 2, Center for International Systems Research, Department of State (Washington, D.C.: Government Printing Office); Andrew Scott, "The Department of State: Formal Organization and Informal Culture," *International Studies Quarterly* (March 1969), pp. 1-18; Andrew Scott, "Environmental Change and Organizational Adaptation: the Problem of the State Department," *International Studies Quarterly* (March

1970); Patrick Linehan, *The Foreign Service Personnel System* (Boulder, Colo.: Westview, 1976), pp. 254-70.

Whereas most of the work applying organizational process and bureaucratic politics approaches has been done on American foreign policy, there is a fair body of literature that uses these models or something roughly similar in discussing other governments. See for instance: Carl Linden, *Krushchev and the Soviet Leadership* (Johns Hopkins University Press, 1966); Chihira Hosoya, "Characteristics of the Foreign Policy Decision-Making System in Japan," *World Politics* (April 1974), pp. 353-69; Arnold Horelick et al., *The Study of Soviet Foreign Policy: Decision-Theory-Related Approaches,* Sage Professional Papers in International Studies, Volume 4, Series No. 02-039 (Beverly Hills, Calif.: Sage, 1975); Herman Weil, "Can Bureaucracies be Rational Actors, Foreign Policy Decision-Making in North Vietnam," *International Studies Quarterly* (December 1975), pp. 432-68; Taketsugu Tsurutani, "The Causes of Paralysis," *Foreign Policy* (Spring 1974), pp. 126-41 (on Japanese foreign policymaking) and also the comments on this article on pp. 142-56; Andrew Cockburn, *The Threat: Inside the Soviet Military Machine* (Vintage Books, 1984); Margot Light, "Approaches to the Study of Soviet Foreign Policy," *Review of International Studies* (July 1981), pp. 127-43; Robert Cutter, "The Formation of Soviet Foreign Policy: Organizational and Cognitive Perspectives," *World Politics* (April 1982), pp. 418-36.

Brief reference is made in the chapter to the notion of a "risky shift" that can occur in group decision-making. For more on this see Dorwin Cartwright, "Determinants of Scientific Progress: The Case of Research on the Risky Shift," *American Psychologist* (March 1973), pp. 222-31; and B. Wilpert et al., "The Risky Shift in Policy Decision Making: A Comparative Analysis," *Policy Sciences* (September 1976), pp. 365-70.

Another subject that was given a brief treatment in the chapter is the idea that Soviet foreign policy (and domestic policies) will change due to a generational shift that is now taking place in the Soviet elite. Illustrations of this sort of analysis include Seweryn Bialer, *Stalin's Successors: Leadership, Stability and Change in the Soviet Union* (Cambridge University Press, 1980); and Jerry Hough, *Soviet Leadership in Transition* (Washington, D.C.: Brookings Institution, 1980).

On the subject of interest groups in foreign policy there is a good deal of literature on specific groups and particular sectors of foreign policy but the theoretical understanding of the subject does not seem to have gone much beyond Lester Milbrath, "Interest Groups and Foreign Policy," in James Rosenau, ed., *Domestic Sources of Foreign Policy* (New York: Free Press, 1967) and the discussion in parts of Bernard Cohen, *The Public's Impact on Foreign Policy* (Little, Brown, 1973). There have been various attempts to apply interest-group analysis to the study of Soviet foreign and defense policy. Two examples: Karl Spielmann, "Defense Industrialists in the USSR," *Problems of Communism* (September-October 1976) pp. 52-69; and William Odom, "The Militarization of Soviet Society," *Problems of Communism* (September-October, 1976) pp. 34-51. In Uri Ra'anan, "Soviet Decision-Making and International Relations," *Problems of Communism* (November-December 1980), pp. 41-47, factions are emphasized rather than interest groups.

On the role of public opinion in American foreign policy the classic source still widely cited is Gabriel Almond, *The American People and Foreign Policy*

(Praeger, 1960). John Rielly has edited three reports entitled *American Public Opinion and U.S. Foreign Policy* (Chicago Council on Foreign Relations)—in 1975, 1979, and 1983—which provides a good deal of information on the nature and structure of public attitudes. Similar reports include Daniel Yankelovich, "Farewell to 'President Knows Best,' " *Foreign Affairs: America and the World 1978* (Council on Foreign Relations, 1979), pp. 670-93; and Daniel Yankelovich and Larry Kaagan, "Assertive America," *Foreign Affairs: America and the World 1980* (Council on Foreign Relations, 1981) pp. 696-713. Examples of studies of the relationship between public opinion and policy include Jong Lee, "Rallying Around the Flag: Foreign Policy Events and Presidential Popularity," *Presidential Studies Quarterly* (Fall 1977) pp. 252-56; and Michael Maggiotto and Eugene Wittkopf, "American Public Attitudes Toward Foreign Policy," *International Studies Quarterly* (December 1981), pp. 601-31.

Finally, on elite opinion as opposed to public opinion, there has been a good deal of interest in the shifts in American elite opinion as a result of the Vietnam War. The major survey findings on this are discussed in Ole Holsti and James Rosenau, *American Leadership in World Affairs: Vietnam and the Breakdown of Consensus* (Winchester, Mass.: Allen and Unwin, 1984). For a shorter report on their conclusions see "Cold War Axioms in the Post-Vietnam Era," in Ole Holsti et al., *Change in the International System* (Boulder, Colo.: Westview, 1980), pp. 263-301.

5

A System, a System, the Kingdom is a System

In the study of international politics, more analysis is probably attempted at the level of the nation-state than at any other. For some time world affairs have been essentially the affairs of nations, and so this appears to be an eminently sensible place to start one's investigation.

Nations are a blessing and a curse. The blessing has been largely domestic in nature. The oldest political problem of mankind is maintenance of a community large enough to meet the needs of its members yet small enough to command their emotional attachment. These two requirements pull in opposite directions. A large population and territory are exceedingly useful when it comes to security vis-à-vis outsiders or the resources for economic development. In fact, civilization has usually been a matter of many people clustered together, associated with large societies. To tip the scales of man's fate away from the Stone Age, a lot of people have usually been sitting together on one end.

Paradoxically, people have historically been most deeply attached to communities extremely limited in size, so small that all the members could practically confront each other face to face. Most primitive societies seem to have been no more than about five hundred souls in size, which is perhaps near the upper limit for a community based fully on the personal interaction of its members. The appeal of small town and city neighborhoods remained strong throughout the modernization of the West, while in the rest of the world village and tribal loyalties are often stronger than national ones today. It is commonly held that in modern societies people pay a price in terms of the decline of small communities. Modern life has its charms but psychological support via membership in an intimate community is seldom one of them.

The nation more or less successfully bridges the gap between these conflicting requirements. In terms of territory and population its only historical rival among alternative political communities is the empire. Yet the phenomenon of nationalism can enmesh the citizens in a web of attachments as profound as those in a tribe. The distinctive feature of nationalism is the citizen's commitment to leaders and ordinary people he will never personally know. His attachment is to an abstract conception of a community because he cannot personally experience its further dimensions every day. This is not easily achieved, as the persistence in established nations of attachments based on seemingly less abstract things—like ethnicity or religion or race—attest. But when it works this combination of size and abstract commitment results in an immensely powerful community, able to bend nature and individual effort to collective purpose on a scale beyond anything achieved before. Thus the national has been and remains the preeminent vehicle for the societal facelifting we call *modernization*.

The nation as a curse is the nation in its dealings with the rest of the world. Its ability to galvanize human and material resources permits the consistent development of new and improved wars. Marshalling emotional attachments has allowed great nations to display the ferocity of the Mundurucu on a monumental scale. Short of societies where war was the only real business, the peoples of today's leading states have, in my lifetime, spent a larger proportion of their total resources on preparations for wreaking violence than any in history. Arms spending today is approaching $1 trillion per year and there is no sign that wars and insurrections are about to go out of style.

Thus when we turn to the study of national foreign policy we take up a subject fascinating in its complexity and dreadful in its consequences. Once taken up it is hard to put down, for, like the accident at the corner or a good murder mystery, it has the lure of calamity. Civilization used to be regularly threated by barbarians or plague or famine; today the only real danger to its existence is foreign policy.

All of the approaches considered in the earlier chapters could be and usually are applied to the study of foreign policy. What distinguishes this level of analysis from the earlier ones is the broad sweep of the approaches it encompasses. Here is where contributions from studies of individuals and groups are often melded with assessments of the role of the international system in attempts to produce sophisticated theoretical constructs that make sense of it all. Why here? Why concentrate on the nation? To begin with, our subject is, after all, international politics—the nation is literally at the heart of it. Many analysts assert that the behavior abroad of national governments

> is the key subject in the study of international relations . . . and the only one which can provide a natural and unifying center of investigation.

or that "international politics remains the politics of states."[1] If domestic factors affect world politics it is mainly via their impact on particular nations' foreign policies; if the environment is important it is so mainly in terms of the ways it is perceived by national governments and modifies their actions.

It also seems important that nation states are the focal point of loyalties and commitments in the modern international system. Nationalism, a central fact of international politics, would seem best comprehended by examining the behavior of the communities which it creates. For example, the nation is now the anchor of our self-identity, so much so that it is a serious emotional matter to leave one nation in favor of permanent residence in another. National governments insist on being such a focal point; they resist encroachments on sovereignty, and they make far more strenuous efforts than they once did to retain their citizens (Compare today with the huge population migrations in the nineteenth century, especially to the United States).

Finally, we may concentrate on nations for the same reason others choose to emphasize individuals, because they appear to be the atoms of the relevant universe. The world is composed of nations these days, and it can be asserted that individuals and organizations count only in belonging to and influencing some particular nation. We might decide that each nation is different, making international politics a giant fluid jigsaw puzzle, the pieces of which we try to put together as best we can. Conversely, we may think that all national governments are roughly similar in their problems and processes, and the object would be to generalize about how they all cope. In the former, each nation is of interest, though some more than others; in the latter, particular states would be investigated mainly as examples of the rest. In either case the nation is the fundamental unit under study.

Judging by the previous chapters, we have a veritable alphabet soup of factors that may determine a government's behavior—bureaucracies, genetics, committees, neuroses—enough to overwhelm and mystify. Obviously we need a framework that integrates and organizes these factors—a political version of chemistry's periodic table of elements. We could also stand a good theory that cuts through the clutter to offer a simple, clear explanation of foreign affairs decisions and actions. With a little luck and a decent theory we could even prescribe a bit, telling governments what to do and how, thereby living out the secret ambition of most every theorist.

The Concept of a System

In terms of appeal the most powerful integrating organizing framework for the study of foreign policy has been supplied by the notion of a *system*. Few social scientists have not been deeply influenced in recent years by this. A great many students of political science subscribe to the view that out there somewhere beyond the walls of the academy is the political system, which they can discuss at some length. The term readily crops up in everyday discourse too, as when radicals talk about going up against the system while other folks allow as how the system is something unconquerable.

A systems approach can be used at every level of analysis and in a wide variety of fields. In international politics, systems approaches have been employed mainly to analyze either national-level foreign policy and behavior or the operation of the world as a whole, i.e., the "international system." This chapter concerns only the first of these; the latter will get plenty of attention further on.

A great many definitions of *system* are available. In the broadest sense, a system is simply a set of interrelated elements. However, to deal with complex social entities like nations and their governments we want a definition that takes us a bit further. John Lovell's is particularly useful for the purposes of this chapter; he cites the following as the core elements in a system (and I have added elaborations in brackets):[2]

1. A set of component parts which together can perform some purposeful activity ("Purposeful" is important for us here. Technically, many systems are purposeless, but rarely will study of a foreign-policy system not be concerned about its goals.)
2. Functional interrelationship of the parts (the components work together. If some are absent or do not work properly, the system will fail to work to capacity or might even break down.)
3. An ongoing interrelationship between this set of component parts and the environment (The system monitors the environment, responds to it, may even be able to influence it.)

The first thing you should notice is that to approach a national government or its foreign policy process as a system is to talk about it as if it is something you could take out of a box and hold in your hands. It's an abstraction, an intellectual construct or a theoretical idea—we hold it in our minds, not our hands. We invent this construct and apply it because we find it useful—it makes things simpler, clearer, more organized.

Next, you can readily see that the concept of a system might be applied at any level of analysis. Any individual can be seen as a system, as can any organization (like the State Department). The government can be treated as a system, as can NATO or all the states in the world and their interactions. The concept of a system will permit the application of a great many theoretical approaches and research methods. In fact, it was originally developed in the study of foreign policy to better organize much of the work going on in the field.

Among the most highly touted for illuminating foreign policy are systems approaches of the input-output variety. These are some of the concepts that commonly crop up in this type of analysis. An *input* is the injection into the system of some information or resource (like money or political demands). *Memory* consists of the facilities, faculties, and processes by which information is stored and recalled. A *decision* is a commitment, based on a reading of available information and resources, to take some action vis-à-vis the environment to achieve some goal. An *output* is the system's action. Finally, *feedback* is new information about the results of the previous action, on the basis of which the system can go through the cycle all over again. There are many possible refinements and elaborations of these basic elements, but this will serve as a sufficient introduction for the moment.

If this seems like a rather abstract or static outline, you might breathe some life into it by thinking of yourself as a system. You regularly take in resources and you constantly receive a vast amount of information through your senses, to which you add information summoned from your memory. Life is a succession of decisions—to eat lunch, turn left at the corner, leave town, propose marriage. In each case you pull together your resources with information about your present condition and about the world around you. You take action, saying "marry me," and you start getting feedback, like "Don't be ridiculous!"

One attraction of system analysis is its movie-camera effect. The processes it identifies are constant and ongoing, so this way of thinking seems to capture the dynamics of existence. The processes are serial, one step leading to another, and through the memory they are cumulative so that what happens partly reflects what went before. Since people can be a part of many systems simultaneously, with most systems containing lesser- or sub-systems, we see that systems nestle inside each other like a set of Chinese boxes or Russian matrioshka dolls. In other words, our analytical camera has captured the world in motion and its parts in their interdependence. But at the same time it has segmented the world and its processes into a series of steps, just like movie frames, so we can (analytically) stop the action and get a closer look at each one.

In short, we seem to have grasped the essence of reality in a few simple concepts. Not only that, the physical and biological worlds can be seen as systems too, as are many mechanical contrivances, such as our automobiles. This gives us a whole universe to draw upon for concepts, ideas, analogies, which sounds exciting. Well, when this hit the social sciences, primarily after World War II, staid political scientists went on a bit of a systems binge. No fireworks and wild parties, mind you, just the wine of new ideas that is academia's strong drink. An explosion of systems analysis hit political science, soon dominating the field, and resulting in many interesting studies in international politics.

This was particularly attractive for the analysis of foreign relations. It is important to be able to distinguish a system from its environment, and the boundries seem nice and clear where nations are concerned—so much so that some national boundries are even visible in photographs taken from outer space. Some inputs come all nicely measured, as in budget figures, armed-forces statistics, or votes in elections. Word on what the world is up to pours into governments every day through reports from diplomatic and intelligence sources, the wire services, even direct communications between heads of state. In fact, we can think of an embassy as something like a vary large ear permanently stationed abroad. Other concepts seem equally applicable. A nation has a memory—in its history books, its files and archives, its culture and traditions, and in the personal recollections of its leaders and citizens. It has mechanisms and processes for making decisions. Its outputs range from diplomatic notes to war.

Development of a Systems Model

How can we begin to use the concept of a system to facilitate theoretical inquiry? Maybe the best way to see how to do this is to do it. We can develop a systems model in outline form, starting with something simple, then making it more complicated, and tossing in comments about how we might use our model as we go along.

The simplest system for our purposes would be as depicted in Figure 5–1, MISS (Morgan's Idiotically Simple System) There is nothing complicated about this. But how would we use it? One possibility would be to compare changes in inputs to changes in outputs, hoping to find that regularities in variations in the first are invariably followed by regularities in variations in the second. We could use a few simple, aggregate measures of inputs like gross national product, populations, an index of military power to rank the state against others and some overall characterization of the international system (highly structured

FIGURE 5-1
MISS

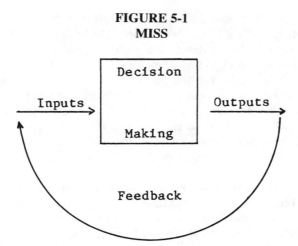

or not, stable or unstable). The result would be, in a primitive way, an explanation: we could say, when asked why outputs vary, that it is because of variations in inputs. (Why does a light bulb shine more brightly now than a few minutes ago? Because the electricity (the input) was increased.)

Notice that nothing is said about that thing in the middle; it is black-boxed and we do not need to refer to it. Next, the explanation offered is indeed very primitive. It doesn't say why variations in inputs lead to variations in outputs—hence there is almost nothing in the way of a theory here. Thus our next step might well be to devise an explanation as to why—a theory. However, there are any number of theories that can be generated to explain why changes in inputs are related to changes in outputs—by itself, MISS cannot help us at all to sort through them and pick out the best one. Finally, we might very well suspect that not all inputs are of equal importance for changes in outputs. Thus we are likely to want to make our model more elaborate to disaggregate or break into pieces some section of it, for the purpose of testing and refining our theories.

How can this be done? Well, with respect to inputs we could start by distinguishing internal from external inputs. We could assert that domestic inputs consist of the following clusters of things: government resources—military, economic, natural, human; societal contributions—the national culture and its dominant elements, the social structure, the feelings and wishes and views of the citizens (this would include elements of memory); political inputs—the nature of the political system, the roles and nature of available organizations, the demands of interest groups or other groups, etc; individual inputs—the personality traits, belief systems, skills and judgment, etc., of individual officials (including elements of memory. You might well choose to add, or substitute, others but the point should be clear. We can do the same for external inputs—clusters of things pressing on our system from the outside. Examples could include the external nonhuman environment (climate, the oceans, the whole biosphere); the nature and structure of the international system; the status or rank or relative position of the nation in the international system; the acts of other states;

This means we have modified our model in roughly the way it is depicted in Figure 5-2 (MMISS-Morgan's Modified Idiotically Simple System) By itself, this does not drastically complicate matters for theoretical purposes: we are still black-boxing decision making and still associating changes in outputs with changes in inputs. We are somewhat better equipped to try to assert that some inputs, or some mixes of inputs, are more important than others. On the other hand our measurement problems just grew appreciably—we now have to sort out and identify lots more inputs.

On reflection, we might want an even more elaborate conception of the input side. For instance, lots of inputs have to be transmitted—

FIGURE 5-2
MMISS

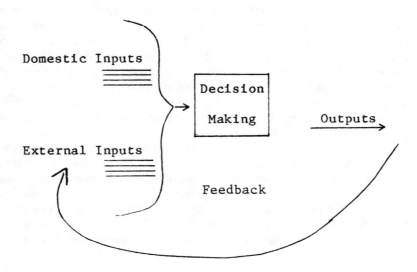

actions by foreign governments, feedback, political demands and support, etc. And we know that communications can be uneven, imperfect, irregular—that systems vary in terms of their communications processes. Then there is the sticky subject of perception—inputs must be seen. What if the government thinks it has more political support or military resources than it does; what if it concentrates on internal inputs and ignores those from external sources? Early in this book we emphasized the perception is always selective. Think of all the things that can affect it: ideology, culture, experience, personality.

Thus we might emphasize that inputs are immersed in communication and perception processes, with their effects are partly (even wholly) shaped by those processes, and therefore we had best include this. It is not easy to depict this on paper, but to keep things simple I will use Figure 5-3—Morgan's Carefully-Modified Idiotically Simple System (MCMISS). This allows us to devise a more elaborate theoretical explanation, something along the lines of "outputs vary according to variations in inputs as mediated by processes of communication and perception." Notice also that our framework now allows us to try to take into account many of the things which approaches in earlier chapters sought to emphasize—organizations as resources and their impact on communications and perceptions, or the effects of character and human cognitive processes. We have not said anything about how to do this, just that there is room in the model to try it.

FIGURE 5-3
MCMISS

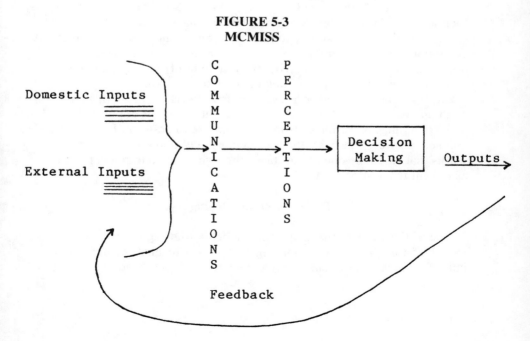

What we have done in the input side we can also do on the output side. For instance, it might seem important to distinguish policy from implementation, and both policy and implementation from action. To take an ordinary example, you decide you want the salt; in reaching for it you get near it but in doing so you topple your glass of wine into the hostess's lap (with plenty of feedback as a result!) and your seeking the salt is abruptly suspended, maybe for good. Governments decide to do things, but what they actually do only partially resembles what they decided should be done, and sometimes they do things no one decided should be done. As this suggests, things like communication and perception could very well be considered as making a contribution on the output side just as they do on the input side. We might also want to categorize actions—in fact, we would almost certainly want to do this for we will want, in the end, a theory that tells us when certain kinds of actions take place rather than others. Actions can be labelled in terms of their intrinsic nature, and as an example I have included the classification scheme used by the World Event Interaction Survey (Table 5-1).[3] As you can see, there are twenty-two large categories broken down into sixty-two narrower ones. We might, alternatively, separate actions by the geographical area at which they are directed, or the particular nations which are the targets, or the type of issue (economic, security, environment, etc.) with which they are concerned.

Trying to put all this together gives us Figure 5–4: MICS (Morgan's Increasingly Complicated System) Thus we have actions of various sorts, sometimes the result of policies and implementation mediated by communication and perception, sometimes the result of implementation without reference to (maybe even in spite of) policy, and sometimes with neither policy nor implementation very evident.

Once we have arrived at a systems framework such as this, how might investigation and analysis proceed? There are lots of possibilities and a rich range of examples from the literature to draw on. I think you will see, as we go through them, how they rely upon systems frameworks that resemble one of the stages through which our model passed as it went from MISS to MICS.

Perfect Decision Making

One of the ways to use a systems model is to design it as a perfect model of foreign policymaking, against which to analyze our sadly imperfect world. A systems approach lends itself quite readily to being

TABLE 5-1
World Event Interaction Survey Events Categories

1. **YIELD**
   - 011 Surrender, yield to order, submit to arrest, etc.
   - 012 Yield position; retreat; evacuate
   - 013 Admit wrongdoing; retract statement

2. **COMMENT**
   - C21 Explicit decline to comment
   - 022 Comment on situation-pessimistic
   - 023 Comment on situation-neutral
   - 024 Comment on situation-optimistic
   - 025 Explain policy or future position

3. **CONSULT**
   - 031 Meet with; at neutral site; or send note
   - 032 Visit; go to
   - 033 Receive visit; host

4. **APPROVE**
   - 041 Praise, hail, applaud, condolences
   - 042 Endorse others policy or position; give verbal support

5. **PROMISE**
   - 051 Promise own policy support
   - 052 Promise material support
   - 053 Promise other future support action
   - 054 Assure; reassure

6. **GRANT**
   - 061 Express regret; apologize
   - 062 Give state invitation
   - 063 Grant asylum
   - 064 Grant privilege, diplomatic recognition; de facto relations, etc.
   - 065 Suspend negative sanctions; truce
   - 066 Release and/or return persons or property

7. **REWARD**
   - 071 Extend economic aid (for gift and/or loan)
   - 072 Extend military assistance
   - 073 Give other assistance

8. **AGREE**
   - 081 Make substantive agreement
   - 082 Agree to future action or procedure; agree to meet, to negotiate

9. **REQUEST**
   - 091 Ask for information
   - 092 Ask for policy assistance
   - 093 Ask for material assistance
   - 094 Request action; call for
   - 095 Entreat; plead; appeal to; help me

10. **PROPOSE**
    - 101 Offer proposal
    - 102 Urge or suggest action or policy

11. **REJECT**
    - 111 Turn down proposal; reject protest demand, threat, etc.
    - 112 Refuse; oppose; refuse to allow

12. **ACCUSE**
    - 121 Charge; criticize; blame; disapprove
    - 122 Denounce; denigrate; abuse

13. **PROTEST**
    - 131 Make complaint (not formal)
    - 132 Make formal complaint or protest

14. **DENY**
    - 141 Deny an accusation
    - 142 Deny an attributed policy, action, role, or position

15. **DEMAND**
    - 150 Issue order or command, insist; demand compliance, etc.

16. **WARN**
    - 160 Give warning

17. **THREATEN**
    - 171 Threat without specific negative sanctions
    - 172 Threat with specific nonmilitary negative sanctions
    - 173 Threat with force specified
    - 174 Ultimatum; threat with negative sanctions and time limit specified

18. **DEMONSTRATE**
    - 181 Nonmilitary demonstration;[walk-out on
    - 182 Armed force mobilization, exercise and/or display

19. **REDUCE RELATIONSHIP (as Neg. Sanction)**
    - 191 Cancel or postpone planned event
    - 192 Reduce routine international activity; recall officials, etc.
    - 194 Halt negotiations
    - 195 Break diplomatic relations

20. **EXPEL**
    - 201 Order personnel out of country
    - 202 Expel organization or group

21. **SEIZE**
    - 211 Seize position or possessions
    - 212 Detain or arrest person(s)

22. **FORCE**
    - 221 Noninjury destructive act
    - 222 Nonmilitary injury-destruction
    - 223 Military engagement

applied in this fashion because it attempts to abstract from reality a set of reasonably neat processes. That is, its categories are already ideal types analytically. All we have to do is assume a government perfectly performs the activities in question and we have our model. Judging by the frequency of its use, this procedure seems to be well nigh irresistible when it comes to teaching, and many textbooks now start their analysis of foreign policy in this fashion.

John Lovell has done this in one of his works, outlining an "Imaginary Ideal Machine for Making Policy," or IIMMP. In doing so he has chosen to set up an ideal system that has many concepts and processes you will recognize from the preceding discussion. This results in IIMMP as it appears in Table 5-2. As you can see, he combines various kinds of inputs with a decision making step and then the categories of policy, implementation, feedback, and memory.

We can quickly think of how things can go wrong in a national foreign policy system. Consider the handling of information. The nation's eyes and ears may miss something important, as when the American and Israeli intelligence agencies failed to conclude that the Arabs were going to attack Israel in October 1973. Or transmissions may be garbled or impeded: some officials who knew Henry Kissinger would not believe an Arab attack was imminent and would be annoyed at those who said so, simply delayed telling him of their suspicions. Or key information may be deemed untrue or unreliable: Stalin dismissed

FIGURE 5-4
MICS

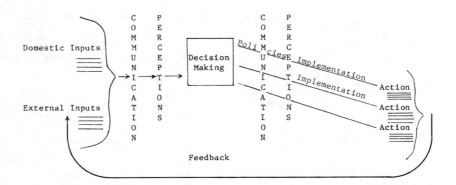

TABLE 5–2
Capabilities of an Imaginary Ideal Machine for Making Policy

TASK	CAPABILITY
Goal Setting	Identification of national needs, interests, and priorities
Intelligence	Thorough, rapid, accurate gathering interpreting, and reporting
Option Formulation	Comprehensive search for options; tallying of probably costs and benefits of each
Plans, Programs, Decisions	Selection of option most likely to provide optimal ratio of gains to costs
Declaratory Policy	Effective articulation of policy and rationale, so as to enlist domestic and foreign support
Execution	Allocation of resources in a manner to ensure effectiveness of each action element and minimize waste; clear coordination and control of all action elements; decisive
Monitoring and Appraisal	Thorough and continuous assessment of the effects of policy actions and commitments; flexibility in correcting for error and adjusting to changing circumstances
Memory Storage and Recall	Learning from experience; quick and accurate recall.

Lovell then reviews the performance of real governments and, needless to say, they do not look good. Lovell's results are outlined in Table 5-3.[4]

TABLE 5–3
Foreign Policy "Machinery" in Practice: Characteristic Limitations

TASK	CAPABILITY
Goal Setting	"National interests" are the object of competing claims; goals are established through political struggle
Intelligence	Always incomplete; system susceptible to overload; biases and ambiguities in interpretation
Option Formulation	Limited search for options; comparisons are made in general terms according to predispositions rather than according to specific cost-benefit items in
Plans, Programs, Decisions	Choices are made in accordance with prevailing mindsets, influences by "groupthink" and political considerations
Declaratory Policy	Multiple voices, contradictions and confusion; self-serving concern for personal image and feeding the appetite of the media
Execution	Breakdowns in communication; fuzzy lines of authority; organizational parochialism; bureaucratic politics; delays
Monitoring and Appraisal	Gaps; vague standards; rigidities in adaptation; feedback failures
Memory Storage and Recall	Spotty and unreliable; "lessons" from experience are remembered selectively and applied imprecisely

all warnings that Hitler was about to attack in June 1941, warnings from other governments and his own intelligence sources. Or available information may be misinterpreted: Japanese military preparations in 1941 were detected but Washington took this to mean a possible attack on Southeast Asia or the Phillipines, not Pearl Harbor. Finally, information has to compete for the attention of the harried decision maker. Hints of missiles in Cuba in 1962 had to get past other information to the contrary (assurances from Moscow that it would not do such a thing), information about other problems (a Chinese-Indian border war broke out that week), and conflicting recall (the Soviets had never shipped offensive missiles out of the country).

We can think along the same lines for other input elements. And the same kinds of problems can appear on the output side—orders may be unclear, distorted, ignored, or misinterpreted at each stage down the line. Thus, at the height of the Cuban missile crisis when avoiding undue provocation was vital, a U.S. plane inadvertently flew over part of the USSR. As President Kennedy snorted when given this chilling piece of news, "There is always some s.o.b. who doesn't get the word."

Intensive Investigation of a Single State

Generally speaking, systems approaches have been designed to facilitate comparative analysis, to foster and organize studies which look at several or many governments, on the grounds that this is going to be much more rewarding theoretically. We want a theory that tells us primarily what is true about the behavior of any government in foreign affairs, not a different theory for every government. However, it can be useful to concentrate on one government within a systems framework meant to apply to any government because scholars lack access to many of the world's governments, and because the careful study of even one government can be a formidable task. Let us look at studies which draw upon a broad systems perspective but focus on just one government.

In 1954, three scholars published what became a widely cited monograph setting forth a decision-making framework along systems lines.[5] Since Richard Snyder was most responsible for this and was most closely associated with it thereafter, I shall refer to it as his for the sake of convenience. Snyder started with the assertion that research in international relations lacked a clear focus and a framework within which concepts and their interrelationships could be effectively studied. In short, he suggested people in the field did not know what they were doing (something each of us readily admits is possible but assumes is most likely true only of everyone else!) Snyder then assumed that the best way to proceed was to develop an approach applicable to any state, so as to generalize about all of them, not emphasize the peculiarities of each. Next, he assumed that for purposes of research the nation at any given time is its decision makers. In fact, it is only those officials actually involved, not those supposed to be involved by law or the constitution. Obviously this limits what we are to look at very severely. Snyder went even further by suggesting that our analyses be built on the decision-maker's view of the world; the external environment or other factors were relevant only to the extent and in ways he perceived them to be.

In chapter 1 we reviewed very briefly the idea that everyone makes do with a complex and subtle, yet invariably limited perspective. This being the case, there are grounds philosophically for doubting that "reality" exists—each of us simply has his or her own. Even if reality does exist, when it comes time to assess a government's performance we want to be able to say something about whether or not the government had a good grip on it and thus should have acted as it did. The question is, why is our "view of the facts" a good basis for judgment, since we must admit our perspective is limited and partial? Also, we may know (or not know) something the goverment did or did not know. Obviously, Snyder was attempting to offer a way out by suggesting we ignore our own perspective and analyze a government's decisions and actions solely in terms of its officials' perspective instead.

Snyder listed a great many variables that could influence the behavior of decision makers. In the original version this resulted in the diagram in Figure 5-5, which lists clusters of factors and, by means of the arrows, suggests likely relationships among them. Look carefully and you will see much that is familiar; essentially it is another version of MCMISS (Figure 5-3) an elaboration of the input side of a systems model (the output side being left simply as "action"), with A, B, and E constituting domestic and external inputs. Left undetailed in figure 5-5 are the elements that fall under C, which contains some more old friends:

1. The decision makers' perception of the situation
2. All the formal and informal elements that determine which officials participate and how, including such things as organizational behavior
3. Communication and information flows, including feedback
4. Motivation, including organizational objectives and personality factors

Later works clustered the variables somewhat differently as: the decision situation, participants, organizations, process, and outcomes.

FIGURE 5-5
Snyder's Decision Making Model

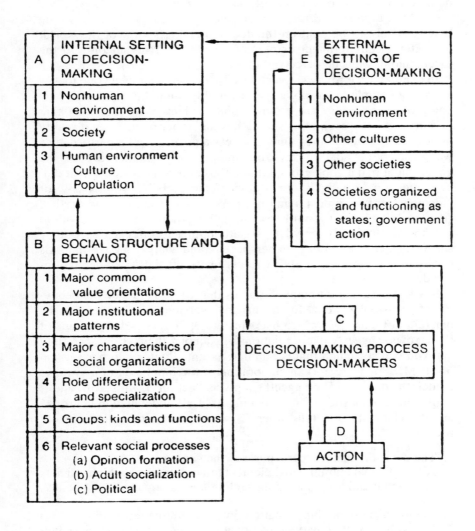

Analysis could then be described as an attempt to trace the effects of the first four on the last one. This did not involve abandoning the basic framework, however. You can see how this framework has room for a great many different kinds of studies, and how it was designed to pull together work going on at many levels of analysis. The personal qualities of statemen are covered in C. Boxes A and B cast a wide net over public opinion, groups, institutions, and the like. Box E takes in the external environment, whittled down by deeming relevant only those elements which decision makers actually perceive.

The one detailed investigation within this framework was *The Korean Decision* by Glenn Paige. It not only used the Snyder approach on a single government reaching specific decisions, it also compared to what happened with what perfect decision making would have produced in order to point out how officials might do better in the future.

Paige started by classifying the American decision to intervene on South Korea's behalf in 1950 as a "crisis decision," and this became the focal point of his analysis. Snyder's scheme listed variable clusters that probably affected decisions. Paige backed up to consider the impact of crisis on these variables. For example, the first proposition he derived was that "crisis decisions tend to be reached by ad hoc decisional units," meaning the decisions emerge from an almost impromptu group rather than an established one like the National Security Council. Why is this important?

> The significance of the nature of the decisional unit immediately becomes a focus of attention because of the fundamental assumption of decision making analysis that decisions vary with the composition of the decisional unit.[6]

Notice that Paige was not testing that "fundamental assumption." He sought to uncover the impact of crisis on the composition of a group; whether that composition had any effect on the nature of the decision was left for other studies.

Another important point is that, as we might suspect, a crisis decision really turns into a bundle of smaller decisions. Paige uncovered six stages in the overall decision, each of which was a decision in itself. The study proceeded by means of a very detailed review of the external and internal settings (inputs), the perceptions of the decision makers, and the day-to-day steps in the decision process. Paige deliberately sought to obtain a series of findings that could be tested in future studies, and some of his more interesting propositions are as follows:

The greater the crisis, the greater the accentuation of positive affect relationships among decision-makers. [Something Janis holds can lead to Groupthink]

The greater the crisis, the more the leader's solicitation of subordinate advice.

The more limited the information, the greater the emphasis placed upon the reliability of the source.

The greater the crisis, the greater the propensity for decision makers to supplement information about the objective state of affairs with information drawn from their own past experience.

The greater the crisis, the more the directed scanning of the international envisionment for information.[7]

Paige noted that U.S. officials consistently overestimated their side's strength and undervalued that of North Korea, a finding later confirmed in studies of many governments in similar circumstances. He also found officials were very unlikely to seek the advice of their habitual critics, foreclosing some potentially useful perspectives. Using such findings he suggested how mistakes might be avoided or at least reduced in future crises.

A second illustration of a systems approaches applied to the analysis of a single state is the framework used by Charles Kegley, Jr. and Eugene Wittkopf in their textbook on U.S. foreign policy. If nothing else, their input-output figure (Figure 5-6)[8] has more visual appeal than my clumsy efforts. Each of the input categories covers many things we have discussed before. The external sources include the structure of the international system, the nature of other states, the existence of important nonstate actors, etc. Societal sources cover national values, public opinion, interest groups, and the like. And the other categories take into consideration the personal qualities of leaders, the dynamics of bureaucracies, and the nature of basic institutions like the Congress, White House, and State Department.

They find that the hallmark of U.S. foreign policy since World War II has been its continuity—it has changed very little, and then only slowly. They ascribe this to factors in each category. For instance, only certain kinds of individuals tend to be recruited to fill foreign policy positions, and once in office their behavior is strongly conditioned by their roles and by political and bureaucratic pressures. The bureaucratic environment is so fragmented and inertial that little change in foreign policy ever results. But the continuity also rides on and reflects a substantial public and elite consensus that cannot easily be disturbed. Finally, as an enormously powerful country, the United

FIGURE 5-6
Kegley-Wittkopf Framework for Foreign Policy Decision Making

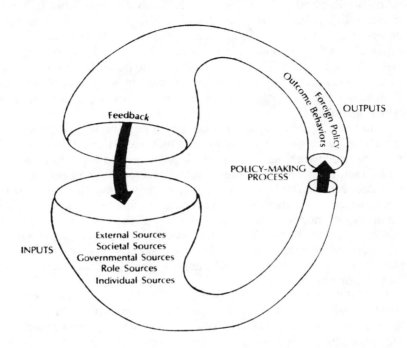

States has been able to be less moved by the external environment than other states might have been.

They also attempt to rank the input categories in order of importance in two ways. First, in normal situations they find that role variables are most significant, followed in order by governmental, societal, external, and individual variables. Role variables are important because

> Each role in the decision making machinery carries with it certain expectations, obligations, rights, and images of appropriate behavior, pressures which tend to make a new occupant think and act like his predecessor. Whereas an individual's style may be markedly different from that of the person who held the job previously, the individual's position on crucial issues tends to be very similar to his predecessor's proposition.[9]

However, in a crisis situation the ranking gets shuffled in their view to individual, then role, then governmental, and finally societal—with external factors falling somewhere in there depending on the nature of the crisis and how it is perceived. In other words, who minds the store in day-to-day matters is not very significant—presidents and other officials come and go while business is much the same—but in a crisis the qualities of the individual decision makers loom much larger in determining what the U.S. government does. In theory this means a crisis allows for much more innovation in foreign policy, but even in a crisis the factors working for continuity are so powerful that innovation rarely results and "crisis most often appears to be 'managed' in a way that keeps existing policy intact and preserves the assumptions on which it is based."[10]

No review of systems approaches could be complete without examining the award-winning studies of Professor Michael Brecher. His systems framework has been used, through penetrating studies of India and Israel, to test many of the hypotheses about foreign policymaking that float around the field and to generate new ones. The framework is summarized in Figure 5-7 and the accompanying list of terms.[11] It's an input-output model, moving from the top to the bottom and then, by feedback, up to the top to start the process over. Inputs (external and internal) are communicated to decisionmakers, being filtered through their perceptions (attitudes and images), and this leads to a decision and its implementation.

Some details are worth discussing briefly. The "operational environment" is what we call the real world. As we saw earlier, Snyder would have us deal only with the decision maker's view. Brecher rejects this. He argues that the outcome of a decision depends not only on how an official saw things, but on how they really were, and it is our place to evaluate the accuracy of his perceptions. Thus the diagram has two kinds of feedback arrows, one for the operational environment and one for the psychological environment—the latter as shaped by officials' personalities, images, ideologies, and culture.

The external components of the environment include the "global system"—the current pattern in which the world's nations are arranged—and the "subordinate system" which is the regional group of states the government mostly deals with or worries about. "Dominant bilateral relations" is Brecher's term for a government's relations with the two superpowers, and "bilateral relations" then pertain to its dealings with any other state. Internal elements cover national military and economic resources, the nature of its political structure, key interest groups, and the maneuvers of those out of power who want to push the present crop of officials into retirement.

On this basis Brecher has intensively investigated major and minor foreign policy decisions in Israel. Remember that Glenn Paige found

FIGURE 5-7
Brecher's Research Design

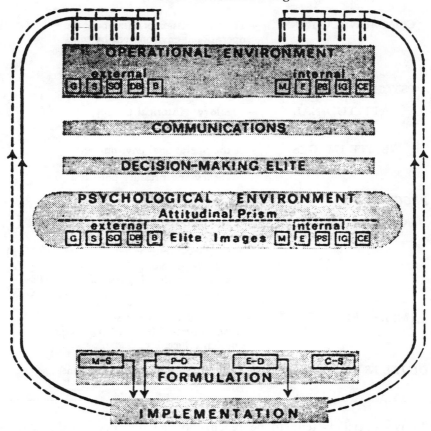

INPUTS

OPERATIONAL ENVIRONMENT

EXTERNAL	—Global System	(G)
	Subordinate System	(S)
	Other Subordinate Systems	(SO)
	Dominant Bilateral Relations	(DB)
	Bilateral Relations	(B)
INTERNAL	—Military Capability	(M)
	Economic Capability	(E)
	Political Structure	(PS)
	Interest Groups	(IG)
	Competing Élites	(CE)

FIGURE 5-7 (Continued)

COMMUNICATIONS   —The transmission of data about the
operational environment by mass
media, internal bureaucratic
reports, face-to-face contact, etc.

PSYCHOLOGICAL ENVIRONMENT

ATTITUDINAL   —Ideology, Historical Legacy,
PRISM   Personality Predispositions

ÉLITE IMAGES   —of the operational environment
including competing élites'
advocacy and pressure potential

PROCESS

FORMULATION   —of strategic and tactical decisions
in 4 ISSUE AREAS:
    Military–Security   (M–S)
    Political–Diplomatic   (P–D)
    Economic–Developmental   (E–D)
    Cultural–Status   (C–S)

IMPLEMENTATION   —of decisions by various structures:
Head of State, Head of Government,
Foreign Office, etc.

OUTPUTS   —The substance of acts or decisions

"crisis decisions tend to be reached by ad hoc decisional units." Brecher's findings do not support this—crises in Israel were typically handled by the cabinet and other standard groups. One of the field's classic assumptions is that states are primarily motivated by a desire to expand their power; Brecher finds the Israeli government often put other considerations first. On crisis decision making, something with which Israel has had all too much experience, Brecher confirms others' conclusions that great stress makes officials see time as very pressing and their options as very limited. His findings support others' that in a crisis officials seek out more information about what is going on, want more face-to-face contacts with each other, and rely heavily on past experiences to interpret the present one (the last being something Kegley and Wittkopf found true in the United States).[12]

Comparative Foreign Policy

The basic idea behind comparative analysis is simple enough. What we want to know is why the actors in international politics do what they do. Let us decide that we must first look at what they do. Then we compile a list of factors that possibly affect their behavior. Then we use comparative analysis to sort out the relative influence of those factors under various conditions. In the end we have a theory that tells us what actors will do under various conditions due to the influence of the factors involved, i.e., it explains international politics.

The trouble is that none of these steps is easy to take. Getting a clear fix on what the actors do is hard work—there is a plethora possible actors to look at performing an amazing amount of acts! As you already know, diligent scholars have turned up lots of possibly relevant variables. At this point we are trying to match a broad range of international behaviors with a somewhat open-ended list of relevant factors via comparative analysis or well over one hundred actors—and our task has assumed outlandish proportions. Naturally this overstates things a bit (but just a bit) in order to make the point that the comparative study of foreign policy is challenging to say the least. Fortunately, scholars appreciate a challenge as much as anyone else, and in fact more than most.

We may start by examining what the analyst calls the "dependent variable," that is, the thing or things he wishes to explain. The first point to make is that the subject, *comparative foreign policy,* is misnamed, hardly an auspicious beginning. Definitions of the term *policy* normally refer to it as an overall strategy or a set of directives designed to guide a government's actions, but there's many a slip between policy and action. Quite often those who study comparative foreign policy are really interested in behavior. Others are truly interested in policy. Still others define policy solely in terms of explicit behavior. Naturally enough, confusion results. The solution is to reserve behavior as the dependent variable and treat foreign policy as one independent (or at least intervening) variable.

The first requirement for comparative analysis of foreign behavior is a classification scheme or typology of that behavior. If we wish to explain what governments (or even other actors) do, our first question is: just what do they do? Strangely enough this question has not, until relatively recently, been approached very systematically. Typically scholars lumped policy and behavior together and produced an astonishing variety of terms and concepts to label what they thought they saw. And very frequently terms designed to describe foreign behavior were also regularly used to identify the factors that caused or shaped it, which is a very circular way of doing things.

One possible antidote devised some years ago is called *events data collection*. The central idea is to go through a source (or sources) like the *New York Times, Facts on File, Deadline Data, Keesings Contemporary Archives,* etc., for a particular period and record every international event. The goal may be to record all the events, or only those pertaining to a particular area like the Middle East, or a specific subject like the Cold War. What is an event?

> Events data is the term that has been coined to refer to words and deeds—i.e., verbal and physical actions and reactions—that international actors (such as statesmen, national elites, intergovernmental organizations . . . , and nongovernmental international organizations . . .) direct toward their domestic or external environments.[13]

This definition was designed to encompass a variety of ongoing projects. An "event" occurs when someone does something to someone else: issues a statement, offers praise or blame, breaks diplomatic relations, opens hostilities.

At the same time it is detecting an event, each of these projects attempts to classify it, to put it in a category with other, similar, events. This is sticky business because there are lots of things being done and lots of different ways to categorize them. Table 5-1, included earlier, is just such a classification scheme and illustrates the complexities involved. You can perhaps appreciate this better by considering the parallels in another field. Say we wanted to explain the world's weather; one possibility would be to collect weather events from all over the world over some period—rain in Bombay, sleet in Minneapolis, sun over the Atlantic, and fog in Moscow. But in order to do that we would need to describe all the possible weather conditions and the rules to determine which event goes in what pigeonhole: just exactly what is the difference between rain and sleet, sleet and hail, hail and snow, etc.?

One possible use of events data is sketching behavior profiles of nations over time. Not only would this allow us to compare the behavior patterns of several countries, it would also permit comparisons of changes in behavior patterns with changes in the factors we think might be relevant in shaping those patterns. That is, after all, the ultimate objective of our efforts.

When we turn to why the actors do what they do, the obvious next step is to select some basis for comparison. In our system models this means moving over to the input side. However, it is possible to do a comparative analysis without reference to a systems framework so, while we will shortly turn to systems approaches again, the following discussion touches on the broad considerations in any comparative analysis.

Consider the problem for a moment and you will see there are a fair number of plausible starting points for comparison, quite apart from ones we discussed in chapters 3 and 4. Assume the actors of interest are national governments. We might decide that their behavior can best be explained in terms of their objectives, the goals they have set. This requires that we devise a typology of objectives, something that has often been attempted. A typical list often includes such goals as self-preservation, territorial expansion, economic development, and so on. The trouble is that governments pursue many different goals at the same time. Not only that, they frequently conceal just exactly what they are after so we are unable to determine what they want just from what they say they want. Sometimes they are severely divided internally on what goals to pursue, making the available clues even more difficult to read. Attempting to infer their objectives from their actions is not necessarily reliable either; we have already noted the gap between actions and policy makers' intentions, while internal divisions may lead to contradictory actions. Also, any one action can be plausibly interpreted in different ways—a conciliatory gesture can be seen as reflecting peaceful objectives or as a deceptive move covering hostile objectives.

Another possibility is comparing states in terms of their capabilities, by assuming that what a state wants and does is based on its resources. This commonly gives us a list like this: superpowers, great powers, middle powers, little powers, and nobodies. Once again, this is more easily said than done. Capabilities are notoriously difficult to measure accurately; leaders have often confidently opted for wars that turned into military disasters because of erroneous capability estimates. One reason is that capability is inseparable from objective. The query: "How much power do I have?" is best answered by another: "What do you want to do with it?" Power, skill, wealth, knowledge and other capabilities are all relative, both to the task at hand and to the ability and willingness of others to get in one's way. And it is often difficult to determine what the task at hand will require. If proof of the pudding is in the eating, international politics serves up an assortment of brand new puddings every day. Did Iraq have the capacity to invade Iran and cause the collapse of its government, or vice-versa? The only way for the two to find out was to fight a long and vicious war. But who wants to eat such puddings?

Often, though not always, related to capabilities is size and thus we might think that size has much to do with how nations behave. But there are contrasting interpretations as to what it means to be large or small. It could be that a small nation must limit its activities accordingly, that it must champion international moral and legal norms and rely heavily on international organizations, avoiding force and threats and trying to keep on the good side of big states. Thus a small state will be circumspect, and a good many certainly are. But it can also be said that small states lack the resources to keep abreast of events, which leads to ignoring problems and failing to spot threats until it's almost too late. This will lead it to having to take the risks of being threatening and obstreperous and, lacking the conflicting responsibilities of big states, a small state will be volatile and prone to conflict. Some small states certainly fit this pattern as well.

Elements of each have been detected in studies using events data. It does appear that small states are less active in general world affairs and thus stay out of many conflicts that embroil big states, while more of their actions are directed at and through international organizations. But small states seem to push more of their conflict behavior beyond verbal levels, taking riskier actions in conflict situations and making more use of coercive steps. Yet another approach sees weak, underdeveloped states as deeply penetrated—politically, economically, culturally—by great powers, as not independent in any real sense. Most importantly, ties among the elites of great and small states are as much or more significant than those among governments, which would mean that some events data collections do not readily capture the real influences and interactions that drive weak state behavior.

Still another possibility is analysis according to type of government (or even type of society). It is a commonplace belief in this century that democracies pursue different foreign policies than other states. It was Woodrow Wilson's belief that democracies would be less aggressive, more peaceable than nondemocracies, a belief many others have shared. Numerous analysts have also suggested that, peaceful or not, democracies are singularly inept in foreign affairs, an assertion as old as de Tocqueville's classic study of America. Of course we find the first conclusion a lot more comfortable than the second! Comfortable or not, the first lends itself more readily to investigation. Studies have, in fact, found that democratic systems seem to engage in less conflict than closed societies. And I know of no real war in this century between democracies, as the term is generally used; democracies do seem to be able to work out their conflicts in some other fashion, a point which deserves more attention than it has received in the field. On democracies being foreign policy bumblers, the rub is that it is hard to define and measure success or failure. What results are hard-to-assess conclusions that public opinion, interest groups, and domestic politicking often present problems foreign policy versus the opposite view that lack of public debate, critical opinions, and competing sources of information cripple the foreign policies of authoritarian states. Most analysts of Soviet foreign policy tend to come down about as Kegley and Wittkopf do on U.S. foreign policy: there is very considerable continuity, not much room for initiative and new ideas, because the role and governmental variables overwhelm the personal quirks and inclinations of individual Soviet leaders. That would mean Moscow and Washington are about equally inept.

You can now see the procedures and complications involved and can, no doubt, imagine other bases for comparison that have been or could be proposed. Level of economic development/modernization is a favorite, as in the following:

> Wherever modernized societies exist, their foreign policies are more similar to each other than they are to the foreign policies of nonmodernized societies, regardless of the scale of the society or its type of government.[14]

Geographical location might be the key (island versus inland), or the nature of the economic system (the core of foreign policy analysis as done by Soviet scholars). Even race has been suggested—recall Hitler's pernicious stress on that, a primitive theorizing that had deadly consequences.

All such approaches compare states in terms of "national attributes" for purposes of theory, and certain comments are in order about this. One is that the number of possibly relevant national attributes is very large—goals, size, nature of political system, resources, and whatnot. This strongly suggests that rather than testing for possible connections between one or more attributes and a states' behavior in order to build a theory, what we need is a theory that tells us what the connections are and only then should we turn to investigation. First we need a good idea, Kenneth Waltz would say, and then we can proceed; when we come to review his theoretical approach later on we will see why he says that looking into national attributes is a waste of time. Many an analyst disagrees; I raise the matter here only to prepare the way for that later discussion.

Another matter we should touch on concerns the elaboration of typologies. To compare states in terms of goals or capabilities or size or political system is to shuffle them into analytical boxes. But reality is always messy and quite often a state is hard to classify—it is sort of half in one box and half in another. That invites trying to develop an index, a measuring stick that either has lots of gradations (more boxes) or tells us more precisely where a country fits. You should always be alert to the index that an analyst is using and be ready to ask hard questions about it: is it very precise? Does it seem suitable? Does it appear reliable? Indexes abound in the literature, with countries being ranked in terms of power, military strength, economic development, degree of democracy, and any number of other things.

A good illustration is the thorny subject of national power. Because power has often been depicted as the central factor in nations' behavior, frequent attempts have been made to rank nations in terms of their power. Peter Beckman has utilized a composite index[15] consisting of

$$power = \frac{\% \text{ of world's steel production} + \text{political stability score} \times \% \text{ of world's population}}{2}$$

He applied this to the major states in the system in order to compare them in terms of power (because he explains states' behavior in terms of their relative power). To derive the political stability score he used the following:

Condition	Score
Civil War, anarchy	0.0
Major uprisings, coups, government authority slipping	0.2
Major uprising, coup, lesser trouble	0.4
General strike, agitation, government paralysis	0.6
Agitation, officials frequently ousted	0.8
No serious challenges	1.0

Then he added a calculation of a state's ability to project power (since power is less significant if it cannot be applied where needed), which he defined as the number of days it took to move war material to the central arena of world politics which, at the turn of the century, was Europe. Hence

$$\text{Projectable Power} = \frac{\text{Power}}{\text{Days needed to deploy power}}$$

For the world after World War II he added two more components to his index: percent of world energy production and percent of the world's nuclear weapons that a state could deliver on other states' homelands.

It is worth noting that, calculated in this way, the Soviet Union had slightly surpassed the U.S. in national power by 1975.

Ray Cline, a former high official in the CIA, offers a different and more complex index but reaches the same conclusion.[16] His formula is

Pp = $(C + E + M) \times (S + W)$ where:
Pp = Perceived Power
C = Population + Territory (size plus critical location, if any)
E = Economic Capability (GNP plus a bonus for special energy, food, etc., resources)
M = Military Capability (Nuclear plus conventional, by various measures, plus "strategic reach")
S = Strategic Purpose (Degree of clear-cut strategic plans for national aggrandizement)
W = Will (National integration, strength of leadership, relevance of national strategy)

Cline boils all the factors taken into consideration into numerical values, though he emphasizes that this often means using rough estimates for qualitative, even subjective judgments. In the rankings that result for 1977, the Soviet Union's overall power surpassed that of the United States by about 25 percent.

The difficulties these scholars have tried to surmount can be readily ascertained if, say we set out to assess the relative power of nations in the Middle East. If one component of our index is military strength, getting reliable figures on armed forces and equipment is not too difficult but by themselves they are not very helpful. In men, tanks, planes and other hardware the Arab states lost several wars they should have won. We find we must take into account training, the quality of military leadership, morale, and other factors not so readily measured. We might find that levels of education and economic development, degree of political stability, and other factors are probably also involved, with the index of national power becoming steadily more complex as it tries to grapple with elements less and less readily measured.

Now we are ready to turn to the investigation, via comparative analysis, of the simultaneous impact of numerous factors. This brings us back to systems frameworks, for the complications of trying to organize such an investigation often seem to analysts to be manageable only with such a framework in mind. We will start with some simple comparative systems frameworks and work our way through to more elaborate ones.

Charles McClelland attempted to provide a way to study states' behavior in crisis situations through a systems approach that focuses almost entirely on the output side, and which he labeled interaction analysis. A state's action is deemed to call forth a reaction which in turn provokes a further reaction, and so on, so that a crisis involves a long chain of interactions between the two sides. McClelland concentrated on behavior because he believed that state actions are an important form of international communication. He also saw it as a way around the complexities of probing the inner elements of states and their decision making which, as we know, can call for monumental amounts of hard-to-come-by information.

> In other words, the research bet of an interaction approach is that a large amount of the work of decision-making study can be by-passed safely in arriving at explanations of international behavior. The contention is that the performances of the participants—the interaction sequences—are reliable indicators of the active traits of participating actors.[17]

Which is to say, what states are is reflected in what they do. One assumes flows of information about actions are fed into the state machinery, processed, and contribute directly to follow on actions, but it is not necessary to track this in detail. This is really the way in which a simple arms race model works—each state's step provokes the next one by the other state—and the conception of an arms race has had a powerful appeal in the field and in everyday conceptions of international politics. If we stick rigorously to this view we can essentially confine ourselves to working with some version of MISS in Figure 5-1, our simplest systems model.

But suppose we think that this overdoes the simplification and omits important things, that some things inside a state have an important effect on what that state does when it receives some jolt from the external environment. In other words, what if an arms race is really more like this: one state takes a step (say it increases its defense budget) and the second state eventually responds but exactly how it responds depends on its leaders' perceptions, on its domestic politics, and on its organizational processes; then the first state also responds, but again only in a way affected by all these factors. Thus there might be a certain amount of action-reaction but it would be uneven, hard to see and even harder to explain unless we took these internal factors into account.

This is roughly how one would sketch the development of analysis of arms races. After World War I, a first attempt was made to see arms racing as a simple action-reaction process, one that could be described with a few equations. Ever since then, but especially in the last two decades, analysts have tried to refine those early equations or to devise new ones that would fit the data about arms competitions. But other analysts have asserted that arms competitions are never just action-reaction in nature; they have tried to uncover and evaluate other factors involved. Still other analysts have asserted that in some cases there is no arms race at all—the internal factors that drive arms spending and production are so powerful that the so-called rivals are often not really reacting to each other at all. They are not keeping up with the Jones'; they are only vaguely aware of what the Jones' are up to.

As an illustration of how to move away from a simple action-reaction systems model, we can look at a project that examined both actions and perceptions. Robert North at Stanford was the guiding figure in this work, which was initiated by studying the great crisis that led to World War I. Things did not go exactly as planned!

> When the overall project was begun, the intent was to complete the World War I study and then move on to another crisis. That was in the autumn of 1958. By the early 1960s we were still plowing our way through the six weeks between the assassination of Francis Ferdinand in late June 1914 and the outbreak of war in early August. It was a vastly larger undertaking than we had anticipated.[18]

A few months' work turned into twenty years'.

Initially there was some poking around in the crisis and the discovery that there was a lot more to it, and to making any sense out of it, than was originally anticipated. The first studies to come out concentrated on the perceptions of the major leaders involved in the 1914 crisis and the effects those perceptions seemed to have on their actions. These perceptions were explored by the use of content analysis. Thousands of documents were translated and studied, their themes extracted and then coded (given an appropriate number or numbers) in terms of such things as whether they were perceptions of another government's strength or hostility, or were assertions of hostility, and if so of what intensity.

These studies tried to grapple with a puzzle. Several states in 1914 felt militarily inferior to their opponents. Why, then, were they willing to go to war? The working hypothesis was that a state that feels injured to a sufficient degree will consider going to war, irrespective of its strength vis-à-vis its opponents. This eventually led to the question of how such perceptions of injury are shaped and how they affect a state's actions. One result was the two-step mediated stimulus-response model which is really a simple input-output systems model (see Figure 5-8).

FIGURE 5-8
The Interaction Model

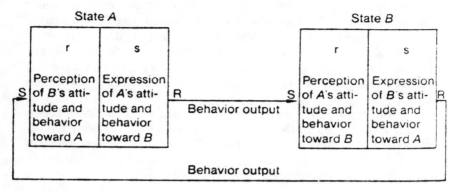

Looking carefully at the model we see that for each state the flow is S-r: s-R, in which a stimulus (S) is perceived (r) leading to an expression of attitudes(s) which produce actions that become the response (R). Each state's R becomes the S for the other but only as mediated by perceptions and attitudes. A hostile S (say a nasty note from Germany to England) produces a perception (r) of hostility by the recipient. This leads the recipient to develop an attitude(s), maybe hostility too, and to decide to do something (R) as a result (perhaps send a similarly nasty note to Germany). At various points the data should be correlated—changes in S's should produce changes in r's, and studies found a modest degree of correlation of the sort expected.

One particular finding of Professor North and some of his colleagues is of interest. They concluded that in August 1914 the German and Austro-Hungarian leaders consistently perceived the actions of the Triple Entente (Britain, France, and Russia) as more violent and threatening than they really were. By the same token, Triple Entente statesmen saw their opponents' actions as less threatening or violent than they really were, so they misperceived the gravity of the situation. When the authors later probed the 1962 Cuban Missile Crisis they found a rather different picture.[19] There the perceptions on both sides, judging from the documents, were relatively accurate. This may be why Soviet and American actions were closely correlated; neither's reactions were way out of proportion to the S's that provoked them. This may be why Washington and Moscow were able to successfully get through the 1962 crisis, while the earlier one was mismanaged right into perhaps the worst disaster of the twentieth century.

As you can see, this type of analysis results in comparing foreign policy actions but only in a limited way. First, only perception is explored as a contributing factor; our earlier discussion in this chapter and, in fact, in Chapters 3 and 4 suggested that many other factors may be involved. Second, there is nothing in the way of an explanation as to why in some states—in some crises—perceptions were reasonably accurate but not so in others. In line with our earlier discussion we would expect analysts to have developed more complex systems frameworks to try to remedy these problems and, sure enough, they have.

Figure 5-9 is the basic framework employed by the Interstate Behavior Analysis (IBA) project, the work of Jonathan Wilkenfeld at the University of Maryland and his associates.[20] Down the left side are listed five sources of foreign policy which roughly correspond to the five levels of analysis used in this book. Each category is really a cluster of variables. Thus the first psychological component covers such things as the phychological drives of decision makers, their personality traits, and their belief systems—the sorts of factors at the individual analysis we discussed in chapter 3. The political component includes the institutions involved in foreign policy, small group dynamics, bureaucratic politics, public opinion, and foreign policy elites.

FIGURE 5-9
IBA Framework for Comparative Analysis of Foreign Policy

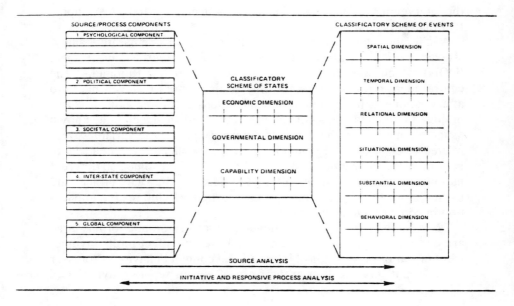

Under the societal component we find national culture, social struc-ture, economic and social change, and the nature and degree of domestic conflict. The fourth component is meant to take into account the many economic relationships a society has with others (in trade, energy, food, etc.) which create interdependence and/or dependence and the interactions these relationships stimulate. The final category is for characteristics of the global system and the state's position in it.

On the right side we have "dimensions," which are simply the categories for arranging types of foreign policy actions ("events"). The spatial dimension concerns the geographical area involved, such as an American action in the Middle East. "Relational" dimension has to do with the number of parties involved in an event, their nature, and their role in the event. "Substantial" refers to the kind of issue involved (economic, political, etc.) while "behavioral" touches on the specific nature of the action. Of course every event has a "temporal" dimen-sion, a time period.

In between are some other things analysts have suggested as impor-tant, some relatively static characteristics of a nation such as the basic nature of its economic and political systems and its capabilities for taking action (such as its military power). The framework reflects the view that all the things covered on the left-hand side work in and through the dimensions in the middle to produce foreign policy actions as described and measured on the right-hand side. Early research with the framework turned up findings that seem to fit with this view, with the intervening variables—in the middle—turning out to be less impor-tant than expected.

A still more elaborate list of relevant factors for comparative analy-sis was developed and applied in the Dimensionality of Nations project (DON) which was primarily the work of Rudolph Rummel.[21] The central idea, however, was not only to list factors believed likely to affect nations' behavior but to rank all nations accordingly by measures of these factors, so that a computer and the statistical technique known as factor analysis could be used to determine how these variables were related to each other. Eventually data were collected on over eighty nations in the international system of the 1950s, on some 230 different national attributes. I will not attempt to describe the DON project and its findings, other than to refer to one particularly interesting applica-tion in comparative analysis.

Does the fact that a nation is developed, or democratic, or has large armed forces, or is internally unstable have any affect on its involve-ment in war or other kinds of international conflict behavior? Professor Rummel put this question in the form of eleven separate hypotheses which asserted that a nation's foreign conflict behavior would be highly related to the nation's:

1. level of economic development
2. level of international communications or transactions
3. amount of cooperation with others
4. being totalitarian or not
5. power
6. domestic instability
7. military capabilities
8. psychological motivations of its people
9. values
10. number of borders
11. combination and interaction of many of the above factors

Many of these hypotheses are plausible. Indeed, many statements can be found in the literature asserting that one or more of them is true. Rummel subjected each to testing on the basis of his data and also reviewed the empirical findings of others. The results came as something of a shock: not one of the hypotheses was confirmed! None of these factors seemed to be consistently related to the conflict behavior of nations.[22]

A well-developed theory of foreign policy would not only point out the relevant variables, such as in the Wilkenfeld framework, it would also rank them in order of their importance or magnitude of impact, such as the way Kegley and Wittkopf try to do for the United States. It would be nice to know that a nation's population, the quality of its armed forces, and the size of its economy determine its foreign policy. It would be far nicer to know which of those factors is the most important and by how much more than the others.

From this point of view, foreign policy is not a very nice subject. As of now we have no generally accepted theory of foreign policy. We must still make do with what James Rosenau calls "pre-theories," extremely primitive theories that have yet to be adequately tested. An elaborate pre-theory has been developed by Rosenau himself, one of the most diligent and respected analysts in the field.

Rosenau has clustered what he thinks are the relevant variables into several categories. (It was these categories that were then applied by Kegley and Wittkopf in the U.S.) They are:

1. individual variables—the personal characteristics of the decision makers
2. Role variables—the impact of the office, and its position in the government, on the office-holder

3. Governmental variables—the structure and nature of the government
4. Societal variables—is the society industrialized, unified, etc.
5. Systemic variables—the nature of the international system

Rosenau believes it is possible to rank these five categories in order of importance for shaping any government's foreign policy. However, he suggests that the ranking will vary depending on the nature of the country. Systemic variables, for example, should be more important for small states than large ones because the former will be more at the mercy of the environment. Thus when the United States reached the culmination of its monetary difficulties in 1971, President Nixon moved to force a change in the whole international monetary system; a small nation in similar straits can only adapt as best it can to that system.

Nations are not only large or small, they are also developed or not, and relatively democratic (open) or undemocratic (closed). Rosenau wants to take these things into account and others as well. He notes that societies are often penetrated from the outside, which could easily affect a government's foreign policy. In addition, we know from studies of domestic politics that different issues are handled by different sets of officials and in varying ways within a government. If this is true of foreign policy then we would probably find that the five variable clusters are of different relative importance depending on the issue at hand. Thus Rosenau worked out a typology of foreign-policy issues—over territory, status, human resources, and nonhuman resources—to round out his analysis.

Pulling all of these things together results in Figure 5-10, which is the complete version of Rosenau's pretheory.[23] Selecting an example from the figure and reading from the top down, we see that in a small, developed, and democratic society that is penetrated from the outside (a country like Belgium), the most important variables will be systemic ones no matter what the issue, while individual variables will be the least important. In such a country, no matter who is in charge of foreign policy, their actions will be shaped by what the rest of the world is up to more than by anything else. Compare this with a large, underdeveloped, undemocratic nation (Indonesia for instance) where Rosenau anticipates that individual variables would be most important.

All this is on the input side of a systems model. Still left is the problem of describing and categorizing foreign policies, i.e. the output side. Rosenau has also been hard at work on this as well, having generated an "adaptation" model of foreign policy.[24] It begins with the assumption that foreign policy is best thought of as adaptive behavior

FIGURE 5-10
Rosenau's Pretheory

Legend:
sy = systemic variables
so = societal variables
g = governmental variables
r = role variables
i = individual variables

The figure presents a large matrix classifying countries by size (Large Country / Small Country), economy (Developed Economy / Underdeveloped Economy), polity (Open Polity / Closed Polity), and penetration (Penetrated / Non-penetrated). For each combination, three areas are ranked — status area, nonhuman resource area, and other areas — using the variable abbreviations sy, so, g, r, and i.

in an increasingly interdependent world. Rosenau asserts that a society relies on four essential systems—physical, political, social, and economic—that must be kept in reasonable repair. But the world outside presses on and strains these systems and adaptation is needed to keep the world and these systems in a tolerable relationship to each other.

There are four kinds of adaptations, which reflect the impact of the factors listed in Figure 5-10. A preservative policy is used by a government very sensitive to the global environment and pressure from domestic sources. An acquiescent policy is that of a government responding primarily to its environment, such as a very small, weak state living next to very powerful neighbors. Opposite this is a government that ignores the environment in favor of attention to demands from inside, leading to an intransigent foreign policy. Finally, a government may be headed by individuals and elites who pursue only their own goals, largely ignoring the environment and their own citizens, which results in a promotional foreign policy.

Problems and Difficulties

This chapter concludes in the usual fashion by reviewing some of the problems and difficulties that beset the analyst who adheres to a systems perspective. Before turning to these matters, a few other comments are in order. One concerns the second question listed at the end of chapter 2, namely "What conception of the nature of man is employed?" Critics of systems approaches have not been entirely in agreement on this point, some saying that systems approaches tend to depict governments and officials as far more rational and orderly than they really are, while others have held that systems approaches downplay the rational calculations of officials and states too much in order to stress many others factors. Systems approaches cannot very well be guilty of both, and the important point is that they do not have to be seen as doing either. A systems approach generally assumes the system has goals and is trying to reach them—it has purpose. But it does not necessarily assume rationality.

One other question in the list at the end of chapter 2 was: "How unique is international politics?" On the whole a systems approach is unlikely to see international politics as involving special problems and conditions. The Snyder scheme was believed to be "equally applicable to the study of domestic politics or comparative politics, not just foreign policy."[25] On the other hand many systems approaches may well allow for some differences—at least at the margins—such as the greater difficulty in getting reliable information, and thus the pervasive uncertainty, that the foreign policy actor must face.

Now we are ready to turn to some difficulties and problems, the rocks in the stream of a systems approach. Lets plunge right in by recalling the all-important point that a framework, model, or theory is supposed to simplify our task in significant ways. How does the systems framework perform in this regard? It is fair to say that the results are meager; we are left with a subject that looks nearly as complex and multifaceted as ever while the intellectual tasks of analysis look almost as daunting. In tracing the various studies we found the categories and possibly relevant factors proliferated like analytical rabbits.

As we saw, one way to get around this is to try to concentrate on only one or two key factors. However, it is very difficult to do this successfully. For instance, to assess the foreign policy differences between open and closed systems we would benefit from access to each. But a closed system is, almost by definition, not really amenable to this kind of investigation. Thus we are apt to have hypotheses meant to apply to closed systems that can only be tested in open ones.

Also, to measure the effects of any one or two factors we may need to be able to understand the shifting contexts provided by all the others. How will a head cold affect a person's performance on an exam? It depends, we might guess, on the person and the subject and the time of day and the nature of the exam and so on. We are left with the feeling that we have to know everything to study anything. Perhaps this is why studies of the relationship between democracy (or size, or geography, or level of development) have failed to turn up consistently rewarding findings—they cannot fine-tune the contexts within which the comparative analyses are made.

The Paige study illustrated the very detailed work that may be necessary to apply systems analysis to just one case. The same is true for the studies by North et. al. of the 1914 crisis. The need for such great quantities of information brings with it various limitations. As has often been noted, this makes it likely that a truly detailed analysis can ever be anything but retrospective in nature. And there are formidable barriers to crossnational research as a result. The vast Brecher work just to describe and analyze foreign policy in Israel will not be easily imitated.

Another defect of systems approaches is that while they are long on framework they are short on theory. It has often been asserted by critics, and generally accepted by foreign policy systems theorists, that these approaches do not go very far beyond the framework itself. Hence Rosenau labeled his work a *pretheory*. An extended critique of his approach has concluded that it is vague at the many critical points, is inadequate when it comes to generating hypotheses, and ends up being just one more typology. Rosenau himself has, more recently, characterized his pretheory as deficient because it is "time-bound," too "static," and too vague about what exactly constitutes foreign policy.[26]

A more serious way to put this criticism is to assert that simply developing categories and collecting large quantities of data—as in the DON project or events data collections—is not very useful, that we need a theory to tell us what constitutes the relevant data worth collecting in the first place. The crux of this view is that a systems framework will inevitably fall short of developing useful and useable theory.

A final problem with systems approaches is in translating the concepts into concrete terms and developing appropriate measures. In the language of methodology this means making them operational, giving them empirical referents. To consider this, take the concept of feedback. To use it effectively we must be able to distinguish it from other informational inputs. If the U.S. announces a Star Wars defense program and the Soviets then drag their feet in strategic arms control talks, is the Soviet move to be treated as feedback? It is difficult to say, though the answer is vitally important to U.S. officials or to analysts attempting to understand their actions. Perhaps the Soviets had no intention of being very cooperative in the talks anyway. If Moscow criticizes the Sudanese government for its treatment of the local communist party and six months later that government signs an aid agreement with the U.S., is this an illustration of feedback? It would be next to impossible to be certain, what with all the other things that may have affected the Sudanese action in the intervening period.

The most elaborate attempts to make feedback a more refined and useful concept have been mounted by Michael Brecher. By immersion in Israeli affairs, Brecher has been able to trace effects of one action and foreign reactions to it on later decisions and to diagram the flow of the effects within his framework. But the result is not, in the end, any real improvement over the work of the diplomatic historian. The relative impact of feedback in comparison with other variables is never specified with precision, and the hypotheses Brecher tests do not deal with this.

It is measurement problems that have helped make crisis, especially an extreme crisis, such an attractive subject no matter how unusual it is. Time is limited, incoming information and decisions and outputs are more readily delineated, the decision unit is more clearly defined. But trying to do these things for the everyday process of a government or even for important noncrisis decisions is much more problematic. Measuring national power is notoriously difficult, and in many categories of a DON project or an events data collection the coding inevitably involves a good deal of latitude for judgment. And without general agreement on what it is we wish to explain, as with the divergent conceptions of foreign policy, research is not easily made truly cumulative and complementary. Sure enough, we find that various events-data projects cover different actors, use varying sources for their data, have several time frames, employ various classification schemes, and differ according to whether they look for multiple targets of actions by several actors or a single target of action by a single actor.

Measurement problems also beset the findings in much of the research. Taking Paige's study as an example, consider the second proposition that was listed earlier: "The greater the crisis, the more the leader's solicitation of subordinate advice." How would you tell a greater from a lesser crisis? How would you measure a president's solicitation of advice? How do we measure his solicitation of advice over a period of a week (in a crisis) as compared with his seeking advice on a matter he pondered on and off for three months? Yet all this is exactly what we must be able to do to test the hypotheses. Any number of Paige's propositions, and those of others working in a systems framework, are open to the same objections.

Paige was attempting to explore the decision process itself, something I have deliberately neglected up to this point, preferring to leave this to the next chapter. The reason is that it is in the nature of decision making that we find the most sophisticated attempts to develop theory at the nation-state level of analysis and it is better give them separate treatment than to try to include them in an already lengthy and complicated chapter. In effect we have been leaving the actual decision process as a black box. Now we must consider efforts to break into that black box and to characterize what goes on there.

Notes

1. David Vital, "Back to Machiavelli," in Klaus Knorr and James Rosenau, eds., *Contending Approaches to International Politics* (Princeton University Press, 1969), p. 153; and Stanley Hoffman, "An American Social Science: International Relations," *Daedalus* (Summer 1977), p. 56.
2. John Lovell, *Foreign Policy in Perspective* (New York: Holt, Rinehart and Winston, 1970), pp. 211-16.

168   Theories and Approaches to International Politics

3. Philip Burgess and Raymond Lawton, *Indicators of International Behavior: An Assessment of Events Data Research,* Series No. 02-010 (Beverley Hills, Calif.: Sage, 1972), p. 30.
4. John Lovell, *The Challenge of American Foreign Policy* (Macmillan, 1985), pp. 27, 32.
5. Richard Snyder, H. W. Bruck, and Burton Sapin, "Decision-Making as an Approach to the Study of International Politics," in Snyder, Bruck, and Sapin, eds., *Foreign Policy Decision Making* (New York: Free Press, 1962).
6. Glenn Paige, *The Korean Decision* (New York: Free Press, 1968), pp. 283-84.
7. Ibid., pp. 288, 290, 293, 295, 301, 309.
8. Charles Kegley, Jr. and Eugene Wittkopf, *American Foreign Policy, Pattern and Process* 2d ed. (New York: St. Martin's, 1982) p. 13.
9. Ibid., pp. 438-39.
10. Ibid., p. 544.
11. Michael Brecher, *Decision in Israel's Foreign Policy* (New Haven: Yale University Press, 1975), pp. 6-7.
12. Ibid., pp. 546-48, 574-79.
13. Burgess and Lawton, p. 6.
14. Edward Morse, "The Transformation of Foreign Policies," *World Politics* (April 1970), p. 371.
15. Peter Bechman, *World Politics in the Twentieth Century* (Englewood Cliffs, N.J.: Prentice-Hall, 1984).
16. Ray Cline, *World Power Assessment* (Boulder, Colo.: Westview, 1977)
17. Charles McClelland, "The Acute International Crisis," in Klaus Knorr and Sidney Verba, eds., *The International System, Theoretical Essays* (Princeton University Press, 1961), p. 194.
18. Robert North, "The Stanford Studies in International Conflict and Integration," in Francis Hoole and Dina Zinnes, eds., *Quantitative International Politics, An Appraisal* (New York: Praeger, 1976), pp. 350-51.
19. Ole Holsti, Richard Brody, and Robert North, "The Management of International Crisis: Affect and Action in American-Soviet Relations," in Dean Pruitt and Richard Snyder, eds., *Theory and Research on the Causes of War* (Englewood Cliffs, N.J.: Prentice-Hall, 1969), pp. 62-79.
20. Jonathan Wilkenfeld et al., *Foreign Policy Behavior: The Interstate Behavior Analysis Model* (Beverley Hills, Calif.: Sage, 1980), p. 35. For an earlier version of the model see Stephen Andriole et al., "A Framework for the Comparative Analysis of Foreign Policy Behavior," *International Studies Quarterly* (June 1975), pp. 160-98.
21. R. J. Rummel, *The Dimensionality of Nations* (Beverley Hills, Calif.: Sage, 1972).
22. Rudolph Rummel, "The Relationship Between National Attributes and Foreign Conflict Behavior," in J. David Singer, ed., *Quantitative International Politics: Insights and Evidence* (New York: Free Press, 1968), pp. 187-214.
23. James Rosenau, *The Scientific Study of Foreign Policy* (New York: Free Press, 1971), p. 149.
24. James Rosenau, *The Adaptation of National Societies: A Theory of Political Systems Behavior and Transformation* (McCaleb-Seiler, 1970).

25. Snyder et al., p. 20.
26. James Rosenau, "A Pre-Theory Revisited: World Politics in an Era of Cascading Interdependence," *International Studies Quarterly* (September 1984), pp. 245-305, particularly pp. 251-52; Steve Smith, "Rosenau's Adaptive Behaviour Approach—A Critique," *Review of International Studies* (April 1981), pp. 103-26.

Bibliographical Remarks

Much of the literature on systems approaches in international politics concerns work at the international system level of analysis, and examples are cited in the bibliographical remarks following Chapter 8. In elaboration of a systems concept at the national level is Karl Deutsch, *Nerves of Government* (New York: Free Press, 1963).

On comparative foreign policy, the following list covers a variety of the available approaches: Howard Lentner, *Foreign Policy Analysis: A Comparative and Conceptual Approach* (Columbus, Ohio: Charles E. Merrill, 1974); Joseph Frankel, *The Making of Foreign Policy* (New York: Oxford University Press, 1963); Patrick McGowan and Howard Shapiro, *The Comparative Study of Foreign Policy* (Beverley Hills, Calif.: Sage, 1973); Wolfram Hanrieder, *Comparative Foreign Policy: Theoretical Essays* (New York: David McKay, 1971); Roy Macridis, ed., *Foreign Policy in World Politics,* 6th ed. (Englewood Cliffs, N.J.: Prentice-Hall, 1985); Richard Cottam, *Foreign Policy Motivation: A General Theory and a Case Study* (University of Pittsburgh Press, 1977).

Jonathan Wilkenfeld et al., *Foreign Policy Behavior* (Beverley Hills, Calif.: Sage, 1980) contains a good review of various approaches for comparative foreign policy and a good bibliography on the subject, as well as laying out the Interstate Behavior analysis project.

A problem mentioned on the chapter is the difficulty of defining and then measuring the dependent variable—foreign policy. Two examples of discussions about how to do this: Charles Kegley, Jr., *A General Empirical Typology of Foreign Policy Behavior,* Series No. 02-014 (Beverley Hills, Calif.: Sage, 1973); and Patrick Callahan et al., eds., *Describing Foreign Policy Behavior* (Beverley Hills, Calif.: Sage, 1982) which also contains a very large bibliography on the comparative analysis of foreign policy.

Crisis decision-making and nations' behavior in crisis situations can be studied at several levels of analysis, and thus some of the works cited here could also be included at the end of later chapters. But it seemed sensible to put them all in one place: Phil Williams, *Crisis Management: Confrontation and Diplomacy in the Nuclear Age* (New York: Wiley, 1976); Abraham Wagner, *Crisis Decision-Making: Israel's Experience in 1967 and 1973* (New York: Praeger, 1974); Richard Ned Lebow, *Between Peace and War: The Nature of the International Crisis* (Johns Hopkins University Press, 1981); Glenn Snyder and Paul Diesing, *Conflict Among Nations* (Princeton University Press, 1977); Christopher Shoemaker and John Spanier, *Patron-Client State Relationships: Multilateral Crises in the Nuclear Age* (New York: Praeger, 1984); Michael Brecher and Jonathan Wilkenfeld, "Crises in World Politics," *World Politics* (April 1982), pp. 380-417; Ole Holsti, "Theories of Crisis Decision-Making," in Paul Lauren, ed., *Diplomacy: New Approaches in History, Theory and Policy* (New York: Free Press, 1979), chap. 5; Raymond

Tanter, "International Crisis Behavior: An Appraisal of the Literature," in Michael Brecher, ed., *Studies in Crisis Behavior* (New Brunswick, N.J.: Transaction, 1979), pp. 340-74; Jonathan Wilkenfeld and Michael Brecher, "Superpower Crisis Management Behavior," in Charles Kegley, Jr. and Pat McGowan, eds., *Foreign Policy USA/USSR* (Beverley Hills, Calif.: Sage, 1982), pp. 185-212; Gerald Hopple et al., eds., *National Security Crisis Forecasting and Management* (Boulder, Colo.: Westview, 1984); Daniel Frei, ed., *Managing International Crises* (Beverley Hills, Calif.: Sage, 1982); Arthur Gilbert and Paul Lauren, "Crisis Management: An Assessment and Critique," *Journal of Conflict Resolution* (December 1980), pp. 641-64; and the response to the critique in Ole Holsti, "Historians, Social Scientists, and Crisis Management: An Alternative View," *Journal of Conflict Resolution* (December 1980), pp. 665-82.

The literature on events data collections is fairly extensive. Some descriptive materials include Edward Azar and Joseph Ben-Dak, eds., *Theory and Practice of Events Research* (New York: Gordon and Breach Science Publishers, 1975); and Charles Kegley, Jr., et al., eds., *International Events and the Comparative Analysis of Foreign Policy* (University of South Carolina Press, 1975). Evaluations' of the data sets and of events data programs in general include Bo Svendsen, "Foreign Policy as Events: A Critique of an Operational Definition," *Cooperation and Conflict* no. 1 (1980), pp. 21-30; Philip Burgess and Raymond Lawton, *Indicators of International Behavior: An Assessment of Events Data Research*, Series No. 02-010 (Beverley Hills, Calif.: Sage, 1972); Llewellyn Howell, "A Comparative Study of the WEIS and COPDAB Data Sets," *International Studies Quarterly* (June 1983), pp. 149-59; Jack Vincent, "WEIS vs COPDAB: Correspondence Problems" and Charles McClelland, "Let the User Beware," both in *International Studies Quarterly* (June 1983), pp. 161-77.

There are any number of works that make use of events data which could be cited here, and the following list contains just a small sample: P. Terrance Hopmann and Timothy King, "From Cold War to Detente: The Role of the Cuban Missile Crisis and the Partial Nuclear Test Ban Treaty," in Ole Holsti et al., eds., *Change in the International System* (Boulder, Colo.: Westview, 1980), pp. 163-88; William Eckhardt, "Pioneers of Peace Research VII, Edward E. Azar: Apostle of Events," *International Interactions*, vol. 10, no. 2 (1983), pp. 269-91, which describes one events data collection and some of its uses; Charles Hermann and Robert Mason, "Identifying Behavioral Attributes of Events That Trigger International Crises," in Ole Holsti et al., eds., *Change in the International System* (Boulder, Colo.: Westview, 1980), pp. 189-210; Stephen Andriole and Gerald Hopple, "The Rise and Fall of Events Data: From Basic Research to Applied Use in the Department of Defense," *International Interactions*, vol. 10, no. 3-4 (1983), pp. 293-309, which contains an interesting account of an effort to use events data to assist policy makers and of the problems that arose.

On the DON (Dimensionality of Nations) project and studies related to it I can suggest the following: Rudolph Rummel, *The Dimensionality of Nations* (Beverley Hills, Calif.: Sage, 1972); Gordon Hilton, *A Review of the Dimensionality of Nations Project*, Series No. 02-015 (Beverley Hills, Calif.: Sage, 1973); Dina Zinnes, *Quantitative International Politics, An Appraisal* (New York: Praeger, 1976); Raymond Tanter, "Dimensions of Conflict Within and

Between Nations, 1958-1960," in John Mueller, ed., *Approaches to Measurement in International Relations* (New York: Appleton-Century-Crofts, 1969), pp. 180-97; Jonathan Wilkenfeld, "Domestic and Foreign Conflict Behavior of Nations," in William Coplin and Charles Kegley, Jr., eds., *A Multi-Method Introduction to International Politics* (Markham, 1971), pp. 189-204. There is a larger body of work of which the DON project has been a part, reflected in the five volumes that Rummel has produced. For an overview of this work see James Lee Ray, "Understanding Rummel," *Journal of Conflict Resolution* (March 1982), pp. 161-87.

The Stanford studies on the outbreak of World War I have resulted in numerous publications as well as critical evaluations. Examples of the former would include Ole Holsti, *Crisis, Escalation, War* (McGill-Queens University Press, 1972); Nazli Choucri and Robert North, *Nations In Conflict* (San Francisco: W.H. Freeman and Co., 1975); Nazli Choucri and Robert North, "Dynamics of International Conflict: Some Policy Implications of Population, Resources, and Technology," in Raymond Tanter and Richard Ullmann, eds., *Theory and Policy in International Relations* (Princeton University Press, 1972); and Robert North and Richard Lagerstrom, *War and Domination: A Theory of Lateral Pressure* (General Learning Press, 1971).

For evaluations of the Stanford studies see Dina Zinnes, *Contemporary Research in International Relations* (New York: Free Press, 1976), pp. 126-49; Robert Jervis, "The Costs of the Scientific Study of Politics: An Examination of the Stanford Content Analysis Studies," *International Studies Quarterly* (December 1967), pp. 366-93; James Caporaso, "A Philosophy-of-Science Assessment of the Stanford Studies in Conflict and Integration," in Francis Hoole and Dina Zinnes, eds., *Quantitative International Politics, An Appraisal* (New York: Praeger, 1976), pp. 359-63; and Karen Feste, "An Appraisal of the Methodological and Statistical Practices Used in the 1914 Project," in Francis Hoole and Dina Zinnes, eds., *Quantitative International Politics, An Appraisal* (New York: Praeger, 1976), pp. 383-406.

Some relevant works by Michael Brecher include "A Framework for Research on Foreign Policy Behavior," *Journal of Conflict Resolution* (March 1969), pp. 75-101; *The Foreign Policy System of Israel* (New Haven: Yale University Press, 1972); Images, Processes and Feedback in Foreign Policy: Israel's Decisions on German Reparations, *American Political Science review* (March 1973), pp. 73-102; and "Inputs and Decisions for War and Peace: The Israel Experience," *International Studies Quarterly* (June 1974), pp. 131-77.

Finally, on the work of James Rosenau in connection with his pretheory and his adaptation approach, a number of his articles over the years have been gathered together in three volumes, one of which is an updated version of an older book: *The Study of Global Interdependence; The Study of Political Adaptation;* and *The Scientific Study of Foreign Policy*, rev. ed.; each of which has been published by Francis Pinter Ltd. in 1980. Also relevant is his edited volume *Comparing Foreign Policies: Theories, Findings, and Methods* (Beverley Hills, Calif.: Sage, 1974).

For efforts to work with the adaptation approach or critiques of its value one can look at the following: Nikolaj Peterson, "Adaptation as a Framework for the Analysis of Foreign Policy Behavior," *Cooperation and Conflict* vol. 12, no. 4 (1977), pp. 221-50; Peter Hansen, "Adaptive Behavior of Small States: The Case of Denmark and the European Community," in P. McGowan, ed.,

Sage International Yearbook of Foreign Policy Studies vol. 2 (1974), pp. 143-74; Patrick McGowan and Klaus-Peter Gottwald, "Small State Foreign Policies: A Comparative Study of Participation, Conflict, and Political and Economic Dependence in Black America," *International Studies Quarterly* (December 1975), pp. 469-500; Steve Smith, "Rosenau's Contribution," *Review of International Studies* (April 1983), pp. 137-46; Steve Smith, *Foreign Policy Adaptation: Aspects of British and Dutch Foreign Policies* (Gower Publishing, 1981).

6

If Reason Ruled the World

The discussion in the previous chapter was probably long and complicated enough to induce some negative feedback in your head what with all those diagrams and proliferating clusters of relevant variables. Unfortunately, that headache—inducing complexity—does not exhaust the subject of analysis at the nation-state level. As indicated at the end of chapter 5, we still have to consider efforts to break into the black box. As usual, there are preliminary matters to consider before we move to the heart of the subject.

We need to remind ourselves, at the outset, that not everyone feels the need to grope around in that box, which in our systems models was labeled *decision making*. As we saw in chapter 5, Charles McClelland (among others) argued some years back that if we can find a sufficiently regular connection or pattern in the interactions of states, we can explain a lot and predict without having to examine the exact processes that lead to each state's actions. A simple, accurate arms race model might well tell us how much country B will spend on arms if we know what country A just spent. At the individual level of analysis this is roughly the approach taken by Skinner briefly discussed back in chapter 4—grasping the effects of conditioning allows explanation of human behavior without recourse to the concept of consciousness or wrestling with the inner workings of the mind.

However, many analysts insist on trying to break into the box, trying, that is, to characterize the decision process of states on foreign policy matters. This brings us to another point. The subject of decision making has arisen previously in this book. At the individual and group levels we reviewed approaches which tried to get a handle on how decision making proceeds. If we think that what moves individuals (or groups) can in turn explain the behavior of national governments then we have already reached into the box. But if we think approaches at those levels supply only part of the picture, then we must say something else about decision making of a government as a whole. We must come up with something new or else our box will remain black (or at least grey).

Still another possibility, only infrequently considered in the field but worthy of a passing reference at this point, is that governments do not—at least not very often—really make decisions (and thus there is no black box). It is possible that what governments do in foreign affairs is mainly routine, seldom fashioned via conscious choices. Thus the study of decision making has only an occasional relevance. On the other hand, this may be a case where a concept can be usefully applied for purposes of analysis even if it only awkwardly encompasses many details of the subject. Whatever governments mostly do, it may be useful to say that it is decision making, more useful to describe it that way than any other way. This is a point we will return to throughout this chapter.

Let us say that governments do make decisions; let us also say that it is important to know how those decisions are made. How might we then proceed? By far the most influential answer has been that we should start by assuming that governments are rational when it comes to foreign policy decisions. It will take the rest of this chapter to begin to explore what this has meant for the study of international politics.

Rational Decision Making

The conception of rational decision making has been a powerful tool for the development of theory in several social sciences, and this has been particularly true in the study of international politics. Generally speaking, rationality is taken to refer to a *procedure* that takes place within a set of *conditions*. The following list of elements covers both:

1. The decision making unit has a *goal* or several goals. If there are several goals, they are ranked in order of preference or importance.
2. *Information* is available, and is gathered by the decision making unit, about the situation in which it finds itself and how that situation affects its goals.
3. The decision making unit considers the available alternative steps that could be taken to achieve its goal or goals, evaluating them in terms of their costs and benefits as well as their probability of success.
4. The decision making unit then picks the best alternative—in terms of costs, benefits, and probability of success.

If we want to allow for recurring decision making and the possibility of uncertainty we can also include a step to cover feedback, so that the decision making unit gathers information on the results of its choice and alters its future decisions accordingly. Thus within certain conditions—the situation, the information available, and the goal(s)—the decision making unit engages in a process that maximizes its achievement.

There are certain things to note about this conception. One is that what is rational depends on the goal; decision making units in the same situation and employing the same process may well choose different actions because their goals are not the same. Next, a conception of rational decision making can be used at many levels of analysis, not just at the nation-state level. A bureaucratic politics model, for instance, tends to describe bureaucratic actors as rationally pursuing their organizational interests, and some approaches at the regional level which we will take up in the next chapter make use of a rational decision maker conception. Finally, how one employs a rational-decision-maker conception in an analysis depends fundamentally on where the analyst thinks goals come from. This is not a well appreciated point, but it is one to keep constantly in mind. If we think the goals of a decision making unit largely arise from within, we will go at analysis very differently than if we think those goals are primarily determined by the situation or environment in which the unit finds itself.

How can this conception be employed in the study of international politics? There are at least three ways. The first we discussed in the previous chapter and we will just skim over it here. A rational decision maker conception, or model, can readily be used as an *ideal type,* a model of how things ought to be done against which to compare the real world. Not only can this clarify our sense of what actually happens, it can be used to offer advice on how things might be improved. This is done all the time. When the Reagan administration Pentagon turned out to be paying foolishly high prices for ordinary tools or parts of weapons systems, suggestions were immediately offered—such as introducing more competition in defense contracting—to make the weapons acquisition process more "rational." I trust this is all clear and we need not say anything more about it here.

To introduce the second path we might consider the practice of "kibitzing." If you peer over the shoulder of someone playing chess or a foursome at bridge you are likely to start to fidget, as you suffer from the almost irresistible urge to kibitz—to tell at least one of those players what to do next. Think for a moment of the intellectual operations involved in kibitzing. The kibitzer must somehow contrive to put himself in another person's shoes, muttering to himself, "If I were sitting there. . . ." To do so he must size up the situation—what game this is, what the rules are, who is on what side—and decide what the object for the player is at this particular point. He then develops a strategy for achieving that goal in that context and in doing so he tries to take into account what the other players are up to, what their goals and strategies are. In short, he tries to work out the logic of the situation, to detect what rationality indicates should be done next.

The assumption that people are behaving rationally, or at least trying to, allows the kibitzer mentally to get into the game, even if he knows nothing about the players. It offers a short-cut, a simple way to proceed so as to get to the heart of the matter. The inclination to analyze others' behavior in this way (as well as to kibitz) is very compelling, and some con games exploit it. In one, two players—playing for money of course—seem to be skillfully and intently playing a strange game (there are odd terms, inexplicable moves) and the idea is to get the "mark," the kibitzer, to try his hand at it once he thinks he's figured out enough of the game. Actually there is no game; the two made up the terms and rules as they went along. The new player finds that he sometimes wins but more often loses because of rules he never quite understands. He may never tumble to the fact that there was no game at all.

Assuming rational decision making is often an academic version of kibitzing, the analyst goes into action by thinking as if he was one of the players in the foreign policy game. To do this he starts with Graham Allison's rational policy paradigm or a similar model in mind.[1] The nation's actions are assumed to be purposeful, and the decision makers are assumed to be weighing alternatives in terms of costs and benefits and selecting the one that looks best. In an interdependent world, this means they must also be taking into account the goals and strategies of other governments.

Thus the second way of applying this conception involves what we might call *behavioral rationality*—the conception is used because it is believed to accurately describe what actually happens. The contrast could hardly be greater between this image of a government's behavior and those conveyed by many of the approaches we previously discussed. It assumes that, in the main, governments' actions make sense. Leaders normally are not kooks, officials are not trapped in personality problems or organizational/perceptual routines, decisions are not dictated by parochial elite or bureaucratic squabbles. Instead the peculiarities of individuals, groups and organizations are largely ironed out in the process of weighing what to do for the nation. As you can see, this simplifies things considerably. If it works then it ought to be possible to figure out what any government, as a rational actor, is up to.

There is nothing too tricky about all this—one uses a rational decision model because governments are rational. The third way to use a rational decision maker conception is not as easy to grasp, but it, too, has been very influential, particularly in fields like economics. The critical point is that when we make starting assumptions in order to construct a theory, such as the assumption of rational decision making, we do not really care whether the assumption is behaviorally accurate—what we care about is whether the theory that results works better than any other available theory. Thus we might call this *theoretical rationality* (as opposed to behavioral). In effect, the analyst says "I don't know if governments are rational, but when I assume they are as part of devising my theory I end up with a better theory—I can tell you more about what they are doing and will do, more accurately and more easily, than other theories can." This really is rather tricky; for one thing, it is a sophisticated version of black-boxing again—the analyst does not peer into the box, he just makes a useful assumption about what goes on in there. In addition, most of us are uncomfortable with the idea that it does not matter whether decision making is actually rational—we tend to feel that if the assumption is behaviorially inaccurate then the theory will not work. But this is not necessarily true.

Let us turn to some examples of approaches that employ a rational decision maker conception, using them to elaborate on the distinction between *behavioral* and *theoretical* rationality. Generally speaking, the former is more apt to the employed in an inductive fashion and the latter in a deductive mode and we will use this in part as a way of organizing the discussion.

Induction

In an inductive application of a rational decision maker conception, the analyst tries to appreciate someone else's particular situation or unique perspective and in this way grasps the behavior that flows logically from it. Suppose we want to explain how the Iranian government will react in a severe confrontation with the United States (such as the hostage crisis in the Carter administration). Will it back down? Go to war readily? Talk tough but do almost anything to avoid war? An inductive approach would examine that government's behavior in past confrontations with other states, especially with the United States, and explore what appear to be the starting assumptions, objectives, ideological views, and the like that constitute the wellsprings of Iranian international behavior. The question becomes: Given the Iranian way of looking at the world and at the United States, what approach will make sense to that government?

One way to do this is introspective in nature. I know of no study of foreign policy based solely on introspection, and it is relatively infrequently discussed as a technique by academic analysts. However, I include it here because introspection is employed all the time by ordinary citizens and government officials. Many a diplomat, journalist, or intelligence analyst earns his or her daily bread by applying introspection (at least in part) to such questions as what the Russians really want in the Middle East or how likely it is that various governments will try to develop nuclear weapons. Introspection means the "observation and analysis of oneself." If you think like someone else, then analyzing your own thinking should teach you something about his viewpoint. Perhaps the best way to do this is to reproduce in and for yourself the conditions of the other person. Using this approach the analyst tries to become, however temporarily, like those he wants to study. In order to think like a Russian one would visit the USSR frequently and become immersed in the study of Soviet life. This technique is employed by historians, diplomats, and area specialists, and it can be an effective teaching tool. In some classes children have been introduced to the effects of discrimination by having the class treat those with blue eyes or red hair differently. A major text on the "logic of international relations" devotes the first section to a review of world politics from the perspectives of the U.S., Soviet, and Chinese governments and that of a typical Third World country.[2] The object is to get students to see the world as others do and thus appreciate their view of what is rational and why. Finally, the U.S. government (and other governments, I presume) sets up elaborate games of war or crisis to give high level officials some sense of how opponents will perceive the world and behave in real situations.[3] One benefit is to point out that what we intuitively expect other governments to do, without taking their perspectives into account, can be dreadfully wrong.

Introspection has its pitfalls, of course, which are quite readily apparent. One way to bolster such analysis is by *retrospection,* which uncovers the reasoning of governments through the careful study of history. Simply put, if nations act purposefully and rationally, then a study of their actions over a long period of time will allow us to uncover the logic behind them. We must distinguish between the labors of the thorough analyst, such as the diplomatic historian, and studies which only occasionally dip into history or build an analysis on the basis of relatively recent events. Obviously, any analyst will make use of the past to some extent. What we describe here is the one whose entire orientation is to the past.

There are as many ways to approach diplomatic history as there are for contemporary international politics. One involves tracing the pattern of rationality in a state's foreign policy. A good example is the work of Norman Graebner, one of the most influential American diplomatic historians of the post-1945 era. He describes the history of U.S. dealings with the world as falling into two relatively distinct periods, with 1898 as the dividing line. Prior to 1898 the inner logic of U.S. policy was pursuit of the national interest, which in turn derived from the nation's geographic position and its security requirements.

After 1898, however, the nation moved to pursue ideological interests instead. Now the main goals derived from dominant values in the society, such as democracy. The government eventually undertook to "make the world safe for democracy" and to do battle, on ideological terms, with the threat of communism. This required a shift in policy, because

> A nation cannot pursue simultaneously its national interest and what it imagines to be the cause of humanity, for a nation and its ideology are not synonymous.

Professor Graebner imposes these two patterns on the stuff on American diplomacy since 1776. The central purposes of statesmen are seen as a better guide to explaining their behavior than, say, their personal idiosyncracies. Such as approach searches out the grand logic of events, but is not a logic imposed by the events themselves or by the workings of sweeping historical forces. Rather the order is to be sought in the assumptions and purposes of the men who acted.[4]

Before leaving this section I shall once again note that we have been considering approaches which have a behavioral orientation toward rationality. That is, the rationality is not abstractly assumed for purposes of theory but believed to be displayed, more or less, by the governments under study. In the section to follow we will see more of this but also the alternative application of a rational decision maker conception as well.

Deduction

Inductive methods can be applied at various levels of analysis, and the same is true of deductive methods. However, I should note that deductive theorizing is considered by many analysts to be the ultimate form of science; they think it the sort of thing social scientists should be getting around to doing if the enterprise is to be intellectually respectable. Whether or not they are correct, this kind of theorizing has been widely attempted (though seldom with great rigor) and has had considerable influence.

The procedure involved is to construct a model of rational behavior in foreign policy by deduction from a more general theory or set of initial assumptions. We might start with some conception of human nature or the forces of history or the nature of conflict in the international system. The actual events in international politics can then be used both as examples and as evidence to test our deductions.

Once again we can start with introspection. Just a few pages back we described going at it by trying to become somewhat like those who are to be studied. Another way to do it is to assume that someone else is pretty much like ourselves. While this method can be far less reliable, it is also a great deal easier and thus is apt to be employed far more often. No special study, travel, or other experience may be necessary. For example, you ask why the Soviets ever intervened in Afghanistan and in response I suggest the U.S. government is similarly unhappy about political unrest and the prospect of unfriendly regimes in an area as close by as Central America. Same problem, same result.

Political Realism

Obviously this is a very simple form of analysis. But if we assume rational decision making, and if we also see governments everywhere as driven by much the same sorts of goals and concerns in international politics, then we can arrive at a much more complex and subtle version. To illustrate this we can review aspects of the approach developed by Hans Morgenthau and other so-called realists. His work has been so influential that he can be considered one of the founding fathers in the field. His approach merits considerable discussion and we will return to it once more in a later chapter. We noted earlier that for Morgenthau politics is a struggle for power. Given this vantage point, how do we proceed? Morgenthau suggests

> We put ourselves in the position of a statesman who must meet a certain problem of foreign policy under certain circumstances, and we ask ourselves what the rational alternatives are from which a statesman may choose who must meet this problem under these circumstances (presuming always that he acts in a rational manner), and which of these rational alternatives this particular statesmen, acting under these circumstances, is likely to choose.

A better description of a rational decision maker approach would be hard to find. But how do we know what is rational for the statesman? We return to the starting point—the statesman must pursue his nation's interests within an international power struggle. It follows that those interests can only be conceived in terms of the power necessary to achieve them. Thus the truly rational statesman will be guided by "interest defined in terms of power."

Statesmen are not perfectly rational any more than you and I. But, says Morgenthau, they are often either rational or their behavior intuitively conforms to what rationality would dictate. Thus we can put ourselves at the statesman's elbow.

> We look over his shoulder when he writes his dispatches; we listen in on his conversation with other statesmen; we read and anticipate his very thoughts. Thinking in terms of interest defined as power, we think as he does and as disinterested observers we understand his thoughts and actions perhaps better than he, the actor on the political scene, does himself.[5]

Obviously, this approach is meant to be descriptive, telling us what governments actually do, and therefore concerns behavioral rationality. On the other hand, when leaders are not perfectly rational it can tell us what they ought to be doing, what rationality dictates. This allows for prescription as well. For example, in a world of clashing interests, nations should never pursue goals they lack the power to achieve. Many moral virtues are of this sort; governments are tempted to pursue freedom or human rights, as they define them, throughout the world but this is futile for they cannot muster the necessary power. Prescription here calls attention to prudence as the highest virtue, prudence in defining the nation's interests and in selecting policies to attain them.

Not only does Morgenthau subscribe to this approach, he insists that it is the only way to effectively study international politics. It may be true that national governments are not perfectly rational, but a theory must "abstract from these irrational elements and seek to paint a picture of foreign policy which presents the rational essence to be found in experience, ..." We proceed in this fashion because it is the only way to understand reality: "It is these rational elements that make reality intelligible for theory." Recall from chapter 1 that in our thinking we necessarily abstract from "reality," simplifying it by highlighting some elements at the expense of others, and that the key contribution of a theory is to do this in a creative way. Morgenthau advocates abstraction in a particular fashion as critical for our purposes, one that focuses on the rational.[6]

Another way to make use of the assumption of rationality within a deductive process would be to construct an analysis that pertains to only one relationship or aspect of international politics, rather than to all the actions of a state (which is what Professor Morgenthau sought). Much of the rest of this chapter reviews such approaches. They deserve attention because of the hopes they have periodically aroused that the promised land—a good theoretical command of our subject— was finally at hand.

By far the most common application of models of rational behavior to a limited area of international politics has occurred in the study of conflict. Needless to say, conflict is too characteristic of world politics for our own good. When it results in war, it becomes one of the classic scourges of mankind, the one we have made the least progress in controlling. We are interested here in attempts to get a grip on it by studies of rational conflict behavior.

The very idea of such a study may seem foolish. For many of us, the most rational approach to conflict is to avoid it! Conflict is perceived as abnormal, even pathological—anything but rational. War and lesser conflicts often seem to draw from the dark and primitive side of human beings, to spring from defects in human nature or in human societies. Political scientists, on the other hand, usually share with certain other social scientists the assumption that conflict is a natural and normal aspect of human interaction. Many would agree that "the basic prerequisite of a political system is dissensus, disagreement."[7] In any case they seldom see it as innately pathological.

Even if its normal, though, such behavior is not necessarily rational. In war, for example, passions are aroused and terrible emotional strain is imposed by the human losses and responsibilities involved, while patriotic fervor and belligerence distort perceptions. War would seem to be a far cry from rational behavior in action. How then can it be studied in this way?

We will touch on two possible responses. First, behaving rationally in a conflict could maximize one's chances of winning, but we do not often have the time or the inclination to figure out what to do next. The solution is to plot out the proper course of action beforehand. Consider football—an immensely passionate game. Out on the field the coach does not want his players calculating the physics of bodies in motion or what the anatomy of a person's balance tells us about where to tackle; he says (usually with some heat) "I want you to get in there and *hit, hit, hit!*" There's a rational way to knock someone down but players cannot stop to figure it out in the game. Training is the endless practice of fundamentals on how to block, tackle, move on a particular play, so that a player will do the rational thing instinctively, without thinking about it. Highly rational behavior can then take place within the fiercely intense context of the game itself. Armed forces train their units with just this in mind. National governments attempt exactly the same thing through contingency planning and the development of special routines for emergencies. These efforts improve their chances of winning, which is why the U.S. government has financed a good deal of research in the logic of conflict situations.

The other reason for studying rational behavior in a conflict these days has to do with contemplating the prospect of a nuclear war. It would be eminently sensible for great powers to know how to avoid conflicts where both sides will insist on winning to the point of a mutual catastrophe, and how to select strategies that promise to keep conflicts, even wars (especially wars), within limits. How do they do this if the logic of conflict situations is not thoroughly explored and understood?

Game Theory

Game theory is one way to go exploring. Many games resemble international politics: the players have competing interests, there are various possible moves, and strategy requires taking the opponent's interests and actions into account. Game theory is a field in mathematics in which the object is to design a game and then depict, if possible, the most rational strategy in that game for each player.[8]

There are several important starting assumptions. First, the players are perfectly rational and choose the strategy with the most beneficial/ least harmful consequences. Second, the utility of each outcome of the game for the players can be calculated. Otherwise, how could players rationally compare strategies leading to different outcomes and pick the best one? Finally, it must be possible to assign a probability to the outcomes, so players can choose among strategies in terms of chances of success. One can have serious doubts about whether any of these assumptions is valid in the real world. However, the game theorist's reply is a familiar one: these are powerful simplifying assumptions that allow us to construct a useful theory, a logical skeletal structure on which is draped the flesh and blood of reality.

Four very simple examples follow. If we can find the most rewarding strategy for each player in each example, then we have solved the game and we know what the outcome between two rational players will be every time (just like all of us as children "solved" the game of tic-tac-toe). We also add one condition, which is that the players play simultaneously, not in sequence.

		Dick's Strategies	
		C	D
Tom's	A	4(−4)	2(−2)
Strategies	B	5(−5)	−3(3)

This first game is as follows. If Tom chooses strategy A and Dick selects strategy C, then Tom wins 4 and Dick loses 4 (Dick's payoffs are in parentheses). However, should Tom select strategy B and Dick choose D, then Dick wins 3 and Tom loses 3. What strategy will each player choose? Tom will think as follows: B gives me the largest payoff possibility but Dick, being rational, will not choose C where he loses no matter what I do. He will choose D, so I must choose A and get a payoff of at least 2. We see that Dick will indeed choose D because if Tom chooses B Dick will win and if Tom selects A Dick minimizes his loss. So the outcome of the game will always be A, D.

In the second game Tom and Dick each have three possible strategies:

		Dick's Strategies		
		D	E	F
	A	8(−8)	−5(5)	−10(10)
Tom's	B	0(0)	−2(2)	6(−6)
Strategies	C	4(−4)	−1(1)	5(−5)

Reading the matrix in the same way we see that if outcome A, D is the result, Tom wins 8 while Dick will lose 8, and so on. What will happen? Tom quickly sees his opponent will not play D and that if he plays A to Dick's E or F he will lose big. So he can only play B or C, the payoffs for which when Dick selects E or F will be.

	E	F
B	−2(2)	6(−6)
C	−1(1)	5(−5)

Now, says Tom, if I can see all this, so can Dick, and he will also realize he cannot lose playing E or win playing F. When he chooses E all I can do is play C to hold my loss to a minimum. Thus the obvious outcome is C, E, which is referred to as the "saddle point" or the "maximum" solution because each player maximizes his winnings or minimizes his losses against the other's best strategy.

These games seem to take us far afield from international politics.

But consider the third game, which is an example of a mixed-motive game—the players have some incentive to reach a mutually acceptable solution, but also some incentive not to cooperate.

		Dick's Strategies	
		Cooperate	Don't Cooperate
Tom's	Cooperate	3(3)	2(4)
Strategies	Don't Cooperate	4(2)	1(1)

Here we see that if the two choose not to cooperate, each does badly. If one cooperates and the other does not, the latter does much better but both are better off anyway. And if both cooperate, neither gets the maximum benefit but both do well. The game is often called *chicken,* where (for instance) two drivers in hot rods go directly toward each other, each trying to get the other to turn off the road first. The penalty if neither turns off (cooperates) is clear; so is the reward if both turn off. The nasty aspect of chicken is that it would be nicest of all to win, so there is some incentive to not cooperate. However, the logical solution is for both to cooperate.

What does this have to do with our subject? The answer is that chicken is usually considered representative of the inner logic of mutual deterrence in a superpower crisis. If each holds out hoping the other will back down the result would be catastrophe, and each might be tempted to do so. Notice that there is some disincentive to go through with noncooperation (at least a player gets a 2 and maybe a 3 and will not risk getting only 1) which is somewhat like the disincentive to retaliate a deterrer may face. Fortunately, the logical solution is to cooperate, hence deterrence can be successful.

Now consider the most famous game in the literature, called the *Prisoner's Dilemma.* Two suspects are arrested in the investigation of a capital crime, but the evidence is such that if they do not confess they can only be convicted on a lesser charge. So the clever district attorney separates them and offers each the following deal:

- If both refuse to confess, then each gets a five-year sentence
- If one confesses, implicating the other, the informer gets a one-year sentence while the other gets the death penalty
- If both confess, they get life sentences

Under our assumption that utilities can be calculated, the game matrix might be as follows.

| | | Dick's Strategies | |
		Don't Confess	Confess
Tom's	Don't Confess	3(3)	1(4)
Strategies	Confess	4(1)	2(2)

Reading the matrix we see that if they both confess each loses (getting a life sentence) and if they both sit tight they do much better (five-year sentences). But if one confesses, the other loses everything. And if each one protects himself from the other's confession he also gets a chance at a very light sentence, which is the biggest payoff. Thus the saddle point, the logical outcome, is that they both confess and get life sentences!

Is there any international situation you can think of in which if two nations trust each other and cooperate they both benefit but where if one cheats it gains a major advantage so that neither trusts the other? How about arms control talks among the great powers? Or the Arab-Israeli conflict? Prisoner's Dilemma can alert us to the fact that a conflict may make mistrust too rational to permit an optimal arrangement. On the eve of World War I both sides are so fearful that they would suffer defeat if they mobilized second, that they were unable to prevent the initial steps that brought on the war neither side really wanted. Some analysts have worried that Prisoner's Dilemma might be the most characteristic game for mutual deterrence, which is a very disturbing thought.[9]

Deterrence Theory

The ultimate example of a rational analysis of conflict that is then used to shape decisions is deterrence theory, for it is chiefly through deterrence that the great powers now attempt to prevent war. It is not going too far to say that we bet our lives, civilization, even the future existence of humanity on deterrence every day. That being the case we would be well advised to have a good theoretical understanding of it.

Deterrence is a psychological relationship in a conflict situation in which one side convinces the other not to attack by threats of a punitive response. Many analysts have attempted to elaborate the theory of deterrence so that statesmen will have some guidance as to how to prepare for or behave in these situations. Stripped to its essentials, classical deterrence theory involves a handful of basic concepts and starting assumptions and a deductive analysis of what logically follows from those concepts and assumptions. The concepts in question are easily grasped. A *first-strike capability* is the ability to attack in such a devastating or effective way that the opponent cannot seriously respond—like getting a knockout on the first punch in a fight. A *second strike capability* is the capacity to absorb an attack and still retaliate effectively. *Unacceptable damage* is a level of harm greater than an attacker would wish to bear. The assumptions are equally simple. One is that governments are rational. The other is that a conflict exists which is serious enough to lead to war if something is not done to prevent it.

As with any good theory, from these simple starting points a host of conclusions can be derived. To begin with, as the prospective attacker is rational the key to deterrence is to convince that government that the response will impose unacceptable damage. This obviously means that the defender must maintain a second-strike capability, and this becomes the first prerequisite for successful deterrence. But if we think more about this, we soon conclude that a threat to retaliate in a (to the attacker) costly way will not work unless it is believed; indeed, the threat is useless unless believed. Remember that it is the threat, not the retaliation, that the defender wants to work. This is the problem of threat credibility. If the U.S. deterrent threat fails to work, we would be left with the fleeting pleasure of saying "we told you so" to the Soviets when, in response to their shattering attack, we proceed with a shattering response. (The Soviets, in turn, have a similar problem.)

A threat might fail because the attacker did not believe you *could* carry it out. We try to deal with that by having weapons aplenty, but a deterrence posture can be credible only if those weapons can survive a surprise attack; otherwise the opponent will be tempted to try just such an attack and emerge unscathed (that is, the opponent would have a first-strike capability). Thus deterrence theory led the way in pointing to the value of missiles over bombers (as harder to destroy in an attack, harder to defend against), of hardened missile sites over soft ones (harder to destroy), of missiles on submarines (harder to find), and of multiple command and communication systems (so an attack cannot paralyze the retaliatory forces)—the last being a particular concern for the Reagan administration and many contemporary analysts.

A threat might also fail because the opponent did not believe you *would* carry it out. This is not an easily solved problem if it would be very costly for the defender to respond, and it arises most often in connection with so-called extended deterrence wherein a government tries to threaten in order to protect a third party from an attack, as in the U.S. alliances with Western Europe or Japan. One possible solution is for the deterrer to work hard at building a reputation for always living up to its commitments, an idea which has had a huge impact on

U.S. foreign policy. Building and maintaining just such a reputation was the basis for U.S. participation in the Korean War and was the essential rationale offered by several administrations for U.S. involvement in Vietnam.

Another solution would be to make retaliation look virtually automatic. How can we convince the Soviets that we would undoubtedly react to their attack on Western Europe even at the risk of losing millions of American lives to their missiles in a general war? The answer has been to make this threat plausible by building an integrated NATO force structure with several hundred thousand U.S. troops stationed in Europe. The idea is to so arrange things that in attacking Europeans the Soviets would have to kill large numbers of Americans too—hence U.S. forces are positioned in Germany in the path of a potential attack, not in Wales or Portugal.

Deterrence theory has also had more startling consequences. Under the logic of *defense,* the weaker your opponent the better off you are. But under the logic of deterrence this is not always true. Suppose U.S. forces are sufficiently indestructible to guarantee retaliation but Soviet forces are vulnerable to a U.S. attack. If the U.S. plans no attack, should Washington be concerned about this situation? Indeed it should. Suppose a huge crisis emerges—the Cuban missile crisis all over again. If some or all of those Soviet forces were used—by accident or because of a misunderstanding induced by the tension—a great many Americans would be killed. Someone would certainly suggest to the president a quick strike to destroy those forces, ensuring the survival of all Americans. Now if you and I can envision this, so can the Soviets. If it is logical for the United States to attack, it might well do so. The Soviets' conclusion: "Attack the Americans while our forces still exist, reducing their forces to save some Russian lives."

At this juncture deterrence has collapsed. The whole point was to *prevent* a Russian attack. Obviously in this case a strong, secure opponent is better than a weak one! Even more astonishing—if you are facing an insecure, nuclear-armed opponent, then logically you should encourage that nation to make itself less vulnerable to an attack. This is exactly what Secretary of Defense McNamara attempted at various times in the 1960s, telling the Soviets we would all be better off if they reduced their vulnerabilities. President Reagan showed an appreciation of the same point when, in proposing the U.S. develop a defense against missile attacks, he suggested the U.S. might well share the technology with Moscow.

Such an analysis can be extended further and lead to still other surprising conclusions. Michael Intriligator and Dagobert Brito have employed mathematical models to devise a better understanding of stable deterrence in relationship to levels of nuclear weapons. Some of their findings can be illustrated by reference to Figure 6-1.[10] Lines M_a and M_b represent the number of weapons (such as missiles with nuclear weapons) that states A and B have. If either has enough more weapons than the other to have a first-strike capability, then it can attack—the lines marked "A attacks" and "B attacks" represent such a situation. Where either has a clear second strike capability then it can deter—as in the lines "A deters" and "B deters"—because it has so many weapons that would survive to retaliate. Now look at point D, where these two lines intersect. The whole area to the left and below that

FIGURE 6-1

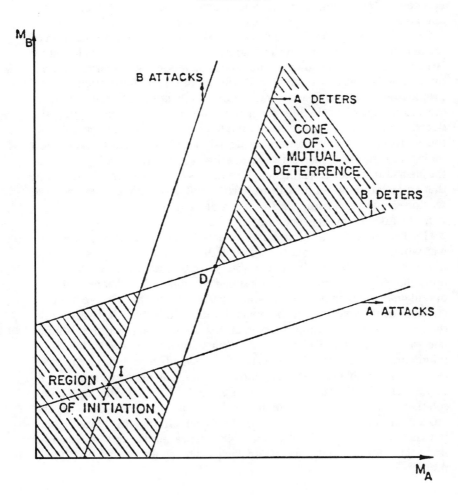

point is highly dangerous and unstable, because either one or both states (at various points in that area) could launch a first strike and emerge unscathed. Only above and to the right of point D do we find a cone of mutual deterrence where it would pay neither to attack.

Intriligator and Brito conclude that mutual deterrence is much more secure if the two sides have quite a few nuclear weapons, so that they have a certain second-strike capability. *It would be foolish to pursue arms control that greatly reduced each sides' nuclear weapons,* for that would move A and B out of the cone of mutual deterrence. In addition, not all arms races are bad. If an arms buildup pushes the two states into the cone of mutual deterrence from any other point outside it, then deterrence is stabilized and the chance of war sharply declines. Hence, under certain circumstances arms reductions are dangerous and an arms race is just what these two governments need!

Our final example in this section, a powerful deductive application of rational decision making to the analysis of war, has been developed by Bruce Bueno de Mesquita as the basis for modeling decisions mathematically. He argues that "for all the emotion of the battlefield, the premeditation of war is a rational process consisting of careful, deliberate calculations."[11] He sets forth the following assumptions: that the decision to go to war is ultimately made by a single, strong leader (thus the state is ultimately a unitary decision maker), that this decision maker is rational ("interested in maximizing his own welfare"), that the decision maker's willingness to take risks influences his decision, that uncertainty about how third parties will behave in the prospective war affects the decision, and that a state's military strength declines with distance from its homeland.

He then develops a theory that asserts that a state decides to go to war when it calculates that the war will bring a net gain. It assesses the harm that another state's undesirable policies are inflicting, the likelihood that those policies can be changed by some other means than war or will change for the better for some other reason, the relative military strength of the two states, the costs it will have to bear if it loses, and the relative strength and probable actions of third parties if they should choose to participate in the war. With allowance for a state's risk-taking propensities and for uncertainty, this leads him to devise a set of equations which predict what choice a rational· decision maker will make. (He also has to make use of a method for calculating states' relative military strength, much like Bechman and Cline did—as discussed in the previous chapter.) Applying all this to 133 conflicts between 1816 and 1965 (51 threats, 48 interventions, and 34 wars) he finds that in the great majority of cases the results are as his theory predicted.[12]

While we cannot do justice to the wide-ranging implications and applications of the theory in the brief space we can allot it here, a few points are worth mentioning. The theory emphasizes that states are interested in far more than power (unlike Morgenthau's analysis)—the roots of war lie in their conflicting policies and preferences. Also, the theory suggests that there is very little possibility of war when neither party in a dispute can perceive any net gain from it, which lends strong support to the view that mutual nuclear deterrence can be a stable solution to the problem of great power wars. In effect, the theory discounts the idea that wars occur accidentally.

We should also note that, once again, the starting assumptions of the theory are justified not because they mirror actual behavior but because they permit construction of a useful theory. As Bueno de Mesquita writes:

> as with any other theory, we should not expect reality to comply precisely with our assumptions. The ultimate test of an assumption's helpfulness is whether behavior in reality tends to be consistent with the expectations of the theory.[13]

Variants of Rational Decision Making

The last remark is a good point of departure for this next section. Many analysts are unhappy with rational decision maker models, whether inductively or deductively applied, of the sort we have been discussing. The objections take various forms. One troubling element is the fact that a procedural conception of rationality says nothing about the goals to be achieved. If people vary greatly in their values and objectives then what is rational will vary too—so that the model does not simplify things at all. Even a paranoid personality could be seen as rational in his or her actions. That makes the concept most readily applicable when the goals and values are dictated from outside—either by the theorist or by the environment. (Then everyone is after the same things).

This problem affects even game theory. As analysts have pointed out, the Prisoners' Dilemma looks quite different if one prisoner is a saint, i.e., always seeks the welfare of others, or if both believe deeply in always seeking cooperative solutions instead of egotistically pursuing their own welfare. And what if both belong to the Mafia and expect to be killed if they ever "squeal?"[14] In the real world, one is reminded of how Anwar Sadat broke through the standard Arab-Israeli Prisoners-Dilemma game in a determined bid for peace.

Then there are those who find the model of rational decision making too much at variance with reality. There are just too many ways in which governments can be irrational. They may lack the capacity to be rational, not unlike a small child. A newly created revolutionary government or one in a severely underdeveloped society may lack the training, experience and resources that are needed. Or a government may not understand the rules of the game—like our kibitzer in the con game. A government may be seriously short on the necessary information. Perhaps there was no time to gather and process it, or the intelligence and diplomatic personnel were inefficient, or the information was lost or garbled in transmission. Or maybe it was noted and then forgotten, as when in the game of bridge one's partner trumps one's ace and then, noticing the glint in that partner's eye, asks what trump is. Or a government can be illogical—the list goes on and on.

Thus for some analysts the problem is that people, groups, and governments are never as rational, as consciously calculating, as the conception suggests. If people are recruited to play the games analyzed mathematically in game theory, it turns out that they do not all behave the same way and often persist in selecting moves that fail to maximize their welfare.[15]

For others, the model is unsuitable for a collective decision-making process—such a process is inevitably shot through with political pulling and hauling, numerous compromises, trade-offs on the issue at hand with an eye to those to come next or as an extension of compromises reached on decisions in the past. Bueno de Mesquita himself persuasively argues that when controversial decisions must be made collectively the result is likely either to be a compromise that reflects no one's interest accurately (including the nation's) or that the decision will reflect the ability of groups and individuals to manipulate the agenda to favor their preferences. This leads him to assume a unitary actor for purposes of theory building, but in a curious nod to behavioral rationality, he also suggests that on decisions for war

> Apparently the internal bargaining and maneuvering that typically precedes most foreign policy decisions is not common to decisions regarding these questions.[16]

This leads right into another criticism. It is one thing to say that we will assume rationality for purposes of theory; it is another to then contrive a deductive analysis which seems to *require* that such rationality actually be consistently displayed. This is what bothers critics of deterrence theory. We desperately need to have nuclear deterrence work every time it is tested and that seems to require an awful lot of rationality. We do not wish to find that the theory, proceeding as if governments are rational, is pretty good at capturing what they usually do but not always. We might not survive the exception that proves the rule.

Naturally enough, critics have alternatives to suggest. Of course, we could simply abandon rationality entirely, but many analysts are reluctant to do so. As Herbert Simon says,

> I think there is plenty of evidence that people are generally quite rational; that is to say, they usually have reasons for what they do. Even in madness, there is almost always method, as Freud was at great pains to point out. And putting madness aside . . ., almost all human behavior consists of sequences of goal-oriented actions.[17]

Yet Simon is most prominent among those who think the application of procedural rationality in a deductive fashion skews analysis and distorts conclusions.

The alternative that has thus far commanded the most attention is to treat decision makers as operating within what Simon, among others, has termed *bounded rationality*.[18] The general idea is this: decision makers simply cannot be rational in the way we have been using the term up to this point—they do not have the time, the necessary information, or the resources. Even the human mind, marvelous instrument that it is, is not up to the task—our attention spans are too short, our ability to hold all the necessary pieces of information together is too limited, our capacities to compute all the necessary calculations are too skimpy. But if we are so "bounded" then how can we be "rational" at all? The answer is that we do set goals, try to work through the problems of reaching those goals in a systematic way, and try to come up with the best alternative. But as decision makers we creatively adapt to our limitations, working out procedures that do "well enough." Given our shortcomings, this is the rational thing to do. Analysts of this persuasion think it possible to model and describe those procedures as an alternative to the conception of rationality we have been discussing. Let us now go back through some of the topics previously raised—game theory, deterrence theory, etc.—and see where these analysts would take us.

Decision Making Revisted

We may as well start with Simon himself, with a model which was not designed expressly for the study of foreign policy but is often cited in the literature. As we noted, Simon was disturbed by the assumption of rationality where it involved maximizing. He criticized models depicting people and organizations as constantly seeking the best possible solution to a problem, the optional decision.

> Most human decision-making whether individual or organizational, is concerned with the discovery and selection of satisfactory alternatives; only in exceptional cases is it concerned with the discovery and selection of optimal alternatives.[19]

In other words, the decision maker is not a maximizer, he's a "satisfier." He looks at alternatives with an eye to finding one that will work reasonably well and does not continue to search until the perfect or very best one available has been found.

Simon's conclusion is that the only way to understand this sort of rationality in practice is to study practice—to study the way decision maker's minds work, the limitations they live with, the adjustments they make to cope with those limitations. In other words, we would move back toward behavioral rationality (Simon's term is *substantive rationality*), emphasizing what is rational given the limitations of humans.

The influential analysis offered by David Braybrooke and Charles Lindblom makes use of a similar insight.[20] Whereas Simon was initially concerned with organizations in general, Braybrooke and Lindblom were particularly interested in political decisions. They proposed that we think of such decisions in terms of the degree of change that the decision maker thinks they would involve. Obviously there is no hard and fast distinction to be drawn, but what we can envision is a continuum:

Incremental change_____Large change

We may also think of decisions in terms of how much information and understanding the decision maker has, which is another continuum:

High
|
Low

Putting the two together we see that decisions would fall into four categories:

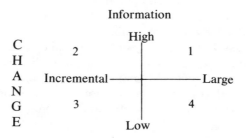

Those that fall in quadrants 1 or 2 produce changes, large or small, based on a good deal of information. They are potentially rational decisions in the procedural sense. Alas, given the impediments to rationality in a government, there are not likely to be many decisions of this sort, particularly in quadrant 1. In fact, Braybrooke and Lindblom felt that quadrant 2 decisions are the only ones where the rationality we have described was within reach of human abilities. Those decisions that fall in quadrant 4 are usually forced on officialdom. Given the large consequences and lack of information, officials will avoid them if they can. In fact, if possible they will try to break such decisions down into ones with smaller consequences. This leaves quadrant 3 as the one in which most decisions will fall. As with those in quadrant 2, only small changes or effects are at stake so they will often be considered routine.

So what decisions are most common? Those involving small effects and made by lesser officials—even major problems will generally be handled this way. This is incrementalism, the slow nibbling away at situations—inevitably unimaginative and unexciting. Sound familiar? Many an "I-was-there" memoir describes this situation; journalists and ordinary citizens often lament the dull plodding involved in government. But they typically blame bureaucracy or particular personalities or officials' preferences. Braybooke and Lindblom saw these as extenuating circumstances, but in general they point to this as a rational adjustment to the nature of the decisions that have to be made—the most appropriate way to accommodate uncertainty within responsibility.

Deterrence Revisited

Simon's suggestion that it is necessary to investigate how decision makers actually go about their work is amply illustrated in the work of Alexander George. He has elaborated what is basically an inductive approach in which specific historical cases of some phenomenon—coercion, deterrence, crisis management—are examined in order to develop theoretical propositions. George has used it in attempting to develop policy-relevant theory, which is theory designed to help the policymakers analyze the situations he faces, giving him in a systematic way the lessons of history as to what works and what does not.[21]

An excellent example is the massive analysis of deterrence by Professor George and Richard Smoke.[22] They begin by reviewing the theory of deterrence in its abstract, deductive form. Then they review ten examples of deterrence failures in U.S. foreign policy since 1945, where another government challenged Washington militarily in a way it wished to avoid, such as the North Korean invasion of South Korea in

1950 or the several occasions when the Russians tried to force the West out of Berlin. They ask the same questions in delving into each case, a method referred to as *focused comparison*. Here are some of their findings.

First, "deterrence *strategy,* as applied by policy-makers bears only a loose resemblance to . . . deterrence *theory.*"[23] The theory does not tell us much about how officials behave, and so is not of much help to them in predicting the behavior of the opponent either. Would we go to war if Taiwan were attacked? Doubt existed about this throughout the 1950s, even though we thought we had clearly promised to do so. It turns out that making a firm commitment and a clear threat is not easy. Would Taiwan be worth World War III? And if the U.S. meant such a threat, would anyone believe it? (Remember the critical importance of credibility). What if the attack came indirectly or in a piecemeal fashion—which is the way, George and Smoke found, clever opponents were apt to design their challenges to such commitments. George and Smoke found that many past U.S. commitments were weak and vague, and that an opponent could find ways to undermine them or to attack in various ways when it appeared that the risks were controllable. And the answer is not simply making one's threats much firmer. Many threats are weak or vague precisely because the defender would have some substantial reasons for not carrying them out. In the Taiwan example, would a war on Taiwan's behalf have been popular at home? How many American lives and dollars was Taiwan's security worth? (If this seems like airy speculation, substitute "Nicaragua" or "El Salvador" for "Taiwan"). George and Smoke concluded that U.S. leaders often respond to a challenge by trying to make the commitment look firmer—talk tough, display U.S. forces in the area, etc.—instead of realistically considering whether it was worth upholding. That can lead to disasters like the Vietnam involvement, where we pay a high price before seeing that the objective is not worth such a price.

Thus deterrence is likely to fail under a variety of circumstances, and George and Smoke identify three kinds of failures:

1. The *fait accompli*—a quick grab of the objective keeps the deterrer from doing anything because his commitment is actually weak.
2. The *limited probe*—using pressure and maneuver to weaken or undermine a commitment.
3. *Controlled pressure*—using pressure and maneuver to weaken or undermine a commitment.

For each of these they point out some correct and incorrect strategies that might be followed. However, if deterrence can fail, they conclude, great states should not rely on it so heavily. Even when it works, it just forces the opponent to retreat without resolving the problem that caused the conflict. Thus they urge that the U.S. government learn to make greater use of other ways of influencing foreign decision makers.

A variety of other studies have been made of the decision making in crises or confrontations, including decisions to go to war, and in many instances it appears that governments overestimate their military strength, underestimate the commitments of their opponents, seriously misjudge the risks they are running, and fail to appreciate how the situation (including their own positions and actions) actually looks to the opponent.[24] These factors can result in a failure of deterrence even when, objectively, it ought to work. This has naturally given rise to critical evaluations of classic deterrence theory itself.

An alternative way to reexamine deterrence theory to the one offered by George and Smoke, but with exactly the same interest in trying to capture what occurs in deterrence situations, is use of a "sensible" decision maker model I have developed.[25] The heart of the argument is that decision makers often consciously or intuitively appreciate the bounded nature of rationality—their own and that of other governments. Thus they are inclined to avoid situations with great uncertainty and grave consequences—the quadrant 4 decisions of Braybrooke and Lindblom—as a sensible way to cope. The point of a deterrence threat is not so much a matter of getting an opponent to add up the costs and benefits of an attack in a precise, rational way as it is to convince the opponent that is in a quadrant 4 situation so that it decides to go to a more incremental step than an attack that sets off a war. That is how deterrence works.

Unfortunately, not all decision makers are sensible in this way. Sometimes governments have great confidence that they know exactly what they are doing. It may be due to arrogance or a profound religious conviction that "God is on our side." It may be because of a revolutionary movement's sense that it is moving with the tide of history. It may be due to overconfidence in sources of information and ability to predict what other governments will do. It may even be due to an overwhelming sense that circumstances leave no other choice. If such a government is thinking of launching an attack, it is far less likely to be dissuaded by a deterrence threat; and it is also more likely to stumble into a situation where it provokes a war when it did not intend to, despite the deterrent threats offered by its opponents.

Ultimately this means that the effectiveness of deterrence depends at least in part on who it is being practiced against. If the "wrong" sort of opponent is at hand, a government that is not very sensible, then deterrence may fail. Given our reliance on nuclear deterrence to prevent a catastrophic war, this is not a very comforting conclusion.

Game Theory—Again

An obvious alternative to the abstract, deductive treatment of games such as those we reviewed earlier would be to develop games that more clearly resemble real situations in world politics. This can include designing games with moves in sequence, rather than simultaneously, with some limited communication between the players, and with some built-in uncertainties as to the moves each player will make. Steven Brams has recently been investigating the design of such games and their implications. He believes that he has developed a new type of game which better explains how deterrence works, because even though the party threatening retaliation would find that action unrewarding (and thus the threat is incredible) there is some autonomous probability that it would retaliate anyway, and this unpredictable risk of a disastrous response is enough to deter a rational opponent.[26] This is an updated, game-theoretic treatment of an older analysis by Thomas Schelling, who argued that threats it would not be rational to carry out could still be credible if a government could not guarantee it would be sufficiently rational.

Schelling pioneered the study of the "theory of interdependent decision-making in situations of less than pure conflict."[27] This refers to the making of decisions in a conflict situation where neither side controls the outcome alone and where some of the possible outcomes would benefit both sides. He was very interested in the strategy of conflict but he insisted that psychological factors are so important that a conception of what is rational must take them into account. He urged that game theoretical treatments be revised accordingly. One subject that has engaged his interest is tacit cooperation and tacit bargaining— that is, the reaching of a mutually beneficial agreement without any formal conversation of other communication. It is quite normal in a conflict for the two sides to markedly reduce or suspend communication. In such a situation—a war, for example—is agreement still possible? Certainly, said Schelling. What each side does or does not do also communicates—Actions speak louder than words.

Schelling used this to shed some light on the subject of limited war. In Korea, did the two sides meet to agree on where the war would be fought and what was out of bounds, or that napalm was acceptable but nuclear weapons were out of order? Obviously not, and yet each side observed certain limits—they cooperated without formal conversation in the middle of a war. How does this happen?

Schelling designed games to illustrate the existence and use of obvious reference points—points on the maps in our minds. It is around these points that such agreements may be reached. If I say to you "divide these 100 $1 bills into two piles in exactly the same fashion as the person in the next room and you each get to keep the $100," what would you do? Most people choose 50-50. No one divides the pile into 77-23 or 91-9. Why not? Mathematically they ought to turn up about as often as any other division. If we were to list the numbers from 1 to 100 that most stick out in our minds, some which stand out reflect the fact that our number system is based on tens. We might include 12 and 24, having to do with the way we tell time, 7 and 21 because of popular gambling game, and 13 for the superstitious. For each of us the list might be a little different but there is enough similarity that if we have to agree with someone else to win the prize we can be fairly certain of success with 50-50, which has the obviousness of symmetry, just as "splitting the difference" does in sales and labor negotiations.

Gas warfare was not used in World War II. Why not? Because of the Geneva Convention? If so, it was the only international agreement the Nazi government held sacred. Obviously the two sides tacitly cooperated in not using gas, out of fear of retaliation. But why the use of none? Why did they not tacitly agree to use a little, or some? Schelling says that where formal communications is suspended it is impossible to agree on subtle distinctions, so tacit agreement will emerge around the obvious reference point if it develops at all. A scale on the use of gas listing major reference points would look something like this:

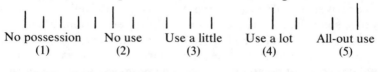

The problem with point (1) is that it is difficult to verify so any tacit agreement will be hard to sustain. Points (3) and (4) are not obvious enough because they require agreement on details. How much is a "little" gas—should the measure be number of shells fired, or the area over which it is used, or the casualties it causes? Points (2) and (5) seem the most obvious, but (5) is the one we want to avoid. Point (2)

has obvious advantages: easily verified, no details, no measurement problems.

The arrow at the bottom reflects Schelling's view that in a conflict the pressure of events tends to force escalation up to obvious reference points. Thus once point (2) is crossed the next really obvious one is (5). Schelling opposed the use of any gas—even tear gas—in Vietnam. The administration argued that use of a nonlethal gas would not erode the restraints on lethal chemical warfare, but he felt nonuse of any gas was much more obvious and thus safer.

Schelling's analysis has many possible applications. The most obvious reference point for nuclear weapons is nonuse, something the critics of strategies for so-called limited nuclear war regularly emphasize. Arms races also have obvious reference points, which are therefore the best places to seek arms control agreements. The concept can also be used to understand how limited wars are kept limited, which is vital in the nuclear age.

Notice that these points are not obvious in an abstract, logical way. Instead they are behaviorally logical—due to geography, culture, history and the like. Unlike pure game theory, Schelling described not a rational world but rational behavior in a somewhat irrational one, and he urged a reformulation of game theory accordingly.

Difficulties and Drawbacks

As in preceding chapters, we will close by reviewing some of the problems and difficulties posed by these approaches. Most center on the two core elements—putting oneself in someone else's shoes and the concept of procedural rationality. Obviously, mentally recreating another government's view of the world is always difficult. Roles can severely shape perceptions. So can culture, education, even illness. How does one take all such factors into account to reproduce the inner perspectives of officials? Presidents insist that theirs is a unique viewpoint and that no amount of training or imagination will substitute for being there. How confident can we feel about strategic analyses of Chinese leaders or Egyptian officials—people from such different cultures and ideological systems?

Of course this is not a problem if governments are simply rational, either inherently or in response to the logic of particular situations. Are governments rational? Obviously not all the time, perhaps never. As we have noted, many analyses take account of this and therefore insist that governments are nothing more than purposeful. They even use models of bounded rationality in action.

The trouble with retreating from the assumption of procedural rationality is that it tends to lead to both a proliferation of ways of describing what people do and a far more complex task for explanation.[28] Consider, for instance, how we might end describing deterrence if we move along this path. It could turn out that every government is a bit different—in values, perceptions, decision making processes, standard perceptual and cognitive errors, risk taking propensities, etc., when it comes to practicing deterrence or thinking of an attack. That would mean we need a study of the American approach, like George and Smoke developed, and the Chinese approach (Allen Whiting looked into this once), and the Israeli approach, and so on. The theory would also prescribe differently depending on the nature of the potential attacker. And the necessary information to properly catalog states would be vastly increased. In the end we would turn out to have little in the way of a useful theory. I am reminded of the way psychiatrists, seeking patterns of personality disorders, can take years to gather information, disagree strongly about just how to catalog patients, and end up being surprised at what those patients do. Critics of deterrence theory have been quite good at pointing out how the assumption of rationality may greviously oversimplify matters but not nearly as successful at devising an alternative theory of deterrence. What holds true for deterrence can readily apply to other areas of decision making (deterrence theory is, after all, an extraordinary effort to model, and thus manipulate, decision making).

It is also worth reflecting a bit on the term *bounded rationality*. I can think of two broad ways to conceive of it. It could be that people (governments) go through a rational process but they are not perfect—they make some mistakes, they do not have all the available information, or they lack the time; thus, they have a kind of restricted rationality. But it could also be that they are affected by passion and bias, their initial preferences distort the very way they gather and evaluate information, they have such limited attention spans and calculating capacities that they fail to assess alternatives systematically, and so on. This is not a restricted rationality, it may be seen as a thin crust of rationality covering a stew of other processes. But descriptions of bounded rationality often seem to lump these two together and the question is, where are the bounds which mean we are beyond rationality?

The other answer to the charge that governments are not rational is to assert that the assumption they are need not be behaviorally correct, just theoretically useful. There are several difficulties here. The gap between the assumptions and reality often seems so great that only a substantially effective theory will justify it, and such theories have yet to emerge as broadly accepted and powerful tools. Normally the theories that we have available are treated as only partially relevant and useful, requiring supplementary perspectives. This is roughly what has happened to political realism. It is not ignored, just qualified. It is applied, but then augmented. It has been suggested that analysts like Bueno de Mesquita are so eager for a broad and parsimonious theory that they adopt assumptions which sacrifice accuracy.

Another difficulty is that rationality is usually treated as a very good thing. In our culture and language it is given a high value. What this means is that if one develops a theory as if governments are rational, people immediately want to begin applying it—what could be better than to be rational? But if rationality is not meant to be displayed, just assumed, then people get leery about the theory. It might be different if we assumed people were green—people would not then set out to get as green as possible.

And if the critics are right, the assumption of procedural rationality, especially when applied deductively, is ultimately pernicious, for our theory tells us a good deal about a mythical world. Many analysts find that such an approach is quite regularly used by officials to explain the behavior of other nations, and that in practice it introduces distorted perceptions. It can make it very difficult to distinguish between offensive and defensive steps by another state; it analytically oversimplifies the process of communication among governments; it leads to officials overlooking how their actions convey "unintended" threats; and it provides a static conception of real situations.[29]

Still other criticisms might be reviewed but it is important that we concentrate on one in particular. It concerns a preceding point about the lure of rationality. The idea is that this attraction is misplaced, that rationality is a mixed blessing, that we can have altogether too much of this good thing. This notion crops up in political theory but is seldom adopted in international politics. We tend to think our troubles stem from the irrationalities of anarchy, or because ignorance and emotion triumph over reason in world affairs.

Consider, however, this criticism of deterrence theory. Following the logic of conflict wherever it leads can take us into hypothetical analyses of how to conduct a nuclear war. It also leads to detailed planning of such wars and the design of nuclear arsenals accordingly, leading to war-fighting options and scenarios. Critics respond that this has the effect of hardening our sensibilities, crippling out emotional response to the inhumane. Pushing things to a logical conclusion can lead not only to thinking about unthinkable things but being more ready to do them. This argument is simply Schelling's analysis in another guise. It asserts, in effect, that there are psychological or emotional defenses we maintain against doing terrible things, defenses that rest precisely on making them unthinkable. To think about them is to breach these defenses, to cross an obvious reference point and start down a road where the next most obvious point is doing those terrible things. This is, by the way, the kind of argument often raised against euthenasia, pornography, even a rapid shift in fashion. Once this barrier is breached—so it goes—where will we stop?

Notes

1. Graham Allison, "Conceptual Models and the Cuban Missile Crisis," *American Political Science Review* (September 1969), pp. 689-718; or his *Essence of Decision* (Boston: Little, Brown, 1971), pp. 10-38.
2. Walter Jones, *The Logic of International Relations,* 5th ed. (Boston: Little, Brown, 1985), pp. 1-223.
3. See Robert Mandel, "Political Gaming and Foreign Policy Making During Crises," *World Politics* (July 1977), pp. 610-25.
4. See, for example, Graebner's two readers: *Ideas and Diplomacy* (Oxford University Press, 1964); and *An Uncertain Tradition* (McGraw-Hill, 1961). The quote is from the former p. viii. Also the recent collection of his essays: *America as a World Power: A Realist Appraisal From Wilson to Reagan* (Wilmington, Del.: Scholarly Resources, 1984).
5. Hans Morgenthau, *Politics Among Nations,* 5th ed. revised (New York: Knopf, 1978), p. 5.
6. Ibid., p. 7. The sixth edition, revised by Kenneth Thompson, modestly revises this passage.
7. Herbert Spiro, *World Politics, The Global System* (Homewood, Ill.: Dorsey Press, 1966) p. 53.
8. Useful introductions: Anatol Rappoport, *Fights, Games, and Debates* (Ann Arbor: University of Michigan Press, 1960); Rappoport, *Two Person Games Theory* (Ann Arbor: University of Michigan Press, 1970); or Barry Schlenker and Thomas Bonoma, "Fun and Games: The Validity of Games for the Study of Conflict," *The Journal of Conflict Resolution* (March 1978) pp. 7-38.
9. Frank Zagare, "Toward a Reformulation of the Theory of Mutual Deterrence," *International Studies Quarterly* (June 1985), pp. 155-69.
10. Michael Intriligator and Dagobert Brito, "Non-Armageddon Solutions to the Arms Race" *UCLA Center for International and Strategic Affairs Reprint No. 1* (UCLA, 1985), p. 9.
11. Bruce Bueno de Mesquita, *The War Trap* (New Haven: Yale University Press, 1981), p. 19.
12. The initial version, presented in Bueno de Mesquita, has been revised in Bueno de Mesquita, "The War Trap Revisited: A Revised Expected Utility Model," *American Political Science Review* (March 1985), pp. 156-73.
13. Bueno de Mesquita, *The War Trap* (note 11), p. 28.
14. See Anatol Rappoport, *Fights* (note 8), pp. 174-77; and Robert Keohane,

After Hegemony: Cooperation and Discord in the World Political Economy (Princeton: Princeton University Press, 1984), pp. 73-75.

15. See the good, brief discussion in James Dougherty and Robert Pfaltzgraff, Jr., *Contending Theories of International Relations,* 2nd ed. (New York: Harper and Row, 1981) pp. 518-20; also, Keohane, *After Hegemony,* pp. 75-76.
16. Bueno de Mesquita, *The War Trap,* p. 16.
17. Herbert Simon, "Human Nature in Politics: The Dialogue of Psychology with Political Science," *American Political Science Review* (June 1985), p. 297.
18. A recent restatement of this is in Simon, "Human Nature."
19. James March and Herbert Simon, *Organizations* (New York: Wiley, 1966), pp. 140-41. Or see Simon, *Models of Man* (New York: Wiley, 1957), part IV.
20. David Braybrooke and Charles Lindblom, *A Strategy of Decision: Policy Evaluation as a Social Process* (New York: Free Press, 1963), pp. 61-79.
21. A recent example of "policy relevant" research and theory: Alexander George, *Managing US-Soviet Rivalry* (Boulder, Colo.: Westview, 1983).
22. Alexander George and Richard Smoke, *Deterrence in American Foreign Policy: Theory and Practice* (New York: Columbia University Press, 1974).
23. Ibid., p. 504.
24. Examples: Richard Ned Lebow, *Between Peace and War* (Johns Hopkins University Press, 1981); Robert Jervis et al., *Psychology and Deterrence* (Johns Hopkins University Press, 1985); Klaus Knorr and Patrick Morgan, *Strategic Military Surprise: Incentives and Opportunities* (New Brunswick, N.J.: Transaction, 1983).
25. Patrick Morgan, *Deterrence, A Conceptual Analysis,* 2nd ed. (Beverley Hills, Calif.: Sage, 1983), pp. 103-26.
26. Steven Brams, *Superpower Games* (New Haven: Yale University Press, 1985).
27. The key works here are Thomas Schelling, *The Strategy of Conflict* (Cambridge: Harvard University Press, 1980); and *Arms and Influence* (New Haven: Yale University Press, 1966).
28. Bueno de Mesquita, *The War Trap,* pp. 32-33.
29. Leon Sigal, "The Rational Policy Model and the Formosa Straits Crisis," *International Studies Quarterly* (June 1970), pp. 121-56.

Bibliographical Remarks

As noted in the chapter there are analysts who see deductive theory as the ultimate objective. For discussions bearing on this I suggest the following: Ronald Rogowski, "Rationalist Theories of Politics: A Midterm Report," *World Politics* (January 1978), pp. 296-323; Kenneth Waltz, *Theory of International Politics* (Reading, Mass.: Addison-Wesley, 1979); Bruce Bueno de Mesquita, "Toward a Scientific Understanding of International Conflict: A Personal View," *International Studies Quarterly* (June 1985), pp. 121-36; The last article brought forth several comments by others and a reply by Bueno de Mesquita: Stephen Krasner, "Toward Understanding in International Relations," Robert Jervis, "Pluralistic Rigor: A Comment on Bueno de Mesquita," and Bueno de Mesquita, "Reply to Stephen Krasner and Robert Jervis," all in the *International Studies Quarterly* (June 1985), pp. 137-54.

There are innumerable works that use game theory. Readers can find a good many in a journal like the *Journal of Conflict Resolution*. I will mention only two others here: Glenn Snyder and Paul Diesing, *Conflict Among Nations* (Princeton University Press, 1977); and Arthur Stein, "The Politics of Linkage," *World Politics* (October 1980), pp. 62-81. Of the various works that are designed to introduce people to game theory the following can be consulted: Martin Shubik, ed., *Game Theory and Related Approaches to Social Behavior* (New York: Wiley, 1964); Martin Shubik, *Games For Society, Business and War: Towards a Theory of Gaming* (New York: Elsevier, 1975); Nigel Forward, *The Field of Nations* (Boston: Little, Brown, 1971); Morton Davis, *Game Theory: A Nontechnical Introduction,* rev. ed. (New York: Basic Books, 1983).

On deterrence theory treated in a deductive way there are numerous works to consult in addition to those listed in the notes. For the history of the theory, in American and Western thinking, see Lawrence Freedman, *The Evolution of Nuclear Strategy* (St. Martin's Press, 1981) and Fred Kaplan, *The Wizards of Armageddon* (Simon and Schuster, 1983). Critics of the rationality of recent deterrence doctrine include Robert Jervis, *The Illogic of American Nuclear Strategy* (Cornell University Press, 1984); Michael Howard, "Fighting a Nuclear War" *International Security* (Spring 1981), pp. 3–48; and Desmond Ball, "Can Nuclear War Be Controlled?" *Adelphi Papers* no. 161, International Institute For Strategic Studies, 1981. Works that provide either a useful review or collect varying points of view on deterrence issues include: Charles Kegley, Jr. and Eugene Wittkopf, eds., *The Nuclear Reader: Strategy, Weapons, War* (St. Martin's Press, 1985); Gwyn Prins, ed., *The Nuclear Crisis Reader* (Vintage Books, 1984); Fred Holroye, ed., *Thinking About Nuclear Weapons: Analyses and Prescriptions* (Croom Helm, 1985); Lawrence Martin, ed., *Strategic Thought in the Nuclear Age* (Johns Hopkins University Press, 1979); and Michael Mandelbaum, *The Nuclear Question* (Cambridge University Press, 1983). Several of these works contain discussions bearing on the ethical/moral dimension of deterrence, and this is also particularly true of Douglas MacLead, ed., *The Security Gamble: Deterrence Dilemmas in the Nuclear Age* (Rowman and Allanheld, 1984). Deterrence theory refined via an inductive approach is John Mearsheimer *Conventional Deterrence* (Cornell University Press, 1983). Finally, a valuable overview of the practice of nuclear deterrence is Edgar Bottome, *The Balance of Terror* 2nd ed. (Beacon Press, 1986).

7

Regions: Elusive Targets in Theory and Practice

The feeling that the nation-state is a wholly inadequate, even perni-cious community is about as old as the nation itself. In the twentieth century, particularly in the nuclear era, many have concluded that the liabilities of nationhood outweigh the benefits. They can cite the increasing interdependence of nations economically and culturally. They point out that nations today cannot even pretend to guarantee the safety of their citizens. For every nation there is at least one other possessing weapons against which there is no effective defense and which, if employed, could destroy the first nation more or less com-pletely. Yet, they say, the continued sovereign existence of nations instigates conflicts that endanger us all.

As we saw earlier, this situation has not led to the decline of nations—there are more of them around than ever. One reason for this is a universal aptitude for ignoring uncomfortable facts of life.

> Most of us wish to keep this failure of nationalism *not* at the center but at the margins of our consciousness, like a pain in the lungs after twenty years' smoking. Nation-states are habit-forming, and nationalism has become an addiction for millions of people.[1]

One of the supposed virtues of honest scholarly endeavor is that it breeds people who face up to unpleasant truths and drag the rest of us, however haltingly, into doing the same. Have we been well served in this regard by students of international politics?

Fortunately, we can say almost without reservation that our scholars cannot be faulted on this score. A thumbnail sketch of the history of the field would detect its origins in the conviction that the chief lesson to be drawn from World War I was the dangerous inadequacy of nationalism and the nation, and the futility of relying on power balanc-ing processes among nations to keep the peace. For twenty years analysts promoted international law and institutions only to see this vision shattered by World War II and the Cold War. This led to considerable stock-taking and the general realization that the existing condition of international politics deserved considerably more respect and wasn't about to yield simply to rational argument. The "realist" school stressed that we had best start by understanding the world better rather than simply trying to remake it. A second realization was that alternatives to the nation had to be examined more systematically so that we might know more about how international politics could change.

The end result was to all but kill off expectations that world government was the immediate solution to the problem of world order. The bets of many scholars were placed instead on regional institutions. Statesmen did the same; after World War II they sought to overcome the deficiencies of the nation acting alone by resorting to alliances, regional associations, and preliminary integration in limited supranational institutions.

All of which gives us the subject matter of this chapter—approaches to the study of the international politics that focus on collections of nations; on alliances, regions, international subsystems, and regional integration. For a while there was much vigor and excitement here, in theory and practice, but as we shall see, analysis at the regional level has fallen on hard times. Attention has shifted once again to world government and other schemes and arrangements at a higher level of analysis, which we shall probe in the chapters to come. That makes it easier to live with the fact that we shall only be skimming over some of the relevant thinking about regions. But we cannot neglect it entirely for our field has its recurring fads and fancies and no doubt there will be a revival of interest in the regional level in the not too distant future.

Alliances

Entering into an alliance is one of the oldest practices of statecraft, one that can be traced back many hundreds of years before Christ. This being so, we might reasonably expect to know a good deal about it by now, but this is not the case. While plenty of assertions exist about alliances and how they work, thorough theoretical analyses reviewing the available evidence only began appearing relatively recently, and we can still ask a lot more good questions about alliances than we can answer.

An alliance is a primitive form of community in which states join together for a limited period to jointly pursue objectives they feel they cannot successfully obtain acting alone. The same could be said of the forming of other international associations, such as a coalition or a voting bloc in the United Nations, so we must specify that alliances involve a formal commitment and that they are entered into because of the possibility of war. Some are formed for the mutual profit of the members in forthcoming conflicts; that is, they are offensive alliances. However, many are defensive in nature, and some analysts believe offensive alliances to be inherently fragile.

Studies of alliances generally fall into four categories. One is the detailed examination of a single alliance such as NATO or the Warsaw Pact. There is a flourishing cottage industry in such studies of NATO, which is constantly being described as being in crisis or disarray. (Not the least of NATO's benefits is that it keeps so many people employed in hand-wringing, ocean shuttling, conference sitting, and speech making) Often studies of a single alliance will offer suggestions about the nature of alliances in general, but the theoretical value of work with only one case is rather limited so we will not review these studies here. A second category consists of analyses of alliances within a theory pertaining to the international system, the foremost example being balance-of-power theory. In the third category are studies of alliances as examples of the logic of collective behavior, part of a larger pattern of political man's activities. In the final category are studies that treat the alliance as a separate phenomenon, not as part of something much larger, in order to examine the members and inner dynamics of alliances and thus explain how they work and why they sometimes do not.

Returning to the second category, where alliances are analyzed within a theory of the international system, we may start with the observation that "in one way or another, a conception of alliances is implied in every general and analytical account of international relations."[2] Our best example is that most durable of all approaches, the balance of power. Here the central feature of the international system is the constant, often vicious drive of each state to acquire more power and to offset the power of others. Any dangerous concentration of power in the system is met by creation of an appropriately powerful alliance. Hence alliances are a means of creating and preserving a balance and they exist only as long as the nations involved have certain interests in common. They are born of political expediency, midwifed by rational statesmen, and dissolved when hard-headed calculations dictate.[3]

Most analysts feel this is a useful starting point, but that there are too many elements it fails to adequately explain. Some argue that alliances often undermine peace and the balance of power rather than sustain it, by serving to expand national power and probably interalliance rivalries. Also, too many alliances seem to deviate from paths a balance-of-power view prescribes, so the theory would seem applicable only to certain alliances. This has led to attempts to refine the rational decision-maker approach, as in the analysis by Steven Rosen.[4] He argues that the existence of war is what leads to alliances, so we cannot explain them without a theory of war. Power in war consists of two elements: the ability to do harm and the willingness to accept harm. Alliances can then be analyzed as a pooling of destructive capabilities and a sharing of damages. During World War II the Russians bore the greatest damages (about which they have always complained bitterly), while their allies supplied a good many destruction resources (material to the U.S.S.R., bombing, the atom bomb). But what if the whole point is not to fight a war but prevent it, the objective of many contemporary alliances? Then we would need a model of war-avoidance, not just war.

Well, how are alliances related to war avoidance? We have quite a few answers and not much agreement among them, so on this matter people are certainly in tune with the rest of the field! (The disagreements even cut right across the scientist-traditionalist division.) Under a balance of power approach, the more even the balance the less likely a war is to occur; hence, alliances should (if properly constructed) reduce the likelihood of war. But some analysts argue that a close balance of power has exactly the opposite effect—a war is most likely to be avoided when one side looks very likely to win, i.e., when it is much more powerful. A review of seven different studies on this finds that there is modest support for the argument that a balance prevents war, more support for the assertion that a significant imbalance presents war, and enough weaknesses in the studies to prevent reaching a firm conclusion. Bueno de Mesquita rejects both views, arguing that we have to take into account the propensity to take risks of governments, singly and in combination, and that when we do we can see that wars can occur under both conditions—a balance or an imbalance (". . . the distribution of power is not significantly correlated theoretically or empirically with indicators of the incidence of war.")[5]

Careful analyses of the available data are similarly inconclusive. J. David Singer and Melvin Small initiated the modern study of alliances by drawing on data from their Correlates of War project.[6] Working in the period from 1815 to 1945 they compiled a list of alliances by hunting through the League of Nations *Treaty Series* and various other sources. Dating the start of an alliance was not too difficult, but deciding exactly when it terminated was often a problem; sometimes they had to rely on the consensus among historians.

A related question they also asked was, when is an agreement an alliance? They insisted on the existence of a written, formal agreement. By examining exactly what was promised, relying on the consensus of historians in doubtful cases, they threw out all but three classes of agreements: (1) defense pacts, (2) neutrality and nonaggression pacts, and (3) ententes—where the parties promise to consult or cooperate in a crisis. To see if alliances were related to the onset of war, they excluded all alliances signed during or three months prior to a war (to avoid cases where a war caused alliances). They also ignored broad, vague treaties such as the Kellogg-Briand Pact and the Treaty of Versailles.

Are alliances associated in any way with the frequency of war? Singer and Small reviewed balance-of-power theory, in which flexibility to switch sides is important so that a proper balance can be maintained. Alliances could be a problem in this regard since they commit governments to particular "sides" and thereby limit their flexibility. The less flexibility there is, the more the international system should be beset by war. This led to the hypothesis that "the greater the number of alliance commitments in the system, the more war the system will experience."

In this hypothesis the dependent variable (the thing to be explained) is "more war." Singer and Small computed the amount of war *for each year* in the international system in terms of:

1. the total number of months all nations were at war.
2. the total number of months major nations were at war.
3. the battle deaths of all nations
4. the battle deaths of major nations
5. the number of wars that began

Also required was a measure of the "amount" of alliance in the international system. For each year this was computed in terms of:

a) Percentage of all nations in some alliance.
b) Percentage of all nations in a defense pact.
c) Percentage of major powers in some alliance.
d) Percentage of major powers in a defense pact.
e) Percentage of major powers allied with minor powers.

If you reread the hypothesis you will see that it calls for changes in the second set of variables to produce corresponding changes in the first set—the more alliance, the more war. A couple of comments are in order. One is that alliances cannot be expected to cause wars immediately—if we compare changes in a-e with variable 5 for each year we distort the results. To allow for a lag in the impact of alliances, Singer and Small computed S not only for one year but for three and five years as well, and found a three year lag was the most significant. The other comment is that just because 1-5 moves in line with a-e, showing that they are correlated, does not prove the former are caused by the latter. Some other factor may be responsible for both changes. Thus this kind of analysis is best used negatively—if alliance and war are not closely correlated then obviously alliances do not cause wars. If they are, the alliances may cause wars but we need more research to prove it.

What did Singer and Small find? In the twentieth century alliance correlates fairly well with war. The hypothesis seems confirmed and we may suspect alliances cause wars. But in the nineteenth century the results are different and alliances do not seem related to wars. The authors urged caution in interpreting these mixed results, pointing out that even for the twentieth century the correlations are such that a number of other factors must affect the frequency and severity of war.

Various criticisms of these conclusions have been raised, ranging from the argument that a true balance of power system was rarely in existence between 1815 and 1965 to the assertion that alliances may not restrict the flexibility of governments, particularly if they belong to more than one alliance at the same time.[7] A major objection has been offered by A.F.K. Organski and Jacek Kugler, who find that alliances have had very little to do with the onset of war in their analysis of the available data.[8] On the other hand, a recent study rejects this view, finding that alliances are not irrelevant although they do not appear to be as important for great powers as lesser powers in affecting the likelihood of war.[9] And Bueno de Mesquita's latest work insists that if alliances are meaningful additions to two rivals' military power, not just constraints on nations' flexibility (as Singer and Small argued) then the balance of power theorists are correct and "alliances do make a difference"[10] when one side is given a notable edge over the other. As I said at the beginning, we can ask more good questions about alliances than we can answer.

Another way to study alliances is to consider them not just as a part of international politics but of politics in general. Here alliances may be seen as just another form of political coalition. William Riker began with the idea that since political decisions are primarily group decisions, someone must put together a coalition to dominate the group. Thus the study of coalitions should take us right to the heart of the political process. Riker's starting assumptions is familiar to us by now:

1. people in politics are rational, choosing the alternative that leads to the most satisfactory outcome.

2. political conflicts are zero-sum in nature—what one side wins, the other loses.

This simplification of reality was held to be justified because it allowed the construction of a rigorous theory.

Riker's theory is often summarized in two key principles, the first of which is called the *size principle:*

> In social situations similar to *n*-person, zero-sum games with side payments, participants create coalitions just as large as they believe will ensure winning and no larger.[11]

Those forming an alliance, for instance, will offer a share of the eventual spoils or some more immediate benefits such as foreign aid (side-payments) to potential allies as an inducement to join. Obviously, the larger the alliance the smaller everyone's share of the spoils so the alliance will be large enough to win and no larger.

This conception of rational coalition-building is modified by the *disequilibrium principle,* which concerns the tendency of coalitions to be unstable. Politics attracts people who, as leaders, want to win not only for the spoils but even more for the sake of winning itself. A coalition is likely to be led by someone who looks less at the spoils than he does at the satisfactions, of power and status in themselves. Added to this is the impossibility of making very precise calculations as to how large a coalition it will take to win (an obvious difficulty when it comes to something as uncertain as war) or how much it will take in side payments to add new members or keep the old ones. The result is a tendency on the part of coalition leaders to pay out too much, because winning is important in itself and because they overspend to be on the safe side in holding the coalition together.

Riker specifically applied this (in 1962) to an analysis of the fortunes of the United States in the postwar world. Its huge initial coalition had gradually been eroded or "whittled down" (as we would expect from the size principle). He suggested that the impact of the disequilibrium principle was at hand, that the U.S. and U.S.S.R. faced an era of competition in which they would slowly exhaust their resources in trying to maintain their respective coalitions. The price for converting neutrals would rise, allies would charge more for their allegiance, and the arms race would grow in cost. Allies and armaments would bring on exhaustion in the end, fragmenting the coalitions and leading to the emergence of several other nations as world leaders.[12]

Looking at the world of the mid-1980s, Riker's predictions seem to have been unevenly borne out. In the case of the U.S.S.R. there has been the loss of China (shrinkage of the coalition), very heavy military spending, the high costs of maintaining Soviet allies in Eastern Europe (such as Poland) and elsewhere (Cuba, Vietnam, and others have been heavy burdens), and a broad economic malaise. The U.S. has sustained its coalition better, within a lower level of defense spending (until the 1980s), but it may have paid a great deal in terms of permitting allies to run it into a huge trade deficit (side payments), and has certainly not been able to achieve sustained economic health and growth. There is still no sign of exhaustion for either government. Of course, we cannot ignore the possibility that where Riker's predictions seem to be holding up, this is due to other factors than the ones he suggested.

Riker's logic of collective behavior focuses on building a winning coalition. Mancur Olson's logic concerns getting a (relatively) free ride within a coalition. He once attempted to explain why it is so often the case in alliances that the members' contributions are not equal.[13] Of course some nations have more resources than others so the rich will likely carry a larger absolute burden. But in NATO, for example, the U.S. spends a larger percentage of its gross national product on defense than its allies, bearing a larger absolute, and relative, share of the costs.

Olson's answer rests on the idea that alliances produce collective goods (often referred to as public goods), benefits all members share regardless of their contributions—in the case of NATO the collective good is security. This being the case each member has some incentive to limit its contribution, to gain the benefits at minimum cost. In much the same way, we all like the benefits of government spending yet each of us is tempted to cheat on his income tax. Thus if the U.S. values the alliance and must bear the biggest burden anyway, the other allies will feel free to let it bear a disproportionate share. Worked out in more rigorous terms, this is why alliance costs are unequally distributed.

Just as interesting is Olson's conclusion that an alliance need not seek a minimum necessary size. Alliances typically "provide collective goods, the supply of which should increase as the membership increases."[14] This means an alliance may very well seek to grow, a conclusion that contradicts Riker's size principle. Riker and Olson choose starting assumptions that simplify reality in different ways, resulting in quite different conclusions.

This theory has been discussed and tested in a number of studies. In addition to the pattern in NATO, studies of the Warsaw Pact mostly support it. But the Rio Treaty (the alliance between the U.S. and Latin

America) and the Arab League do not conform consistently to the theory. Also, the theory has not been tested for bilateral alliances, which are much more common than large multilateral ones. Thus

> while the theory . . . as presently developed receives considerable support from the data, it might prove even more fruitful if an attempt were made to incorporate additional concepts into its formulation.[15]

Or: it isn't bad but could be better.

The final category of alliance analyses listed earlier was the examination of alliances themselves, their internal dynamics. Generally speaking, this means more attention to the members and their specific relationships, less to the international system or the supposed logic of political behavior. For instance, it has been argued that alliances are deeply affected by the *national* attributes of the members. Examples include the suggestion that new nations typically avoid alliances and that ideological, religious, or cultural affinities are the basis for most alliances (rather than strictly power considerations).

Most significant in this regard is the work of Ole Holsti and his associates. They used data in alliances from 1815 to 1939 to test propositions about what makes alliances tick. Then they turned to the communist world and NATO to see if alliance cohesion is affected by the nature of the governments involved. They concluded that where the members are democratic, any conflicts among them in one or two issues are not likely to spread and poison all ather relationships. The alliance will be far from monolithic, but will be well equipped to make pragmatic adjustments to handle disputes. But an alliance of authoritarian status will be less flexible and disputes on one matter will likely spread to others. This is why the disenchantment of France and China, in the 1960s, with their respective alliances, turned out so differently— France remained, at least partly, within NATO while China came to be totally at odds with the U.S.S.R.

These findings were perhaps less important than one other conclusion that was reached:

> There is limited theoretical mileage to be gained from efforts to spell out propositions purported to be valid for all alliances, irrespective of the nature of the alliance or its constituent nations.[16]

That is, attempting to develop a theory of alliances will not take us very far.

Regions

For most of us the relevant world is good deal smaller than the real one. We pay taxes to only one national government, live in only one community, concern ourselves with the comings and goings of a relatively tiny portion of the world's population. We are comfortably ensconced (or trapped) in one culture, even subculture, and its geographical location. Unlike people of earlier times we are somewhat aware of the existence of other societies, we read about them or see their people fleetingly on television, we even visit them. But in the core of our being most of us remain part of and partial to one rather small segment of the world.

This is also true of national governments. Each is concerned about and interacts intensively with some group of nations smaller than the world as a whole. The implication is that for many aspects of international politics the world is best thought of as clusters of nations, that much of the business of international politics takes place within these groups and between them. An alliance represents one such group but it can be rather temporary in nature. What we would like is a list of clusters or groups of nations that is more permanent because it encompasses the ways nations habitually distribute their attention and their actions.

The standard name for such a group is *region*. The term is most often used geographically because geography seems a far more permanent factor than many others. The Soviet Union is stuck with China as a neighbor; Israel cannot readily relocate itself from the midst of the Arabs. Thus we frequently talk about regions as if territorial proximity is the chief element, as when we refer to conflict in Central America or the tensions in the Middle East.

Breaking the world into regions, however, is not that simple. Geography can be a fuzzy guide—Turkey and the U.S.S.R. are in Europe and out of it, and is the Sudan best seen as an Arab state in the Middle East or a state in Central Africa? We may also decide that criteria other than geography are more useful. An economic region would consist of a relatively intense pattern of trade, aid, and other economic ties; by that definition Israel is not part of the Middle East at all. A political region could consist of states that have roughly similar political systems, or closely associated foreign policies. There is a communist camp in both senses, but they do not overlap completely, so it makes a difference how we choose to define a political region.

How are we to determine the existence of region? Bruce Russett once conducted an exercise in inductive taxonomy;[17] rather than beginning with a definition of a region, he collected data on various criteria to see what regions would turn up. The criteria around which clusters of nations, i.e., regions, were uncovered, are:

1. Sociocultural similarity.
2. Similar political attitudes and behavior, as reflected in votes in the U.N.
3. Common membership in international organizations.
4. Economic interdependence, measured by trade as a proportion of national income.
5. Geographical proximity, determined by air mileage between national capitals.

The method used was a form of factor analysis known as Q analysis. To indicate briefly how it works, we will look at item 1, sociocultural similarity. There are any number of ways to measure this—number of pupils in school in different states, gross national product, dominant religion, level of government spending, and so forth. In fact, Russett had some 54 of these measures! Working with such a large number is extremely awkward, but a factor analysis can be used to find those measures that are closely related. A set of closely interrelated measures makes up a factor and Russett was able to reduce the 54 to just four factors, a considerable improvement. A second factor analysis was then used to see how the world's nations (82 in this study) clustered in their rankings on these four factors.

Russett called each cluster of nations a region, and in terms of sociocultural elements Russett identified the following regions: Afro-Asia, Western Community, Latin America, Semi-Developed Latins, and Eastern Europe. While he used names reflecting the geographical location of most members in each cluster, some regions contained countries that didn't fit geographically. Thus Argentina, Japan, and Israel all ended up in the Western Community Region, while the Philippines was included in Latin America.

Proceeding in this way Russett accumulated five sets of regions according to the list of five criteria above. He found regions were very different depending on the criteria. However, each set of regions turned out to be fairly stable over time; the regions in the early 1960s based on world trade patterns or U.N. votes or membership in international organizations were roughly the same ones that existed in the early 1950s.[18]

With regard to U.N. votes, Russett considered this continuity to be quite significant. Earlier chapters in this book discuss the view that domestic factors deeply affect the foreign behavior of governments. In the chapters to come we will see the emphasis placed on the international environment as the thing that makes the most difference. Which view is correct? Russett argued that governments came and went, individual leaders rose and fell, and yet the positions on issues that nations adopted in the U.N. hardly fluctuated at all. He saw this as support for the argument that international-system elements determine a nation's behavior more than domestic factors.

Another way to operate is to devise a definition of a region and then use it to determine which countries fall into what regions. Any foreign ministry does this when trying to decide how to organize itself into various sections, breaking the world into regions so the ministry's members can specialize. Michael Brecher some time ago depicted international politics as consisting of a dominant system (the coalitions led by the U.S. and U.S.S.R.) and a set of subordinate systems or regions.[19] He supplied six features of a subordinate system: 1) limited geographical scope; 2) at least three members; 3) recognition by others as a region; 4) considered distinctive by the members; 5) inferior to the dominant system; and 6) more affected by the changes in the dominant system than vice-versa. Brecher suggested that each subordinate system could be described in terms of such things as its members and their location (core, periphery and outer ring), the distribution of power and nature of interaction among the members, their similarities and differences, and their relationships with the dominant system. He concluded that there were at least five subsystems worthy of attention: Middle East, Americas, Southern Asia, West Europe, West Africa.

Brecher made the point that too often analysts are preoccupied with what goes on in U.S.-Soviet or East-West relations, at the cost of ignoring what really concerns many of the world's governments.

> There is an array of interstate problems, conflicts, and relationships among actors outside the blocs that have nothing or little to do with the bloc system.[20]

This is exactly what many Third World governments have been saying for years, and illustrates the danger of having so much of the study of international politics concentrated in a country like the United States.

William Thompson has usefully pulled many of the suggestions and findings about regional subsystems into a "propositional inventory," which is a list of hypotheses that at least someone thinks are relevant.[21] The list is long but the hypotheses are not overly interesting and many lack confirmation. In short, the study of regional sybsystems does not seem to have contributed very much to our knowledge.

Thus we must conclude this section by observing that theory on international regions or subsystems is still at a very primitive level, which is saying something in view of the state of theory in the field as a whole. Analysts have reached no agreement about how to detect or define a region and how to describe one when we find it. The larger questions remain: Are regions each unique or can we generalize about all of them? Is a region a microcosm of the entire world, so concepts and theories from one apply to the other? As of now, who knows?

Regional Integration

Regional integration is the most serious and successful contemporary effort to supersede the nation-state. As such, it once attracted a good deal of attention and in some respects theory on integration was better developed than in most other areas of the field. In what follows we will settle for a far-from-comprehensive review of the efforts of some leading analysts and attempt to get at why those efforts are currently moribund.

Integration theories tackle the problem of analyzing change over time. Often they include a belief in supranational integration as an inevitable or logical "next step" in human-community development. From this perspective human affairs are "going somewhere," they are headed in a certain direction toward a specific future situation. Modern man, surrounded by rapid change in domestic affairs, has often found attractive those currents of thought, such as Marxism, that seek a dynamic analysis of change itself. It has been argued that the very nature of social reality demands such a theory.

> The fact that the social system is a dynamic system means that all problems of social science have an essentially historical dimension and that in effect the main task of social science is to *explain historical development*.[22]

In international politics, the ruinous consequences of the two World Wars and the coming of the nuclear age have added a note of urgency and necessity, a sense that a big departure from business as usual is called for in the interest of the survival of civilization.

In international politics integration concerns mergers among nations into new political communities, but in some sense it is involved in politics at all levels. Many nations have emerged from the melding of smaller units, often at great cost. Governments in the so-called Third World face grave problems in trying to knit tribes and villages into viable nations. Many U.S. officials have striven to integrate cities and suburbs into metropolitan regions because the problems of these areas—transportation, pollution, employment—appear regional in scope.

Thus integration may be the same wolf in the clothing of several different sheep. Many analysts have felt that international integration is not a peculiar phenomenon but part of political integration in general. We would therefore be able to derive insights about international integration from cases of national and subnational integration. One reason this is appealing is that otherwise we should have little to study. If integration is the merger of several established nations into a new one, there are spectacular cases of failure, none yet of success. As such, integration on the international level has barely begun and theories about it must wait on the verdict of history.

In general, integration theorists may it be said to concern themselves with several questions: What is integration? What are the preconditions for it or the factors that affect it? How does it come about? As one analyst puts it, the main question has been: "within what environment, under what conditions, and by what processes does a new transnational political unit peacefully emerge from two or more initially separate and different ones?" These questions initially attracted attention because in the wake of World War II a good many leaders in Western Europe and the United States concluded that integration was the way to get European nations to put aside age-old national differences and the wars that had accompanied them. In other words, a very practical problem incited work on a theory. Nothing is more conducive to theoretical reflection than the prospect that the results can be put to good use.

Our first question was, what is integration? It may come as a surprise that there is no generally accepted definition of integration. Once again international politics involves the study of something the nature of which is not exactly clear. Some consider integration to be a *condition* (as when we say a community is "integrated"), but it is equally plausible to think of it as a *process* (as in saying Western Europe is steadily undergoing integration). In turn, those who think of integration as a condition have different opinions as to just what that entails: a simple "security community" wherein war among the members is regarded as unthinkable, or a community with a sense of identity and elaborate institutions to help coordinate the members' behavior, or a full scale union with a government superior, in power and in the citizen loyalty it attracts, to the formerly independent states of which it is composed.

Definition is further complicated by the fact that there are, presumably, various degrees or levels of integration (as a *condition*) or various stages of integration (as a *process*). One review suggests that integration has four dimensions:

1. degree of collective decision-making
2. performance of functional tasks
3. patterns of social interaction
4. political attitudes

A community must then cross a certain threshold on each one in order to be fully integrated, but measuring just how well it is doing can be extremely difficult.[23] Even more complex is another scheme in which political integration is defined as evolution of a collective decision-making system. Leon Lindberg believes this kind of decision making has at least ten important aspects that must be investigated to decide how integrated a system has become. And any one of these aspects can be broken down into as many as ten additional elements, each of which poses further measurement problems! Remember, this is just to define and measure integration—the task of explaining still remains. When Lindberg tells us that "the image I will have conveyed is that the political integration phenomenon is enormously complex," we are hardly likely to disagree.[24]

Still another difficulty is that integration may occur or be sought in different sectors—economic, political, scientific, military—with varying speeds and success, and it is hard to craft a definition to take all this into account. Given such problems there is the danger our subject will be so amorphous as to evaporate.

> Theory is not sufficiently advanced that there exists either a commonly accepted definition of integration or general agreement on the relevant indicators of integration.[25]

Our second question was: What are the preconditions for or the factors that affect integration? The question mentions both preconditions and factors because theories can treat the same phenomenon either way. In part this results from differing conceptions of integration. If integration is a condition, then an easy flow of people across national boundaries may be a precondition for it. But if integration is a process, then this movement of people becomes a factor that advances or retards it.

In the abstract it would seem possible to distinguish between factors and preconditions—the former relate to movement in a certain direction, the latter make movement possible in the first place. In practice it turns out to be nearly impossible to sort them out. Let us examine the mobility of persons within the European Economic Community. People have readily crossed these national boundaries—as students, tourists, businessmen—for many years. This could well have been a precondition for integration. But formation of the EEC was meant to markedly increase such travel and this in turn has been expected to increase the willingness of Belgians to associate with Germans, of Germans with French, and so in. In short, what was a precondition now becomes a factor.

The last question (How does integration proceed or come about?) is the most important. Integration is not just an abstract idea, it is something people have devoted their lives and energies to. Theory has been sought, as was pointed out above, not only to explain but also to prescribe, to indicate whether mistakes were made in the past, and to advise on what should be done next. A decent theory would also allow us to predict the prospects for success in any particular case and to anticipate what should be or will be the next step.

Ultimately, however, we need to know how integration comes about simply because of a human need to know. Knowledge that something exists, even being able to measure it, is never sufficient. Geneticists long realized the impact of heredity and, within limits, could measure its results, but that only whetted their appetite to know how the passing on of characteristics from one generation to the next takes place and this led to the cracking of the genetic code. The question of how integration comes about or proceeds is the most formidable of the three, but only by answering it would the theorist attain complete intellectual satisfaction.

Integration: The Classic Approaches

We are using the term *classic* in two senses here. In the first, we refer to older approaches that were somewhat influential at one time. The second pertains to approaches that have deeply influenced thinking about integration in the past three decades. In our review we will make use of the lovely summary and analysis that has been offered by Charles Pentland. There are four classic approaches: federalism, functionalism, pluralism (or transaction analysis), and neofunctionalism. Pentland finds that each envisions integration leading to either a unified new state or to a coordinated community of separate states. And each one sees integration as coming about either directly by political decisions, or indirectly by changes in social and economic conditions and relations. This gives us the fourfold typology presented in Figure 7-1.[26]

FIGURE 7-1
Theoretical Approaches to Integration

		End Product	
		State	Community
	Direct-		
Integrative	Via Political Variable	Federalism	Pluralism
	Indirect-		
Process	Via Socioeconomic Variables	Neo-Functionalism	Functionalim

Federalism

We begin by returning to the opening point of this chapter, namely that the nation often appears disturbingly inadequate as a community. One response of thoughtful observers has been to urge the conscious, deliberate creation of larger political communities or even a world state by means of federalism. The historical analogy normally used is the creation of the United States or Switzerland. Proposals for what would amount to a United States of Europe date back several centuries in European history.

Notice that this is to happen as the result of a deliberate decision. The political elites of the countries involved must specifically decide to federate. Presumably this would mean a step akin to that taken by the leaders of the original thirteen states in drawing up and ratifying the U.S. Constitution. Notice also that it involves a rational decision maker conception—the reason for creating a new community would be that it is an eminently sensible thing to do and political leaders (and their constituents) will act accordingly.

Perhaps this is why (although a few eminent scholars have been attracted to this view) it did not have a great impact. Nationalism is tenacious and national autonomy alluring. Few analysts who see integration as the rational thing to do have found in the historical record any basis for confidence that leaders and peoples are up to it. Governments have not been induced to take the drastic (for them) step of stripping themselves of much of their power and independence. Thus, the federalist approach has proven to be of no use in explaining the developments of the postwar era.

> Events since 1954 in Europe and since 1960 in Africa have effectively contradicted these federalists' descriptions, explanations, and predictions. This approach, in its pure form, is probably discredited.[27]

Functionalism

It is against this background that the functionalist approach emerged. Its foremost exponent for many years was David Mitrany. Looking at Figure 7-1, we see that functionalism does not aim at a single world state or at regional ones. Mitrany's goal was not regional integration but the creation of a world political community of states. In fact he was dismayed by European integration efforts in the 1950s and 1960s because he saw this as leading to just another larger nation, which would still be isolated from and competing with other nations. Such a world would remain dangerously fragmented.[28] However, we review functionalism here because this way of thinking has had a powerful influence on regional integration efforts.

The trouble with federalism, Mitrany felt, was that national governments would never directly accept it. But the continuation of a world of separate, autonomous states would inevitably mean the persistence of war. He suggested functionalism as a more practical route to peace. His idea was that a large part of modern society is very complex and technical in nature, and that technical problems can often be separated from more sensitive political ones. At the same time, in a growing number of areas it was becoming clear that national governments could not fully meet their citizens' needs. Rising international interdependence would induce governments to see forms of cooperation as in their national interest, making cooperation on technical matters both valuable and relatively painless. Effective and authoritative international institutions would emerge to coordinate various activities, and as interdependence grew, reliance on still more of these institutions would gradually spread. This would enhance habits of cooperation and strengthen incentives to avoid war. A larger political community would emerge, almost in spite of national governments. Interdependence would

> overlay political divisions with a spreading web of international activities, in which and through which the interests and life of all the nations would be gradually integrated.[29]

Thus functionalism is an odd mixture. It sees structural change leading to a change in attitudes and behavior as governments, in effect, teach themselves to cooperate. But the structural change is, itself, initiated by governments having already consciously appreciated the utility of it. The implication is that governments are very narrowly rational, able to be reasonable on small, practical steps where they could never take the larger one. The latter can only be achieved indirectly, almost by stealth.

While the functionalist approach had a considerable impact on some of those who helped create the movement for integration in Western Europe, it has largely lost ground to other theoretical approaches to explaining integration. It has turned out that when officials directly experience efforts at cooperation in international institutions, and when that cooperation is effective and beneficial, they do adopt favorable attitudes toward it, but they do not seem to become gradually more attached to those institutions than to their own national communities.[30] In addition, a signal defect of functionalism is the belief that politics and national governments can be circumvented, when in fact nothing is more inherently political than the creation of a community to which people give their loyalty.

Pluralism

This approach to integration relies heavily on analysis of transactions—political, economic, social, cultural—across national boundaries, and thus is also referred to as *transactionalism*. The most eminent analyst in this school is Karl Deutsch who pioneered the application of communications theory to the study of politics—work which brought him to the pinnacle of his profession. Deutsch argued that communication is what makes a community, and a community consists of people who talk to (write to, listen to, deal with) each other more, and more easily, than outsiders. One implication is that a community encompasses persons with mutual relevance, something we can detect in rates of communication, or transaction flows, among them: phone calls, mail, travel, trade, etc. This notion triggered a host of studies using data on transaction flows either to detect the potential for integration in an area or to measure the degree of integration attained there.

However, mutual relevance is not enough. People and their institutions must also be willing and able to respond to each other so that transactions result in mutual satisfactions and rewards. In elaborating on this, Bruce Russett suggested that we may depic. the relationship between states A and B in terms of the demands they make on each other's ability to respond. Integration requires that their capacity for responsiveness keep ahead of the demands on it; integration is increasing when "the growth of capabilities is outpacing the increase in loads." Russett examined the relationship between Britain and the United States in this century, using a variety of measures of responsiveness, and concluded that in the 1950s the two nations had not drawn closer but had, if anything, become somewhat less responsive to each other.

Deutsch's investigations were largely confined to Western Europe and the North Atlantic. His initial work (with a number of collaborators) attempted to derive lessons and insights from experiences in building nations or maintaining empires, reaching back into history for rewarding examples. The picture of the process of integration that emerged has recently been described as follows:

> First, functional links develop between separate communities. Such ties in trade, migration, mutual services, or military collaboration prompted by necessity or profit generate flows on transactions between communities and enmesh people in a transcommunity communications network. Under appropriate conditions of high volume, expanding substance, and continuing reward, over extended periods of time, intercommunity interactions generate social-psychological processes that lead to the assimilation of peoples, and hence to their integration into larger communities. . . . [Then] the desires of members and the efforts of the elites may be directed toward institutionalizing, preserving, and protecting the community's integrity and distinctiveness and regulating transactions through the establishment of institutions of government.[31]

People interact, and learn from positive interaction enough to constitute a community, and only then can a state for the community be built.

Perhaps the most influential aspect of the transaction approach was that the concept of community came to embrace far more than tightly knit states. Looking at the categories of Figure 7-2,[32] the bottom two types are not integrated even though the one on the right has a state. The top two are "integrated" but only the one on the right is a single political community, a nation. Deutsch was quite willing to settle for a pluralistic security community (hence the label "pluralist" given to this approach), and the concept (though not the term) has come to be widely accepted in the field. In a pluralistic security community the independent existence of the governments continues, but they feel quite safe with one another—they have reached the point where they can hardly conceive of making war on each other.

Deutsch and his colleagues found nine conditions to be essential for a successful amalgamated security community, including (1) mutual compatibility of main values; (2) expectations of stronger economic ties or gains; (3) marked increase in political/administrative capabilities of some of the participating units; and (4) multiple ranges of communication and transaction. For pluralistic security communities, the re-

FIGURE 7-2
Deutsch's Classification of Communities

	NONAMALGAMATION		AMALGAMATION
INTEGRATION	Pluralistic security community *Example:* Norway-Sweden today	**THRESHOLD**	Amalgamated security community *Example:* U.S.A. today
	·······INTEGRATION		THRESHOLD·········
NONINTEGRATION	Not amalgamated, not security community *Example:* U.S.A.-U.S.S.R. today	**AMALGAMATION**	Amalgamated, but not security community *Example:* Hapsburg Empire 1914

quirements were found to be far less stringent, and they also appeared far more durable as communities.[33]

> The first of these was the compatibility of major values relevant to political decision-making. The second was the capacity of the participating political units or governments to respond to each other's needs, messages, and actions quickly, adequately, and without resort to violence. . . . A third . . . may be mutual predictability of behavior.[34]

Deutsch and other transactionalists pushed on with this work, trimming and adjusting to new findings while tracking the slowdown in Western European integration that became evident by the 1960s, a subject we will return to in a moment. Their approach has a number of attractions. For one thing it envisions a degree of integration that stops short of erasing the power of national governments yet moves us toward a more peaceful and cooperative world. This seems more plausible than either federalism or functionalism—in fact, it appears to be an accurate guide to what has actually been achieved in Western Europe since 1945, a community in which ancient enemies now can hardly imagine going to war. Such an approach is far more likely to appeal to national governments, solving some of their security problems without putting them out of business, and in fact Gaullists and others in Europe seem partial to it.

However, it is not without shortcomings. Once the initial assumption (that communication is the heart of community) is accepted, its strength lies in developing measures of integration. Its weakness comes in explaining integration, which is, after all what we want a theory to do for us. One thing missing from most transaction analyses is the role of politics and political leaders: when, why, and how rates of transactions lead to decisions important for integration is not clear. Also missing is any indication as to when a pluralistic security community might turn into an amalgamated one. We have to settle for tests of probably relevant conditions that encourage and sustain integration.

> Overall, we have come to recognize that regional integration is a multidimensional phenomenon, much more complex than initially imagined. Transaction approaches are appropriate and useful for investigating some aspects of regional integration; they are less useful for investigating others.[35]

Neofunctionalism

This approach is more closely associated with the work of Berkeley's Ernst Haas and Harvard's Joseph Nye.[36] In tracing its evolution we can see the interplay between a theory and its critics, showing us how scholarly discourse aids in theory development but can frazzle the life of the theorist. Haas attempted to correct the functionalists' avoidance of politics. He began with the contention that creation of limited supranational institutions to handle complex technical problems would gradually bring political elites and interest groups of the countries involved to support further integration, because they saw benefits in it for themselves. Thus the pragmatic self-interest of political elites would cause a spillover of integration from one sector to another. That is, integration in one sector of an economy provokes integration of another, and economic integration then spreads into other fields and culminates in a submerging of the governments involved in a larger community, as more and more decision making is transferred to supranational institutions.

By now it should leap out at you that this approach means working with a conception of officials and elites as rational. Their reaction to integration is to ask "what's in it for us?" and integration proceeds precisely because they see it as having better payoffs than the alternative.

Thus integration is a process in which previously created supranational institutions lead key interest groups to organize internationally, to seek greater services from those institutions, and to compromise in conflicts by expanding the institutions so that everyone benefits. It is crucial that elites become convinced integration has something in it for them. Haas defined integration as

> the process whereby political actors in several distinct national settings are persuaded to shift their loyalties, expectations, and political activities toward a new center, whose institutions possess or demand jurisdiction over the preexisting states.[37]

Notice that, unlike Deutsch's view, a certain amount of integration is believed to take place before the formation of a community and, in fact, can help to begin community-building. It is also the case that Haas envisioned a pragmatic form of rational decision making would operate—elites would be guided by their self-interests.

In 1964 Haas and Philippe Schmitter laid out nine variables they believe affected the transition from economic union (such as the European Common Market) to political integration.[38]

Background Conditions
1. The size of the units and their relative power.
2. The rate of transactions among them.
3. The degree of pluralism in these units.
4. Complementarity in the thinking of the national elites

Conditions at the Time of Economic Union
5. Degree to which the governments' economic aims are the same, not merely converging, and the degree to which they are committed to eventual political union.
6. Is the process of integration a series of planned, automatic steps or does each step have to be renegotiated?

Process Conditions
7. Decision making style—is a good deal left to technical experts?
8. Rate of members' transactions as economic union develops.
9. Adaptability—can governments and major groups transcend crisis and conflicts by expanding integration? If so, spillover occurs.

From this viewpoint they expected Western Europe, which they ranked highly on the nine variables, to experience reasonably steady progress toward integration. According to the last process condition even a crisis—where two or more governments could not seem to agree—was likely to lead to more integration. The politicians would fish around for a compromise and end up expanding the reach of supranational institutions.

The first problem with the theory came when it ran into French President de Gaulle, who disliked integration and moved to put a stop to it. Theory or no theory, he did. He provoked lots of crises but they failed to promote integration. How could the theory account for this? In fact, it cound not. Some critics drew a distinction between "high" and "low" politics and argued that integration in the latter, including the economy, would not readily spill over into such high policy matters as national security.[39] A study of Euratom, the effect to integrate nuclear research and development of the Common Market countries found that difficulties and problems did indeed turn into political crises, but that this brought on stubbornness and less willingness to let supranational institutions make decisions. "Crisis . . . led to disintegration, not integration," which is not what the theory predicted.[40]

Other critics weighed in with another objection. If you look back at those nine variables you will see that all of them refer to conditions within the proposed union. What happened to the rest of the world? Perhaps the nature of the international system and the attitude of powerful outsiders such as the United States were important in explaining the progress, or lack of it, in integration. Other studies suggested that the theory needed revision to fit integration among developing nations. There it proved difficult to avoid nationalism and politically volatile matters when anything directly affecting economic development was automatically "political" and received first priority from political leaders. Such leaders often leaned to the heroic pose and personalistic politics, which did little to promote decision making by technicians and supranational bureaucrats.[41]

Donald Puchala set out to test the spillover thesis by comparing public opinion polls in Western Europe during 1957-1962 on the issues of economic and political integration. During these years the Common Market blossomed and soon proved immensely popular. Was there a spillover in the public's mind in each country so that general support for political union also grew? Puchala found nothing of the sort. Evidently people simply separated the two; support for one did not give rise to support for the other. Perhaps this was one of the costs of success. If prosperity surges ahead, then nobody feels a pressing need to wade into the touchy, testy subject of political integration.[42]

All this led Haas to adjust his views toward the argument that pragmatic interests of groups are not enough to overcome the distinction between high and low politics. He added the category of the statesman with "dramatic-political" aims, i.e. DeGaulle, as someone who may get in the way of integration or even foster disintegration. Later he and others added still more revisions, such as moving away from the view that integration leads to only one outcome in favor of seeing three possible alternatives: (1) a regional state—one nation taking the place of several smaller ones; (2) a regional commune—the members are highly interdependent and have lost much authority and legitimacy, yet no firm central government has emerged; (3) asymmetrical regional overlap—members are only partially interdependent so a number of centers of authority exist to which citizens are attached in "infinitely tiered multiple loyalties."[43]

He also began to view the relevant factors as working to affect integration in different combinations—action paths—depending on the issues, the locale, and the prior progress that had taken place.[44] This would give us a multiple dependent variable (several kinds of integrated communities) and a variety of linked independent variables (numerous clusters of relevant factors) for developing a theory of integration (or maybe just a bad headache).

Joseph Nye proposed other revisions in the neofunctionalist model in order to produce a "political" model of regional economic integration. One element of this was a set of seven conditions which together constituted the "integrative potential" of a region. They included such things as the relative size of the participating nations' economies, the ability of the member states to adapt and respond to each other and to new situations (a nod to the concerns of Professors Deutsch and Russett), and the degree to which political leaders see the benefits of integration as being distributed equally or as helping them to deal with the rest of the world (one of Haas' initial starting points.) Nye also detected seven "process mechanisms"—ways in which integration grows or spreads over time. These included spillover and other processes that Haas identified, but also ones other analysts detected such as the impact of external actors or the ideological commitment to (not just pragmatic self-interest in) regional integration. Finally, Nye outlined four characteristics of a true integration process over time: an increasing role for politics, a redistribution of such factors as industrialization, an increased sense that there are few alternatives to integration, and a greater tendency for the member states to mount a common front or policy vis-à-vis the outside world. Overall, Nye emphasized that integration was far from automatic or inertial: sometimes spillover occurs but sometimes not, external actors may help or retard integration, and so on.[45]

Other approaches are still more complex, so much so that an account of each would run to many pages. Here I will mention just one. James Caporaso rejected the idea that integration must, or ought to, culminate in higher levels of well-structured government over a region (or the entire globe). Instead, he anticipated that complexities would develop as highly structured, centralized national governments gave way to complex networks of ties and relationships between groups across national boundries. The decentralization of existing governments, not a new higher level centralized government, would result. The individual would be caught up in a web of cross-pressures and multiple loyalties. Combinations of people and numerous links between groups and governments would form, dissolve, and reform, and this would open the door to maximum flexibility, adaptability, and creativity in meeting the needs and interests of people and their societies. He called this an entropy model, and it has elements of both Haas' asymmetrical regional overlap and the emphasis in the Deutsch approach on interactions and responsiveness on many levels as crucial.[46]

In spite of the modifications, integration in theory has not gone anywhere in the past few years, while in practice it went backward in some parts of the world and made only agonizingly slow progress in Western Europe. The world seems more interdependent all the time, but it's hard to find groups of nations that are becoming much more integrated.

> Whatever had been happening in Western Europe apparently stopped happening. It stopped happening elsewhere as well, and to the intellectual embarassment of scholars involved, integration theory offered no satisfactory explanation for these turns of events.[47]

There are various possible explanations, of course. Perhaps integration slowed in Western Europe because the critical problem with which it was supposed to deal, the periodic warfare among the states involved, was solved—solved by enough integration to create a pluralistic security community, and by the overwhelming presence of the Russians and the Americans, and by the division of Germany. Maybe integration theory is like deterrence theory; that was moribund for a while but it has become pertinent again, and perhaps regional integration may make a comeback in theory and practice.

However, many analysts have opted for a third explanation. Haas took the lead here by suggesting that interdependence itself is making regional integration theory obsolete because it is occurring on the *global* level, a point which sets up the discussion in the next two chapters. Haas asserted that new kinds of global issues were emerging—on the environment, energy, and the like. These issues are not really regional in nature, nor could the solutions be so. Nations are becoming increasingly interdependent even as they pursue conflicting objectives, leading to shifting patterns and confusing ties among them. Thus a nation in the European Common Market may have an energy problem due to OPEC and must look outside the Common Market for solutions. It may have other problems at the same time that arise elsewhere which cannot be approached by the old ways envisioned in regional integration theory. As a result

> The theories we have developed for describing, explaining, and predict-ing regional integration, however, have a tendency not to predict very accurately the events which came about, and not to explain very convincingly why events which were predicted did come about in fact. It has been suggested that we can probably devise better theories which would lead to more dependable findings. But . . . the effort is probably not worth our while.[48]

Haas used the term *turbulent fields* to describe the more fluid international patterns he saw emerging, adding that we needed to subsume integration theory under broader theories of interdependence in international politics. Donald Puchala finds that this is in fact what has happened as "integrationists' earlier curiosities about international collaboration via transnational processes within settings of interdepen-dence have become central concerns of International Relations" on a worldwide scale.[49] This takes us full circle, from the origins of regional integration theory in the primitive barbarism of 1914-1918 and 1939-1945 to the idea that the world has now become too advanced for it.

Problems and Difficulties

Some weaknesses in the approaches reviewed in the chapter have already been discussed, and a major criticism of Russett's study of regions appears in the next chapter, so these closing comments will be brief. It is fairly obvious that a purely regional perspective—on alli-ances, regions, integration—has been inadequate. In each case ana-lysts made reference to the overarching international system. Alliances were discussed with models of the global system in mind, frameworks for regional analysis included slots for "intrusive powers" or the "dominant system," and integration theories were reworked to take account of the international environment as an important factor.

The danger in studies at the regional level is that the influence of the international environment will receive only casual mention instead of careful, systematic analysis. In fact, some analysts have been attracted to regional-level studies precisely because they did not want to grapple with the world as a whole—a position hardly likely to improve their judgment of how the world affects the region.

A second problem that cropped up throughout the chapter was the difficult matter of definition. It was glaringly obvious with respect to identifying regions—depending on the criteria used they seem to grow on trees for, as Russett pointed out, different criteria produce different maps of the world's regions, maps which overlap but do not coincide. Sure enough, Brecher's list varied from the ones others supply. No wonder William Thompson's review of regional subsystem studies found minimal similarity in their basic concepts and little useful theory, which explains the "little progress made, to date, toward the goal of scientific explanations of regional subsystem behavior."[50]

Lack of consensus on what integration was did not keep scholars from getting out there and digging into it. At times this led them to talk right past each other and made it difficult to add the knowledge accummulated by one study to that uncovered by another. The process of definition really involves two steps: first, stating what something is and second, indicating how we can measure or detect it, i.e. the operational definition. We saw integration theorists uncertain about whether integration is a process or something at the end of a process. Haas worked on political integration, Nye on a political model of economic integration, Caporaso on an entropy model. All the theorists agreed that integration was (is) multidimensional, but the measures used to tap its many dimensions varied considerably from one analyst to the next.

Another problem is that the assumption of an underlying similarity in integration at various levels is distinctly implausible. The creation of a viable, developed nation involves having the masses pass through a complex process Deutsch has called "social mobilization," as a result of which they are integrated in a large political community. The level of economic, social and political development that results makes a tremendous difference in many things—but not, we are told, when it comes to integration! It would seem more likely that integration of developed societies is something quite different from the integration that created those societies in the first place. This might also explain why it has been difficult to apply Europe's experience to the developing countries, as Joseph Nye discovered.

I should preface the next comment about integration theory by saying that I like much of the work that was done, particularly the determination to get a grip on something that might well improve the general welfare of mankind. I share the belief that in some respects nations are obsolete. Still, I am bothered by the fact that everyone deeply involved in the theory (or practice) of integration seemed to be strongly in favor of it. They thought integration a good thing, inevitable in the long run and necessary in the near future if we were to make it to the long run. Much earlier we reviewed the point that the more strongly a person believes in something the more likely it will seem to him, or "the wish is father to the thought." Why would this not apply here?

One last comment concerns William Riker's approach. In contrast to other approaches reviewed in this chapter that were cumbersome and complicated even in preliminary formulations, Riker admitted he greatly simplified reality. His critics insist he thereby distorted it. The point of coalitions, to Riker, was to share the winnings and since the more shares there are the smaller each one will be, coalitions will be as small as possible. But what if the winnings consist of security? Increasing the coalition could increase everyone's "take," which is the logic of a world alliance against aggression such as the League of Nations was originally intended to be. Karl Deutsch has expanded on this by suggesting much of politics concerns increasing the size of the pie so everyone's share grows, a politics of growth. Riker may tell us something about situations where rewards are fixed and limited, but are his ideas applicable to coalitions which would enlarge the rewards and people's access to them?

Other difficulties with these approaches, such as the proliferation of variables, will have already occurred to us and this chapter is already long enough. The approaches just reviewed often found it necessary to take the general international environment into consideration. It has recently been suggested that the chief contribution of integration theory was to prepare the way for a sensitivity to the impact of rising interdependence on the global system—that integration theory prepared the way for a radical reformulation of our conception of international politics as a whole. This forces us to consider the possibility that the best place to investigate international politics is at the level of the international system. We turn next to those who attempt to do just that.

Notes

1. Karl Deutsch, "Nation and World," in Ithiel de Sola Pool, ed., *Contemporary Political Science* (New York: McGraw-Hill, 1967), p. 218.
2. George Modelski, "The Study of Alliances: A Review," in Julian Friedman, Christopher Bladen, and Steven Rosen, eds., *Alliances in International Politics* (Boston: Allyn and Bacon, 1970), p. 65.
3. See Hans Morgenthau, *Politics Among Nations,* 5th rev. ed. (New York: Knopf, 1978), pp. 188-200. Also George Liska, *Nations in Alliance* (Johns Hopkins University Press, 1962), p. 27.
4. Steven Rosen, "A Model of War and Alliance," in Friedman et al., pp. 215-37.
5. Bruce Bueno de Mesquita, "Risk, Power Distributions, and the Likeli-

hood of War," *International Studies Quarterly* (December 1981), p. 565. The review of seven studies on this is in Randolph Siverson and Michael Sullivan, "The distribution of Power and the Onset of War," *Journal of Conflict Resolution* (September 1983), pp. 473-94.

6. J. David Singer and Melvin Small, "Formal Alliances, 1815-1939," in Friedman et al., pp. 130-64; Singer and Small, "Alliance Aggregation and the Onset of War 1815-1945," in Singer, ed., *Quantitative International Politics: Insights and Evidence* (New York: Free Press, 1968), pp. 247-86.

7. Dina Zinnes, "An Analytical Study of the Balance of Power Theories," *Journal of Peace Research* no. 3 (1967), pp. 270-88.

8. A.F.K. Organski and Jacek Kugler, *The War Ledger* (University of Chicago Press, 1980), pp. 25-26.

9. Randolph Siverson and Michael Tennefoss, "Power, Alliance, and the Escalation of International Conflict, 1815-1965," *American Political Science Review* (December 1984), pp. 1057-69.

10. Bruce Bueno de Mesquita, "The War Trap Revisited: A Revised Expected Utility Model," *American Political Science Review* (March 1985), p. 163.

11. William Riker, *The Theory of Political Coalitions* (New Haven: Yale University Press, 1962), pp. 32-33.

12. Ibid., pp. 202-43.

13. Mancur Olson, Jr. and Richard Zeckhauser, "An Economic Theory of Alliances," in Friedman et al. (note 2), pp. 175-98. Olson's approach is set forth in greater detail in *The Logic of Collective Action: Public Goods and the Theory of Groups* (Cambridge: Harvard University Press, 1965).

14. Olson and Zeckhauser, p. 189.

15. John Sullivan, "International Alliances," in Michael Haas, ed., *International Systems, A Behavioral Approach* (Corte Madera, Calif.: Chandler, 1974), p. 113. He reviews relevant studies on pp. 108-12.

16. Ole Holsti et al., *Unity and Disintegration in International Alliances: Comparative Studies* (New York: Wiley, 1973), p. 214. See the discussion and findings on pp. 149-213. A brief statement of this view is in Ole Holsti, "Alliances and Coalition Diplomacy," in James Rosenau, et al., eds., *World Politics, An Introduction* (New York: Free Press, 1976), pp. 361-64.

17. Bruce Russett, *International Regions and the International System* (Skokie, Ill.: Rand McNally, 1967).

18. In a later study he confirmed this for regional trade patterns reaching back to the late 1930s: Bruce Russett, " 'Regional' Trading Patterns, 1938-1963," *International Studies Quarterly* (December 1968), pp. 360-79.

19. Michael Brecher, "The Subordinate State System of Southern Asia," *World Politics* (January 1963), pp. 213-35; and "The Middle East Subordinate System and its Impact on Israel's Foreign Policy," *International Studies Quarterly* (June 1969), pp. 117-39.

20. Brecher, "The Subordinate State System" p. 217.

21. William Thompson, "The Regional Subsystem: A Conceptual Explication and a Propositional Inventory," *International Studies Quarterly* (March 1973), pp. 89-117.

22. John Harsanyi (his emphasis), cited in Wolfram Hanrieder, *Comparative Foreign Policy* (New York: McKay, 1971), p. 13.

23. Charles Pentland, *International Theory and European Integration* (New York: Free Press, 1973), pp. 197-204.

24. Leon Lindberg, "Political Integration as a Multidimensional Phenomenon Requiring Multivariate Measurement," in Leon Lindberg and Stuart Scheingold, eds., *Regional Integration, Theory and Research* (Cambridge: Harvard University Press, 1971), p. 113.
25. James Dougherty and Robert Pfaltzgraff, Jr., *Contending Theories of International Relations,* 2nd ed. (New York: Harper and Row, 1981), p. 453.
26. Pentland, p. 23.
27. Ernst Haas, "The Study of Regional Integration: Reflections on the Joy and Anguish of Pretheorizing," in Lindberg and Scheingold, pp. 20-21.
28. David Mitrany, "The Prospects of Integration, Federal or Functional?" in Joseph Nye, eds., *International Regionalism* (Boston: Little, Brown, 1968), pp. 43-73.
29. David Mitrany, *A Working Peace System* (New York: Quadrangle Books, 1966), p. 18.
30. See Robert Riggs and J. Jostein Mykletun, *Beyond Functionalism: Attitudes Toward International Organization in Norway and the United States* (University of Minnesota Press, 1979).
31. Bruce Russett, *Community and Contention* (Massachusetts Institute of Technology Press, 1963), p. 39.
32. Donald Puchala, "The Integration Theorists and the Study of International Relations," in Charles Kegley, Jr. and Eugene Wittkopf, eds., *The Global Agenda: Issues and Perspectives* (New York: Random House, 1984), p. 189.
33. Karl Deutsch et al., *Political Community and the North Atlantic Area* (Princeton University Press, 1957), p. 7.
34. Ibid., pp. 46-67, with the quotations on pp. 66-67.
35. Donald Puchala, "International Transactions and Regional Integration," in Lindberg and Scheingold, p. 128.
36. See Pentland, pp. 100-46; and Dougherty and Pflatzgraff, pp. 430-43.
37. Ernst Haas, *The Uniting of Europe* (Stanford University Press, 1958), p. 16. His early views on spillover are set forth in chapter 8.
38. Ernst Haas and Philippe Schmitter, "Economics and Differential Patterns of Political Integration: Projections About Unity in Latin America," in *International Political Communities* (anthology) (New York: Doubleday, 1966), pp. 259-99. See also Haas, "International Integration, the European and the Universal Process," in *International Political Communities,* pp. 93-129.
39. Stanley Hoffmann, "Obstinate or Obsolete? The Fact of the Nation-State and the Case of Western Europe," in Joseph Nye, ed., *International Regionalism* (Boston: Little, Brown, 1968), pp. 177-230.
40. Lawrence Scheinman, "Euratom: Nuclear Integration in Europe," in Nye, pp. 269-81; the quote is from p. 276.
41. See Roger Hansen, "Regional Integration, Reflections on a Decade of Theoretical Efforts," *World Politics* (January 1969), pp. 242-53; Joseph Nye, "Central American Regional Integration," in Nye, pp. 377-429; Joseph Nye, *Pan-Africanism and East African Integration* (Cambridge: Harvard University Press, 1965); and W. Andrew Axline, "Underdevelopment, Dependence, and Integration: The Politics of Regionalism in the Third World," *International Organization* (Winter 1977), pp. 83-105.

42. Donald Puchala, "The Common Market and Political Federation in Western European Public Opinion," *International Studies Quarterly* (March 1970), pp. 32-59; and Roger Hansen, pp. 253-56.
43. Haas, pp. 23-24. See also Haas, "The Uniting of Europe and the Uniting of Latin America," *Journal of Common Market Studies* (June 1967), pp. 315-43; Joseph Nye, *Peace in Parts* (Boston: Little, Brown, 1971), especially chapter 3.
44. Haas, pp. 26-40.
45. Joseph Nye, *Peace in Parts,* pp. 64-93. A summary of his refinements is offered in Dougherty and Pfaltzgraff, pp. 439-43; and it is tested in Charles Kegley, Jr. and Llewellyn Howell, Jr., "The Dimensionality of Regional Integration: Construct Validation in the Southeast Asian Context," *International Organization,* no. 4 (1975), pp. 997-1020.
46. James Caporaso, *Functionalism and Regional Integration: A Logical and Empirical Assessment* (Beverly Hills, Calif.: Sage, 1972), Series No. 02-004. A similar view: Helge Hveem, "Integration By Whom, For Whom, Against Whom?" *Cooperation and Conflict,* no. 4 (1974), pp. 263-84.
47. Puchala, p. 185.
48. Ernst Haas, *The Obsolescence of Regional Integration Theory,* Regional Series No. 25 (Institute of International Studies, University of California, Berkeley, 1975), p. 1. See also Haas, "Turbulent Fields and the Theory of Regional Integration," *International Organization* (Spring 1976), pp. 173-212.
49. Puchala, p. 198.
50. William Thompson, p. 90.

Bibliographical Remarks

As the chapter suggested, regional analysis is not attracting a great deal of attention these days, so these remarks can be fairly short. Besides the items cited in the footnotes, one other work on regional subsystem analysis is Werner Feld and Gavin Boyd, eds., *Comparative Regional Systems: West and East Europe, North America, the Middle East, and Developing Countries* (Elmsford, N.Y.: Pergamon Press, 1980).

On the subject of regional integration Karl Deutsch, *Tides Among Nations* (New York: Free Press, 1979) pulls together many of Deutsch's articles over the years into one convenient volume. David Mitrany's functionalist approach is reviewed with modest favor in Mark Imber, "Re-reading Mitrany: A Pragmatic Assessment of Sovereignty," *Review of International Studies* (April 1984), pp. 103-23; and there is also the collection on functionalist works by A.J.R. Groom and Paul Taylor, eds., *Functionalism: Theory and Practice in International Relations* (Crane, Russak and Co., 1975).

More general works on regional integration include Reginald Harrison, *Theories of Regional International Integration* (New York University Press, 1974) and Paul Taylor, *The Limits of European Integration* (Columbia University Press, 1983). An interesting approach, partly because it suggests that regional integration must be approached within some conception of the international system—in this case of its capitalist dynamics and development—is Peter Cocks, "Towards a Marxist Theory of Regional Integration," *International Organization* (Winter 1980), pp. 1-40.

On alliances, the degree to which flexibility in alliance relationships has existed under multipolarity is investigated in George Duncan and Randolph Siverson, "Flexibility of Alliance Partner Choice in a Multipolar System: Models and Tests," *International Studies Quarterly* (December 1982), pp. 511-38. Discussions of the relationship between alliances and war can be found in Jack Levy, "Alliance Formation and War Behavior: An Analysis of the Great Powers 1495-1975," *Journal of Conflict Resolution* (December 1981), pp. 581-613; and Charles Kegley, Jr. and Gregory Raymond, "Alliance Norms and War: A New Piece in an Old Puzzle," *International Studies Quarterly* (December 1982), pp. 572-95.

8

Grand Theories and Grander Ambitions

We have come to the top of our ladder. The last available level of analysis embraces what is conventionally called "the international system." Human ingenuity being what it is, we can imagine other worlds and conceive of interworld politics, one of the standard themes of science fiction, but all such ideas remain speculative. We can also speculate about a world politics that transcended the *international* system because one or more communities had developed that superceded nation-states. This is the world George Orwell depicted in *1984* or, in a different version, what an advocate of world government desires. However, people have yet to seriously commit loyalty, life, and treasure to supranational institutions, so nations and international politics are still very much with us. Nevertheless, interest in projecting and promoting new patterns of world politics not centered on nation-states has risen sharply in recent years. Later we shall see where this sort of thinking may take us.

We started with approaches that focus on elements and their interrelationships within nations. Then we turned to approaches that explore the behavior of nations as entities. We went on to the study of limited interactions among nations in alliances and regions. Now we see how one might try to describe the central characteristics and processes of the universe of nations (and other actors) all at once or as a whole. This will take two chapters, as a renewed of interest in analysis of this sort has relevant works tumbling out of ivory towers at a rapid rate. We will be reviewing efforts of those who live up to C. Wright Mills' admonition to always "take it big." These grand theorists constantly risk having their reach exceed their grasp in an effort to generate an all-embracing theory. If the magnitude of their achievements is a matter of controversy, that of their ambition and of the task they set themselves is not.

At this level we need the following things for a theoretical analysis. The initial requirement is a way of describing or characterizing the environment surrounding the nation and other actors. Next we have to assume the environment has a big impact on why governments (and other actors) behave as they do. Then we have to find the links between the nature or shape of the environment and that behavior. Finally, either prior to, simultaneously with, or subsequent to that previous step, we need to come up with an explanation for those links which bears up under further investigation. What could be easier?

Some analysts are partial to the view that a true theory of *international* politics will essentially explain the impact of the world on the behavior of states. But most analysts are inclined to see states' behavior as influenced by both the environment and by factors at work inside the states themselves. In either case, something like the procedure I just outlined is unavoidable. What results is a startling array of theoretical visions and nothing that resembles a consensus.

Preliminaries

We should run through certain reflections before casting ourselves out onto this sea of scholarly speculation. To start with, any attempt to theorize about international politics as a whole assumes that there is some order to the world and that it is within our power to comprehend it. If only we look at the vast panorama before us in the right way certain patterns and regularities will emerge, and common situations and standard relationships will be apparent. Alas, the absence of consensus begins to be apparent right here.

As always, there are people around who say it cannot be done or that it cannot be done now. While the grand theorist probes for a broad understanding of the whole subject, these critics seem to suggest that "you can't get there from here." He regards any advance as a hard-won victory, but they insist on pointing out how far there is yet to go.

One set of critics believes there is little or nothing systematic or orderly about international politics, that it is a series of basically unique occurrences. As we noted much earlier in this book, this involves the question of which factors or elements most determine our behavior—those that make us alike or those that set us apart. The theorist concentrates on similarities and repetitions; no "vive la différence" for him! The critic will respond that history is a record of sole events, a record never replayed or replayable.

Then there are those who want and expect a comprehensive theory to emerge eventually, but who argue that the present state of our knowledge makes such theorizing useless. They see theorizing at this stage as something that at best merely sidetracks some of the finest minds in the field from the business of generating the necessary factual information that is the basis for theory. At its worst, premature theorizing may actually handicap research. Remember the experiment recounted in chapter 3 in which teams pawed through bits and pieces of stories in trying to unravel a mystery? The preliminary theory of the team leader cramped his grasp of the situation, inhibiting his ability to learn more. Better say these critics, to let fragments of data and limited theories emerge, accumulating like coral reefs into islands of theory.

The usual answer to this is that we do not know where to look or what to look at or even what tools we need without theory. In chapter 7 we reviewed Bruce Russett's attempt to delineate regions on the basis of patterns into which seemingly relevant data fall. He believed such a collection of facts was necessary to lay the basis for building a theory. In a highly critical review, Oran Young found this work fatally flawed by the "fallacy of puristic induction: the collection of empirical materials *as an end in itself* and without sufficient theoretical analysis to determine appropriate criteria of selection." Just collecting facts doesn't work. If we collect masses of data and arrange them in patterns we are still left with the task of explaining the patterns. But we can usually think of a number of relatively plausible explanations that fit the data and we have no way to choose among them. Instead we need to deduce an explanation and then conduct research to test it.

> Works such as Russett's are *not* important contributions to a genuine science of international relations. On the contrary, they retard progress in that direction both by distorting the basic relationships among the intellectual tasks involved in the construction of theory and by draining off intellectual (and fiscal) resources into essentially secondary activities.[1]

If we find something it remains a "something" unless we have a theory to tell us what it is. This is why, Stanley Hoffman contends, grand theory emerges fairly early in most fields.[2] It wasn't the calculus that allowed Newton to begin to theoretically understand the universe; he invented the calculus because his theory required it.

At this point we have been presented with two ways in which to retard the study of international politics—theory and research! Needless to say, this overstates the arguments of each side. Do we start by deducing propositions from a general theoretical viewpoint or by gathering what evidence we can about the world? Stated this boldly the question cannot be answered because we do both. A theory must be checked against data and is derived from impressions about information previously on hand; working from data to theory and back to data goes on constantly in a developing analysis.

Also worth mentioning are other possible advantages of macroanalysis, of theorizing at this level. As always there is the matter of forests and trees. Within limits, the farther we are from the forest the more likely we are to see it. A global perspective helps rid us of messy details that can be distracting. In the grand view, daily international trials and tribulations that threaten to absorb our attention recede into insignificance. The idiosyncracies of officials, bureaucratic rivalries, and technical details all seem of less consequence.

Working at this level also helps cut events and people down to size. Nothing is of more impressive dimensions than a vast mountain range, but the earth's seemingly jagged crust, in relation to its total mass, is smoother than the skin of an apple! Measured against the mass of history or international politics as a whole, locally prominent figures and topical ideas similarly shrink in significance.

In many approaches reviewed earlier there is a constant problem of gaining access to obscure or hidden information. By adopting the broadest perspective we circumvent these difficulties since that sort of information will rarely be vital to our analysis. The same is true of predicting change. To predict and explain tomorrow we need to know almost everything about today. But to paint a picture of the next decade and beyond, we can use a broader brush dipped in the flow of a generation or more.

Finally, in pictures of the earth from space all nations tend to look much the same. Nationalism down here poses serious difficulties for analysts, for many a theory is bent by the bias inculcated by this greatest ideological force of our age. Thinking on a global scale can help here, since it makes nations seem more like the emotionally neutral A and B and less like the United States and the Soviet Union. We need lots of help here for many have charged that our theories are too West—or U.S.—centered, much like the way our maps typically place North America right in the middle.

Characterizing the World

You will recall that our first requirement for theoretical comprehension at this level of analysis is to define or describe, in a preliminary way, what it is that we wish to investigate. The overwhelming choice among analysts is the concept of the international system. A system, you will recall, is a set of interrelated entities and their interrelationships. An international system would then be set of nations and the networks that link them together. One might well leave room for some other entities as well, but by referring to "international" we would be implying that nations are the most significant components. Some analysts, as we shall see, dispute this, not by ignoring nations but by suggesting that other entities are important enough that we need terms like "world" system or "global" system instead.

Is there such a system? There are a variety of possible answers. It could be said that this is not a question that requires an answer; we simply assume a system exists for purposes of theory and see whether we get a satisfactory result. However, the usual response in the field is "yes" there is an international system, and most of the theorizing and research we will be discussing is rooted in this view.

Another possible answer is that there is a global or world system in which nations and their relationships play an important role but in which other elements are also significant, even crucial. In this era of environmental concerns, for example, many evoke the existence of one world; an "ecological perspective" sees the world as an "interrelated whole," an ecosystem. Such a perspective turns international politics into a subsystem of a more inclusive global one. We might then describe nations and their political relationships as the dominant political subsystem of today's world.

Of course, if we push matters far enough, everything in the universe can be seen to be somehow related to everything else. Thus, to treat international politics as a subsystem is to, somewhat arbitrarily, pull out certain entities and their linkages for special attention. But what if the key linkages vary from issue to issue, time to time, or place to place? Then we would have to rearrange our thinking to deal with many international systems, not just one. We might decide that at any one point there are several international systems coexisting side by side and perhaps having only a limited connection to each other. Or we might proceed as if history records a succession of international systems, each one distinctive enough to deserve separate description and investigation. This way of answering the question, conceiving the existence of several systems, invites comparison as the obvious way to proceed. Thus, we arrive at the subject of much of this chapter: the comparative analysis of international systems.

There is definitely no shortage of grand theories, and we could use a nice framework to make a garden out of an otherwise bewildering variety of exotic blossoms. Fortunately one is at hand, offered by the distinguished theorist Hedley Bull (who in turn derived it from Martin Wright, from whom much British thinking about international politics descends). He sees three competing perspectives on the international system, each of which can be traced back to an important classical political philosopher—to Hobbes, Grotius, or Kant.[3] By nipping corners and squeezing a bit, we can shoehorn the major approaches into

Bull's three categories. However, do not take the resulting neatness too seriously. Many analysts combine elements of more than one perspective. Our framework is a flexible guide, not a rigid demarcation.

The System as Patterns Amid Anarchy

Thomas Hobbes is renowned in political philosophy for describing man bereft of government as living in a situation of war—each against all others. Such perpetual insecurity, a "Hobbesian" world, is what many (going back to Rousseau and Machiavelli) find in international politics. For several hundred years the chief characteristic of international politics has appeared to be the dominance and independence of national governments. With this as our premise a number of things follow, some obvious and some not. For one thing, governments are not apt to be models of kindness and charity. They respond to external requests and demands only when they stand to benefit or when they must. In addition, they like being free to do as they please and resist encroachments on their independence. But as a result they must see to their own security by their own efforts (just as men on the lawless American frontier carried guns), so the system is beset by constant suspicion and incipient violence, with war the ultimate arbiter of disputes.

How are we to find patterns amidst this anarchy? One example is that this view of the world breeds two extremely influential, and ultimately contradictory, perceptions of international politics. Robert Jervis refers to them as the "deterrence model" and the "spiral model."[4] In the deterrence model, emphasis is placed on the fact that some governments want and will try to take more than others can permit—more territory, more power, more wealth—and must somehow be forestalled. The answer is deterrence, the use of threats and force to contain an aggressor. To make threats plausible, a government needs weapons close at hand and a reputation for backing up its warnings. Thus, it is important to be firm, to avoid concessions for aggressors cannot be appeased. From this perspective the anarchy of international politics breeds aggressors and those who must seek to restrain them. War comes when the latter fail to appreciate this and shoulder their deterrence responsibilities.

The spiral model suggests that in a Hobbesian world, governments must be suspicious and acquire the means to defend themselves. Unfortunately a capability to defend will look to a suspicious neighbor like a capability (and perhaps an intent) to attack. When its neighbors arm, a state's suspicions are confirmed and it responds in kind. The resulting spiral of suspicions, tension, and arms spending often ends in war. International anarchy means that tragedy—in the form of unnecessary but unavoidable war—is the essence of international politics. Only efforts at conciliation might suspend this spiral of grief.

The classic example for the spiral model is the era prior to World War I as a grand and gifted civilization stumbled into catastrophe. For the deterrence model it's the foolish appeasement of Hitler in the 1930s, as a result of which he nearly swallowed the entire European continent. Notice that adherents of each view find the others to be terribly dangerous. For spiral-model advocates, to stand firm, talk tough, and rattle sabers is often the worst possible course, but for deterrence-model folks nothing is more foolish than to look weak by attempts at conciliation. Lest you think the debate esoteric, I should point out that it represents the fundamental perceptual cleavage in the United States over how to deal with the Soviet Union. Spiral-model types push detente and often see further arms spending as counterproductive, making us less secure. Deterrence-model advocates insist we must not be mistakenly conciliatory toward the expansionist Soviets with a misguided pursuit of detente and inadequate defense spending, for weakness can only be fatal.

Both views strongly suggest that the international system is not a community. Instead, semianarchy prevails in and through nations' perpetual rivalries and struggles. But notice that each sees the behavior of states as interrelated, and each detects recurring patterns in those relationships. In other words, there is a system of some sort. But neither really constitutes a full-fledged theory. What other ways can we describe recurrent patterns or regularities so as to give us the first laws or first principles of the system?

Political Realism and Its Relatives

Any review of possible answers must start with political realism and its antecedent, classic balance-of-power theory as expounded in eighteenth- and nineteenth-century Europe. Nations first emerged on the smallest continent, where they seemed to constitute a single system. The most impressive theory regarding this system described and analyzed it in terms of a balance of power. When the system disintegrated in this century, political realism undertook to explain why by restating the basic principles of the theory and outlining the ways it had become outmoded. The realist school arose as a reaction to "idealism" or "utopianism" as it affected thinking about international politics in the 1920s and 1930s. At its core is a deterrence model of the international system.

The best introduction to it is the work of Hans Morgenthau.[5] His ideas have been enormously influential in the field and we have touched on aspects of his thinking in earlier chapters. The basic conception of the international system he employed is that it consists of states living in semianarchy, with a structure that is the distribution of power among those states, and that it has a pronounced tendency toward equilibrium in the distribution of that power. As a result there are regular patterns in state behavior.

Morgenthau started with a dim view of human nature. Like other realists he assumed that people, individually and collectively, are power-seeking, selfish, violence-prone, etc. The trouble in international politics is that anarchy gives these tendencies free rein. Governments have basic needs, or interests, arising from their geographical locations, economic ambitions, desire for security, and so on, but given human nature these are not sought in saintly and cooperative ways. To get what they want, governments need power, so they pursue their interests defined in terms of power in a competitive struggle. Hence "international politics, like all politics, is a struggle for power."

What regulates this struggle? The standard regulator has been a balance of power, which works like this. Out of a determination to preserve its existence and autonomy and to pursue its interests, each nation seeks to avoid falling under the domination of any other. Strenuous efforts are made to prevent the emergence of a preponderant nation or coalition. When the threat of this appears, other nations will seek to counteract it by offsetting the threatening state (or coalition). They may unite in an alliance. They may build up their power by expanding their armaments. They may try to buy off the opponent with limited concessions and compensations. Or they may pursue a policy of "divide and rule," trying to weaken or isolate a dangerous state. Whatever their policy, its aim and normally its result will be a rough balance of power. Hence the balancing of power represents both the equilibrium tendencies in the international system and the policy normally pursued by many of its members.

"Idealist" notions about how international politics can be fundamentally harmonious and conciliatory are silly and downright dangerous. So is any claim that one's own nation virtuously pursues the general welfare and not simply its own selfish interests. Morality consists of appreciating the importance of power, the occasional necessity of using it in war or interventions, the impermanence of alliances or other associations, and the virtue of trimming one's interests to fit the power available.

Notice the powerful way the theory links together several levels of analysis. It starts with a conception of human nature, explains the behavior of states, offers a guide to the formation of alliances and other coalitions, and outlines the basic dynamics of the system as a whole. Notice also its simplicity. It describes only two major kinds of states: those seeking to upset the existing distribution of power and those seeking to maintain it. Morgenthau also described a variant of the second kind of state—the "balancer." This is the swing state in the system, one powerful enough to make a crucial difference to whichever side it joins. Such a state consistently joins the weaker side, whenever necessary, to preserve the balance. The theory greatly simplifies the determinants of state action. We need not refer to the ideologies of officials, personalities, decision-making mechanisms, and so on. The chief determinants of the behavior of governments are their relative power and the state of the system. Morgenthau cited many remarks by statesmen to the effect that they thought and acted primarily in keeping with the dictates of the theory, that they were moved by considerations of the balance of power. Thus, we have a theory that strips matters down to essentials, can be used to explain much of the history of international politics, and has been applauded by statesmen. What more could we ask?

We might ask for a theory relevant to today, because Morgenthau concluded that classic balance-of-power theory was not very useful in our time. To see why, we must review certain facets of a balance-of-power system in operation. For one thing, such a system cannot flourish if the members consist of a giant and a bunch of pygmies, because balancing the goliath would be impossible. Next, nations have to feel free to shift alliances—to regard yesterday's friend as today's enemy but tomorrow's ally—as the situation warrants. Third, members must be ready, willing, and able to go to war to uphold the balance. Finally, statesmen must be able to compute the distribution of power in the system reasonably well so that they will know when to do what.

Reviewing these requirements, Morgenthau noted that hardly any are now fulfilled. The U.S. and U.S.S.R. are giants, turning many former great powers into near pygmies. If a third country shifts from one side in the U.S.-Soviet rivalry to the other, it alters the distribution of power between those giants only marginally, so there's no such thing as a balancer. Fierce nationalisms make for unrestrained wars and in the nuclear age total war means disaster, so war is no longer an acceptable mechanism for maintaining the system. Morgenthau put special emphasis on the highly ideological nature of contemporary international politics. The confrontation of ideological opponents makes the system rigid. Each great power jealously guards its sphere and feels a moral compulsion to avoid giving an inch to the heathens on the other side. This makes it extremely difficult for states to shift sides, a standard maneuver in a balance-of-power system. Not that they could readily shift anyway, since modern nationalism coupled with the influence of mass public opinion has given foreign policies a messianic cast. Allies are not temporary friends but those to whom a moral commitment has been made, while embracing today's enemy tomorrow seems cynical and immoral.

Finally, Morgenthau always insisted that power, while central to politics, is not readily measurable. This means the statesman is always uncertain as to the exact distribution of power and the trends affecting it, making miscalculations inevitable. Unfortunately, that also leads to wars, a good many of them in classic balance-of-power systems. Periodic outbreaks of warfare among great powers were once tolerable but this is hardly true in the nuclear age.

Ultimately, this theory presents us with a way of abstractly ascertaining the *rational elements* of reality. It tells us that the nature of the international system, in combination with unchanging elements in human nature, imposes certain kinds of behavior on governments as rational, and that they behave in this fashion much of the time. The defects that Morgenthau identifies in the balance of power for our day all have to do with *limitations on the capacities of governments to be rational*. War is no longer the recourse of the rational statesman (at least for great-power conflicts). Ideology interferes with cold calculation and too much citizen participation invites moral absolutism and utopianism. Power is so difficult to measure that mistakes occur and uncertainty paralyzes the statesman's judgment. Bipolarity means there is too little flexibility in the structure of the system.

There are at least three major problems with realism as it has just been described. Numerous analysts have demonstrated that its key concepts—power, national interests, and balance of power—are fuzzy. For instance, multiple meanings are attached to the idea of "balance" and realists often shift unconsciously from one meaning of the term to another. There is a tendency for people to treat the balancing of power sometimes as operating automatically and, at other times, as something clever statesmen have to attend to or it will not occur. This makes the theory often hazy or inconsistent.[6]

Another inconsistency is that Morgenthau starts describing the international system as the main determinant of governments' behavior, but then turns around and lists changes in nations and their behavior (ideological commitment, messianic nationalism) as partly responsible for altering the system. In a classic balance-of-power analysis domestic factors are important only insofar as they add to or detract from a nation's power. But Morgenthau stressed that domestic factors had also come to affect how nations used their power, altering the perceptions and behavior of governments.

The final problem, one recognized by Morgenthau, is that the theory as he formulated it seemed not very useful in today's world. How then shall we respond to this situation? The alternatives boil down to two: revise the theory or abandon it. Let's see where each one takes us.

Realism Revisited

The most spirited revision of the realist perspective has been the one offered by Kenneth Waltz, and in some ways it has also been the most influential—at least it has the virtue of having attracted widespread attention. His starting point is the assertion that a theory of international politics must, above all else, pick out what is distinctive. For Waltz the distinctive feature of international politics is the nature of the system and the way it drives the behavior of governments; that's where we have to start. If we explain why a state behaves as it does by personality factors or domestic or bureaucratic politics, or by whether the society is capitalist or not, or even by the rationality or irrationality of states themselves (in short, by any of the ways we explored in chapters 3 through 6), we are guilty of "reductionism"—we explain what happens in the *international* system by citing factors located somewhere else, inside nations. As Waltz stated: "Blurring the distinction between the different levels of a system has, I believe, been the major impediment to the development of theories about international politics."[7]

For Waltz, international politics is anarchical and it consists primarily of states. There is some degree of cooperation and there are other actors besides states, but if we concentrate on the essence of the system we come back to anarchy and states. Because the system is anarchical, states must care for their security and survival themselves. Essential for describing the system and how it affects behavior is its *structure,* and a system's structure consists of the distribution of capabilities among the members—that is, the distribution of power. Changes in the system's structure leads to changes in members' behavior, behavior that is always preoccupied with survival and autonomy.

How does the system's structure do this? Waltz cites two elements.[8] One is competition; in an anarchical system states are in constant competition. The other is socialization. Living/competing within a system leads to learning about how best to get along in it, so that structure subtly shapes behavior. The result is that "international politics is the realm of power, of struggle, and of accommodation" with precious little of the authority, administration, and law that we enjoy in domestic politics.

Waltz offers the following as a starting assumption, with the familiar caveat that it is a simplification for purposes of theory: states that "unitary actors who, at a minimum, seek their own preservation and, at a maximum, drive for universal domination." In an anarchical system this leads to the formation of balances of power out of the uncoordinated actions taken by states. Another result is that states tend to imitate each other, following the lead of the most powerful.

> From the theory, one predicts that states will engage in balancing behavior. . . . From the theory, one predicts a strong tendency toward balance in the system. The expectation is not that a balance, once achieved, will be maintained, but that a balance, once disrupted, will be restored in one way or another. . . . [O]ne predicts . . . that states will display characteristics common to competitors; namely, that they will imitate each other and become socialized to their system.[9]

Waltz finds plenty of evidence that balances of power regularly form and that states do indeed imitate each other.

Waltz is as proud of what the theory omits as of what it contains. There is no assumption of rational decision-making. There is no reference to states consciously and deliberately following a policy of balance of power—the balancing is something that comes about, whether states consciously strive for it or not. In short, there is no theory of foreign policy and no reference to the peculiar qualities of states and their leaders—no reductionism.

We could carry this discussion further at this point. However, it may be better to put off considering some of Waltz's conclusions until we have laid out other approaches to which his view can be compared, including approaches about which Waltz has been quite critical.

Comparative Analysis via Structure: Hypothetical and Historical Systems

Analysts of a balance-of-power persuasion have typically proceeded, at least in part, by comparing (mainly contrasting) international politics with domestic political systems. Another way to proceed is to imagine or to find in history other types of international systems and then do a comparative analysis. This has been tried in a number of approaches that emphasize system structure as a key factor.

Morton Kaplan has been a prolific contributor to the literature on international politics and you should keep in mind that the following cursory review hardly does justice to the complexity of his thought. Kaplan's primary concern is analysis at the level of the international system, which he characterizes as more or less "subsystem-dominant." What he means by this is that the essential rules of the system are not treated as "givens" by the major subsystems, the nation-states. Within limits, they do as they please. This is his way of describing limited international anarchy. Finally, he believes the following is a good starting assumption: "If the number, type, and behavior of nations differ over time, and if their military capabilities, their economic assets, and their information also vary over time, then there is some likely interconnection between these elements such that different structural and behavioral systems can be discerned to operate in different periods of history."[10] I hope that you can make your way through this prose thicket. In brief, if we specify all those things listed in the first part of the sentence, they should be related in some way so as to form a distinctive international system. As they change over time so should the nature of the system. This means there is not one system, but several.

Kaplan sought to outline different international systems, to uncover the manner in which each maintains itself, and to evaluate its chances for stability. Originally he distinguished six:[11]

- Balance of power: At least five essential actors (states) and no system government.
- Loose bipolar: Two major blocs, some states outside the blocs, and some "universal actors" like the United Nations.
- Tight bipolar: All the essential actors are in the two blocs.
- Universal: An operating world government along federalist lines, so national governments are still important actors.
- Hierarchical: The world government operates directly on individuals; national governments are weak, if they exist at all.
- Unit-veto: Each state could destroy any other, as if nuclear weapons had proliferated widely.

Notice the Universal and Hierarchical systems are not "Hobbesian" like the others.

Kapan suggests we analyze each system in terms of five sets of variables. The first set consists of the essential rules of the system. In the balance-of-power system, for example, the rules are:

1. Act to increase capabilities but negotiate rather than fight.
2. Fight rather than pass up an opportunity to increase capabilities.
3. Stop fighting rather than eliminate an essential national actor.

4. Act to oppose any coalition or single actor that tends to assume a position of predominance with respect to the rest of the system.
5. Act to constrain actors who subscribe to supranational organizing principles.
6. Permit defeated or constrained essential national actors to reenter the system as acceptable role partners or act to bring some previously unessential actor within the essential actor classification. Treat all essential actors as acceptable role partners.[12]

Recalling our earlier discussion of balance-of-power theory, we see that Kaplan is trying to define the characteristic behavior of the member states, behavior necessary if the system is to continue. Rule 4, for example, concerns moving to prevent any member from becoming dominant; Rules 3 and 6 refer to keeping the minimum number of actors necessary for the system and treating each actor as a potential ally.

A second set of variables embraces transformation rules, ways a system changes. Actor classification variables concern the characteristics of states. Kaplan believes the different kinds of actors—such as authoritarian as opposed to democratic states—will behave differently. The fourth set of variables concerns states' capabilities, such as territory, population, and armaments. Finally, there are information variables, which include actors' information about each other's aspirations, capabilities, and actions.

The first two sets concern the nature of the international system, while the last three cover the sorts of things that are investigated at lower levels of analysis. "Aha," says Professor Waltz, this is really a reductionist approach and does not qualify as a true theory of the international system.[13] "Not so," replies Kaplan, it is not reductionist to include characteristics of actors that are directly relevant for the nature and operation of the international system.[14]

To summarize briefly, Kaplan listed six systems described in terms of five sets of variables. The list of systems was not exhaustive and Kaplan later outlined several more that he considered as less inherently stable than the first six:[15]

• Very loose bipolar: Weak blocs, bloc leaders have some overlapping interests.
• Detente: Bloc leaders and blocs are more open, less in conflict.
• Unstable bloc: Tension between blocs rises, violence breaks out in places, and four or five states have nuclear weapons.
• Incomplete nuclear diffusion: Like the previous system except that fifteen to twenty states have nuclear weapons.

Attempts have been made to add to the list, or to test or apply Kaplan's ideas by both computer explorations of hypothetical systems and historical case studies of real ones.[16]

Kaplan considers the first of his systems not unlike the real world in the nineteenth century. Which of Kaplan's models would we pick to describe the world of the 1980s? We can reject all but one of his original models—only the "loose bipolar system" looks like it might be relevant. Of the ones added later on, in the 1970s at times it looked like we had shifted to a "very loose bipolar" or "detente" system, but now these seem far less applicable.

One of the most compelling objectives in the field is to get an analytical grip on international politics here and now. How do we translate the basic assumption of Morgenthau, Waltz, and Kaplan— that the structure of the system is crucial to the members' behavior— into understanding our world today? This leads to the two broad questions that preoccupy theorists with respect to the structure of the system. One of course is: What is it? The other is: What difference does it make? These are not the sorts of questions we would be asking if our theoretical equipment was very refined, but at least they are the right questions with which to start.

Postwar observers quickly discerned that the old balance-of-power system involving a number of major states had disappeared. The chief element in the new system appeared to be the emergence of the U.S. and the U.S.S.R. as superpowers. This came to be known as bipolarity—the two superpowers heading blocs of states clustered around them. Then in the 1960s the Sino-Soviet dispute grew severe, Japan and Western Europe grew stronger, the Cold War dissipated, and the nuclear club expanded. States seemed to display more maneuverability. Debate ensued as to whether bipolarity was being eroded and, if so, what was taking its place. As we shall see, even the idea that bipolarity ever existed came under fire.

Generally speaking, the analyst who emphasized raw military power or the sheer size of an economy was apt to see the world as still largely bipolar. But others saw the world moving toward mutliple centers of significant power, i.e. multipolarity. The trouble with being a superpower was that each was not the only one—each deterred the other, nullifying much of their raw military strength. And in economic matters new centers of power were obvious—the West Germans and the rest of the European Community, Japan, OPEC. Coming up fast was the Group of 77, the term for the (now more than 77) developing countries that negotiated as a bloc in trying to squeeze greater concessions from the developed nations. Multipolarity would take us back toward a classic balance of power as the regulatory mechanism.

Thus, it could be that we live in a bipolar world, but then again maybe it is really multipolar. So what? The reason theorists were interested was that they wanted to know how stable any particular system was—would it be flexible and able to maintain itself or would it eventually decay? In more practical terms for the nuclear age, can the international system sustain order and keep the peace or will it break down and kill us all?

Kenneth Waltz has taken one side of the debate. In an earlier work he noted a remarkable number of changes in the world after 1945—the breakup of empires, revolutions in military technology, two shifts in the allegiance of China—with no great war and no real disturbance of the superpowers' dominant position or the rough balance between them. All this was not a coincidence. The world was bipolar and would continue that way for some time to come, and it was a good thing, too, for bipolarity provides stability. To quote Waltz: "It is to a great extent due to its bipolar structure that the world since the war has enjoyed a stability seldom known where three or more powers have sought to cooperate with each other or have competed for existence."[17] Waltz has more recently reiterated this argument and developed it at length. He sees the superpowers as far less dependent on other societies— economically and militarily—than great powers of the past. As giants they are less sensitive to ebbs and flows in their foreign policy fortunes, less dependent on precise calculations of power or fickle allies, less in need of fighting to preserve their position. Using oligopoly as an analogy, he asserts that the fewer the number of great powers the easier their competition is to manage, the more that bargaining and collusion is facilitated to maintain order.[18]

This is not a widely accepted view. Usually bipolarity has been seen as too rigid, competitive, and tension ridden—too much like the Cold War—to be stable indefinitely. Some prefer multipolarity, and one of the more interesting arguments to this effect was offered by Karl Deutsch and J. David Singer.[19] They started from the premise that the opportunity for interaction among nations is important; the more actors there are, the more possible interactions among them. This means a multipolar system would be characterized by pluralism— many points of view, cross-pressures, no simple love-hate relationships. There would be many alignments on many different issues all at the same time. Under bipolarity, by contrast, there are two actors (blocs) and so interactions are very limited and focused on the conflict between the blocs. The gap between them would tend to widen under their competition, steadily pushing the system toward collapse.

Deutsch and Singer developed a second, related argument. Interaction requires that states pay attention to one another. For two states to go to war they must pay extreme attention to each other. Now states, like people, have only so much attention to distribute at any one time. As the number of major powers increases, each state finds itself tending to pay less and less attention to any other states. Like the amorous man amid a bevy of beautiful women—too distracted to make headway with any one. Again, bipolarity looks more dangerous; the contending forces can spend entirely too much time and effort cultivating their mutual hostility. To the virtues of multipolarity they added only one note of caution. In a multipolar system a statesman sooner or later goofs and gets his state eliminated, or once in a while the others can agree to divide up one of the members. Thus, a multipolar system will move toward bipolarity—that is, it is unstable in the long run.

Result: flat contradiction so far. If we turn to analysts who have tried to make sense of the available data, things do not improve much. The question of how system structure is related to war has no firm answer. (We began to get into this in the last chapter when discussing the impact of alliances on war, since alliances play a prominent role in balance-of-power systems.) A recent summary based on a careful review of the available studies finds that "the empirical relationship between polarity and war is neither simple nor always consistent. . . . It differs according to historical periods, the methods and data used by the analysts, and the measurement and meaning given to concepts."[20]

Another analyst has explained this by arguing that system structure, whether bipolar or multipolar, is not crucial in bringing on war. Waltz, Deutsch, and Singer assume that system structure determines the level of uncertainty of governments and their willingness to risk war, but in fact their willingness to take such a risk is unrelated to system structure while uncertainty is connected not to bipolarity or multipolarity but to the degree that either system structure is rapidly changing.

If there is a consensus position on how the world is best described these days it appears to be that neither bipolarity nor multipolarity fits exactly, but neither is completely irrelevant. One way to express this is to think of the international system as a game table and to ask: Who gets to play? In a bipolar world just two play; nuclear deterrence is pretty much this kind of game, as are superpower arms-control talks. In a multipolar world several more states get to play; the rest of the members kibitz a bit and occasionally sit in for a round or two but basically it isn't their game. A good example would be the management of the international monetary system. But some analysts see a world that has lots of other games as well, played for varying stakes. Every player participates in one or two, but some play in a great many games simultaneously. Many of the games are interdependent, so that play in one often influences play in another. Some are systemwide, but many are regional or local. The latter seem to be growing in number, and the systemwide games are changing from largely security issues to other sorts of concerns (food, environment, etc.).

This makes the international political system look increasingly subtle and complex, and breeds awkward terms like "bimultipolarity," "complex conglomerate system," and "cascading interdependence" to describe it. Many analysts now feel that it is no longer possible to make much headway by sticking to the core elements of a Hobbesian perspective: national actors in an anarchical environment whose interactions result in, and turn on, power balances of either a bipolar or multipolar sort. Some analysts do not like the emphasis on national governments. Some do not like the notion of anarchy. Some do not like focusing on power. Some do not like the whole thing! What do they offer instead?

The System as International Society

The Hobbesian view sees few signs of an international community; rather, international politics is the absence of community. However, it is not easy to accept this. After all, states do not seem constantly at war with each other; many get along rather nicely and some pretty complex cooperative ventures among nations can be found. A Grotian view of international politics, according to Hedley Bull, stresses these elements and thus assumes the existence of an international "society." The members of this society are the nation-states and they constitute a society because they are conscious of certain common interests and values, accept some common rules, and share some common institutions. As societies go, this is not a very well-developed one, and it is sometimes touch-and-go as to whether it will continue, but there is certainly much more to international politics than anarchy.

A couple of comments might be in order here. One is that this is a society of *states;* we will move in the next chapter to analysts with an inclination to refer to a global society of *people* (a Kantian perspective). There is a radical difference between the two. A second point is that this approach is almost certainly closest to the views of governments themselves and of people directly engaged in foreign affairs. Often accused of being Hoffesian at heart, mercilous competitors in a nasty world, they mostly behave in a more Grotian fashion.

If there really is an international society then perhaps it might best be studied like domestic ones. This has led a British scholar, Evan Luard, to propose that we conduct a sociological analysis, because "societies of states possess many of the characteristics of smaller human societies, and are governed by many similar forces."[21] While we cannot review his findings here, we can at least summarize the approach. His comparative analysis involves systems ranging from the Chinese and Greek city-states before Christ to the contemporary world, in terms of the following as the key factors in each system: the nature of the elites; elite motives, particularly the dominant one for elite behavior; means employed, particularly the dominant one; stratification—the degree of dominance and dependence; structure—types of interactions among system members; roles performed by the members; norms of conduct; institutions; and prevailing ideology or aspiration of the members.

He finds that state systems are not alike. In some, the members are relatively contained and not easily penetrated—the system looks a bit like billiard balls on a pool table, hard-shelled units that bounce off each other. But in others the members have flimsy boundaries and are readily penetrated by outside influences. In some systems the members are mostly expansion-minded while in others they are relatively satisfied and self-sufficient; obviously the former have more competition and conflict.

As an illustration of how a sociological concept can be applied to a society of states, a possible cause of war that has received some attention is the idea that, like people or classes in domestic society, nations arrange themselves in hierarchies of rank or status and that this causes them to behave in ways that lead to conflict and war. The hypothesized villain here is status discrepancy. If states are ranked by different measures—power, wealth, population, prestige—status discrepancy would exist when a state's position in the rankings varied greatly, particularly when its prestige was not parallel with its power or wealth. (The domestic society parallel would be the nouveaux rich who have money but little or no status, or the scion of old nobility who has lots of social standing and no cash in the bank.)

In one study Maurice East was interested in three kinds of rank: economic position, power, and prestige. His hypothesis: "An international system in which high prestige is allocated to the more powerful and more economically developed nation-states is less likely to exhibit international violence than is a system where prestige is withheld from these nations."[22]

East measured economic power by gross national product figures and military power by defense expenditures, while prestige was assessed as the number of embassies or legations in a nation's capitol. The violence in the international system was calculated by using data from J. David Singer's and Melvin Small's Correlates of War project and from an Office of Naval Research (ONR) project. Concentrating on the years 1945-1964, East computed the total annual status discrepancy in the international system and the amount of war. He found "a general and consistent pattern supporting our hypothesis," especially if status discrepancy for one year was compared with the amount of violence one or two years later.

A study by Michael Wallace reached roughly the same conclusion. Wallace generated two hypotheses; (1) "The greater the amount of status inconsistency in the international system as a whole, the greater the level of conflict . . . within it." (2) "The greater the differences among national rates of change on the capability and reputational status dimensions, the greater the probability of conflict in the system."[23] The second hypothesis reflects the view that status inconsistency may be an unsettling factor leading to war only when it is changing rapidly, as for example when the rapid arms buildup of one state disturbs a balance of power.

Wallace explored the period 1825-1965 and certain subperiods therein. He investigated only the states at the heart of the system from 1825 to 1920 and, after 1920, only states with diplomatic representatives from at least 30 percent of all nations. Like East, he drew on the Singer-Small data on war. He used five measures of "capability status"—total population, urban population, iron and steel production, military personnel, and defense spending—to compare a state's power with its prestige. In general, status inconsistency was clearly linked with war, and the evidence suggested (on the second hypothesis) that "status mobility appears to lead to status inconsistency which in turn predicts to war." The findings were not completely uniform; they varied depending on the index of national capability used and the time lags (Wallace used lags of up to 15 years).

Also interesting was Wallace's superb discussion of the limitations of his study and of the complexities involved in interpreting the findings. He noted the unreliability of some of the data. He pointed out how others could challenge the validity of his measures, for instance by arguing that national powers has more to do with political unity or government effectiveness than with population or defense spending. He also emphasized that it was impossible to say that status inconsistency *caused* war because changes in both might be related to some third factor, or it might even be that war caused status inconsistency and mobility.

Treating the international society of states like a domestic society may be carrying things too far. After all, states are rather different from individuals and groups in very significant ways, and the typical domestic society is certainly more organized and institutionalized. Hedley Bull himself prefers a Grotian conception of the international system but stops short of a highly sociological approach. Bull asserts that the major object and regular product of the society of states is *order,* a condition in which states can pursue certain common goals: preservation of the society of states, preservation of states' autonomy, and peace, among others. Order results from the application of various rules. For instance, a dominant rule is that governments are the major actors (not international organizations or multinational corporations) and are to be treated as such. There are rules on coexistence and cooperation, including ones associated with balance-of-power mechanisms. International law, diplomacy, the great powers, and sometimes even war all play a part in creating, interpreting, adjusting, and enforcing the rules and thus sustaining the society.

Given this perspective it becomes important to understand the "rules of the game" as perceived by the members of international society, the conventions—formal and informal—that direct interactions and shape the members' expectations about each other's behavior. This is the subject of various works. In one case an effort is made to track down the origins of international society's conventions in the historical experiences of governments, the myths and metaphors they use and cite, and the doctrines they espouse.[24] Another study contends that in an international society negotiation is no longer simply a way of settling disputes, instead it is a "management process" used by governments to reduce the uncertainty in international affairs.[25] Thus, negotiations become more important for shaping common perceptions—and rules—than for exchanging concessions to get agreements. And Raymond Cohen has updated the old idea that there are "rules of the game," In his words, they are

> "general norms of behavior, aspects of international law, and rules which are created by formal and informal understanding, or are contained in the "spirit" of agreements, verbal 'gentlemen's' agreements and different kinds of tacit understanding."[26]

The most influential treatment of this has arisen in the recent development (since 1975) of the concept of "regimes," a subject about which there is a growing body of literature. The most common definition of regimes holds that they are "principles, norms, rules, and decision-making procedures around which actor expectations converge in a given issue-area."[27] This is at once broader and narrower than the idea of rules, broader in that it extends to decision-making procedures (often via an international organization) but narrower in that a regime applies to only one issue or activity.

Robert Keohane and Jospeh Nye set forth the first major analysis of regimes.[28] In that early work, and in others since, the emphasis is often on melding regimes with political realism as outlined by Morgenthau and Waltz. The structure of the international system is important, and that system has anarchical elements, but regimes intervene between the structure of the system and the way states behave. Keohane has argued at length that in a world of competitive sovereign states it is still rational to set up and maintain those intermediate forms of cooperation, and that this also holds true if states display only limited or bounded rationality (as we discussed in chapter 6). Elements of the concept of regimes are also to be found in approaches to integration (reviewed in chapter 7). Since basic elements of a realist perspective are still employed, this use of the concept of a regime is rather like inserting Grotian chocolate chips in a Hobbesian cookie.

Others, who have been expressly described as Grotian in orientation, see regimes everywhere: "A regime exists in every substantive issue-area in international relations where there is discernibly patterned behavior. Wherever there is regularity in behavior some kinds of principles, norms or rules must exist to account for it."[29] This would mean there are regimes aplenty, and the concept has been used to describe and analyze U.S.-Soviet relations, the SALT process, balance-of-payments financing arrangements, the world oil situation, the world food situation, the law of the sea, and even European colonial rule from 1870 to 1914.

Taking the last in the list for illustrative purposes, this is how Raymond Hopkins and Donald Puchala describe the colonial regime.[30] To start with there was a regime—there were patterns to the flows of people and goods between mother countries and the colonies, there were frequent conflicts and constant competition among the colonial powers but always within certain rules and a sense of restraint. All the colonial rulers shared certain norms:

1. The world was divided into civilized and uncivilized peoples—naturally the former were entitled to take charge of the latter.

2. Such alien rule over the uncivilized peoples was right and proper (today, by contrast, the norm is national self-determination).
3. Expansion of a state's domain was a proper way to seek to bolster one's international power and status.
4. European states must be governed by a balance of power.
5. Controlling one's imperial domain for one's own economic benefit (no free trade) was legitimate.
6. It was improper for one colonial power to interfere in, even criticize, the colonial administrative behavior of another.

On the basis of these norms it was possible to contain colonial rivalries, to construct compromises in international conferences to achieve some order, to arrive at general acceptance of spheres of influence, and to use offsets in colonial holdings to help balance power in Europe.

Although the scale and diversity of the regime literature makes a summary very difficult, the whole point of this book is to provide useful summaries, so I've got to make a stab at one. We can arrive at an overview of sorts by concentrating on these questions. What are the causes of regimes and how do they come about? What causes them to change or collapse? What difference do they make?

Stephen Krasner has identified at least five suggestions in the literature on why regimes emerge.[31] There is self-interest—states form regimes when each figures it will do better with one than without it. There is also power, in particular when a leading state is in a position to lead others to a regime or even impose it. Regimes may also grow out of some larger shared norms or principles. Then there is custom and usage, which is the basis for much of international law. Finally, knowledge may be important, such as when a scientific discovery of a previously unknown health hazard leads states to accept new rules to contain it. The last three are generally given less attention than the first two in theorizing about regimes.

As to how regimes come about, Oran Young offers a useful distinction between those that emerge spontaneously, those that are created by negotiations, and those which are imposed (by, for instance, a very powerful state).[32] What analysts see as causing regimes to emerge also affects their views on why regimes change or disappear. In particular, if self-interest is back of it regimes change when interests change. "Regimes are maintained as long as the patterns of interest that gave rise to them remain."[33] If a leading state has been in a position to impose a regime, when its relative power declines the regime will be in trouble. Of particular interest is the view that, in a realist sense, when the structure of the international system (i.e., the distribution of power) changes, then regimes will also change.

The final question, as to what difference regimes make, is a bit more thorny. We have already noted that the concept of regime has been employed by some analysts as part of their effort to step away, partially or completely, from a realist/Hobbesian conception of international politics. This means rejecting an orientation toward power politics and issues of state security as the crucial elements. In effect, the existence of regimes is treated as evidence that states readily cooperate on many matters, develop patterns of cooperation that represent a good deal of stability and order. Looking at international politics as all fang and claw, therefore, badly distorts what really goes on. Regimes reflect how international politics has changed and they also change it.

On the other hand, many analysts of regimes see them as deeply affected by shifts in the distribution of power in international politics. This is especially true of those who see regimes as primarily flourishing under conditions of hegemony, when one dominant state helps greatly to maintain order. By emphasizing the distribution of power as important, this view is pretty much in keeping with a realist perspective. Regimes do not make a big difference, they just reflect the things that do.

Somewhere in between is the view that regimes, once they exist, can take on a life of their own and become a somewhat independent factor in international politics. For instance, a regime may, over time, contribute to altering the distribution of power or induce states to alter the ways they perceive their interests. This would mean that regimes can (but need not) make a difference, contributing to the way international politics will develop over time.

A good illustration of this last view is Robert Keohane's *After Hegemony*[34] Keohane asserts that even if we just stick to a Hobbesian conception, we can readily show that states may have mutual interests that lead them, as rational actors, to institutionalize some level of cooperation via regimes. And if we relax the assumptions that states are always rational and thoroughly selfish it becomes even easier to show why regimes come about. How do regimes make a difference? Keohane lists a number of services that they provide. For one thing, by facilitating flows of information and regularizing the behavior of states they make it cheaper and easier for states to reach agreements of mutual benefit—they reduce the costs and difficulties of cooperation. They help link issues together, which also facilitates cooperation; on any one issue states are likely to hold out for the maximum benefit to themselves, but if issues are linked together then they can trade off benefits on one for benefits on another, and simply demanding the most for oneself on one issue will set a bad precedent for the settlement of lots of others. Finally, a set of leaders who fear that they will be replaced (in an election or a coup) by others who do not like their policies can make it harder for their successors to change those policies by incorporating them into regimes. In other words, regimes are useful.

Keohane then extends this argument to conclude that since they are useful, regimes—once established—can prove fairly durable. States may be reluctant to discard them and plunge into the uncertainties of less cooperation. He thinks this is very relevant today. The decline in American dominance has made order and cooperation more difficult, threatening existing regimes with collapse. But this is not inevitable; we may be able to sustain order and cooperation to a significant degree if we have a better theoretical understanding of why, and how, it is possible.

Hegemony

One of the most intriguing concepts that has been highlighted by regime theory has been the notion of the hegemonic state. As we saw, one way to explain the rise and fall of regimes is by reference to the fortunes of a dominant state. In fact, a major branch of regime theory is the "theory of hegemonic stability" which, roughly speaking, asserts that many regimes are likely to arise and be accompanied by a high level of cooperation, management, and order in the international system when one state is in a very dominant position (i.e., a "hegemonic state"). This is a state with great military and economic superiority. It is in a position to impose order and it does; regimes emerge, coordination flourishes.

Two other distinguished analysis have made use of the notion of a hegemonic state in influential macroanalyses of international politics: Princeton's Robert Gilpin and George Modelski at the University of Washington. Both have also developed a conception of how the international system changes, in each case by emphasizing the role of major wars. Gilpin begins by asserting that "international relations continue to be a recurring struggle for wealth and power among independent actors in a state of anarchy."[35] Those actors enter into relations with each other and thereby create a system, with the interests of the most powerful members having the most to do with how the system is arranged. Within the system there are a number of things that make for control and management: the domination exercised by the great powers, a heirarchy of prestige among states, division of the world into territories, numerous rules of state behavior, and an international economy. Hence even in the absence of a world government "the relationships among states have a high degree of order."[36]

What gives any international system its characteristic features is the distribution of power among major states, and Gilpin finds that there have been three typical structures in international systems. The imperial or hegemonic order has, as we have seen, a single state dominating all the others. A bipolar structure has two dominant states, and a balance-of-power structure has three or more. All three are familiar. What is new is Gilpin's view that at least until modern times, an imperial system has been the most prevalent, which would mean that an analysis stressing balance-of-power processes is only of limited relevance.

Gilpin assumes governments are rational. Their societies are far from static, subject to major change due to technological, economic, military, even demographic factors. As societies change so do the interests of their governments, i.e., what those governments want and expect out of the international system. This leads one or more governments to contemplate trying to change that system. When it looks profitable to do so, that is, when the benefits appear to outweigh the costs, then such an effort will be undertaken. Normally the changes sought and achieved are incremental, and result from pressure, bargaining, threats, and small wars. Under such circumstances the system is relatively stable. But when a state seeks a major shift in the structure of the system—a shift in the rules, a bigger slice of territory, a much-enlarged sphere of influence—the hitherto dominant state will resist and the system becomes unstable. Often the dominant state fails to strengthen itself or suitably appease the rival and thus restore stability. The result? "The historical record reveals that if [the dominant state] fails in this attempt, the disequilibrium will be resolved by war."[37]

The war that develops is a "hegemonic war," a struggle of monumental proportions. It is a total war and either at the start or eventually it involves all the major states and most of the lesser ones. And the stakes are enormous, too, nothing less than the nature and distribution of power in the system. With so much at stake the war tends to become unlimited and little is held back. Out of it comes a new distribution of power and therefore a new structure for the international system, accompanied by new rules, a redistribution of territory, a new hierarchy of prestige, etc. "In short, hegemonic wars have (unfortunately) been functional and integral parts of the evolution and dynamics of international systems."[38]

Turning to the world of today, Gilpin sees the United States as having ruled a hegemonic system after 1945 (*not* a *bipolar* system) until relatively recently. Now the dominance of the United States has slipped and an ambitious rival (the U.S.S.R.) is eager to adjust the system. The American reaction has been to try to strengthen itself and to distribute some of its burdens among allies. All this may work. Gilpin sees none of the signs that have, in the past, indicated that a hegemonic war was near—at least not yet!

George Modelski has constructed a preliminary theoretical analysis that, while it shares several elements of Gilpin's approach, differs from it in some important respects.[39] To start with, Gilpin's analysis is meant to apply to all historical systems of autonomous states; Modelski focuses on the "global system" that has existed only since about 1500, the time when interactions among states first began to be sustained and developed on a global scale and some states came to have the capacity to operate worldwide. Modelski distinguishes this global system from the European nation-state system, especially in terms of its dynamics and structure.

This is the theory of "long cycles." The global system is seen as having passed through a recurring cycle of a little over 100 years in length, with each cycle consisting of four phases. In one phase the global system is dominated by a "world power," a government with a huge advantage over others in its ability to operate globally, particularly in its global military capacities (which until well into this century were predominantly naval capacities). It has a powerful, innovative economy and the organizational and leadership skills to supply direction and order in the system. Modelski's list of the states that have played this role starts with Portugal, includes Holland and Great Britain, and ends with the United States. But this phase only lasts for 25 to 30 years; then the capacities of the hegemonic state begin to ebb, other states' capacities grow, and a serious rival begins to emerge. Over the next two phases, up to 50 years or so, the system slides into multipolarity, conflicts increase, and order declines. System management decays. In the final phase the system collapses into global warfare, a series of conflicts involving all the states in the system that may last up to 30 years. Out of the chaos and wreckage a new "world power" emerges, and the cycle begins again.

Less clear than the cycle is what causes it. Modelski has suggested that the cycle may be linked to certain other processes, some cyclical, that seem to weaken the reach, flexibility, and dynamism of dominant states and their economic, social, and political systems. However, as yet, the cycle itself is unexplained. This bothers his critics, who suggest that cycles are one of those things that exist in the eye of the beholder—if we can't explain them, then everybody can spot cycles and everybody's cycles are likely to be different.

Much clearer are the implications of long-cycles theory. Much like Gilpin, Modelski sees global wars as having played a critical, *functional* role in world politics, as the only way yet devised for shifting from what has become a disorderly, unstable system to one with sufficient leadership to be modestly managed. Thus, again, like Gilpin, Modelski concludes that there can be order in international politics (in this case the global system), the order associated with the dominance of one state. Applying this to our time, the dominant state since 1945, the United States, has now begun to experience the slow erosion of its capacity to manage. What is ahead is more of the same and, if the long cycle runs its course, another global war, which is indeed a dreadful prospect. He hopes we can rise to the challenge of understanding this cycle sufficiently to either break out of it or find a functional substitute for global war, for it has been a process for selecting a world leader we can no longer afford and maybe no longer survive.

Difficulties and Drawbacks

I hope you have found, as I have, that sweeping analyses of the entire international system can be quite stimulating, and that this will lead you to push on into the next chapter for more of the same. Operating on such a grand scale provokes our imagination and almost compels us to be bold in our thinking. Still, there are problems and difficulties, deficiencies and flaws in this work, and it would hardly be proper to end this discussion without reviewing some of them.

Let us begin with approaches that make a distinction between the international system and its environment. Morton Kaplan's definition refers to a system as a "set of variables so related, in contradistinction to its environment. . . ."[40] The problem is to envision the environment of the international system. What lies outside it? If we start by defining a system as something apart from an environment, then if we cannot find the environment we cannot find the system. Of course, we could use a definition in which the system has no environment: "An international system is a power structure in which the weight of external pressure approaches the vanishing point."[41] Unfortunately we are then embroiled in a nasty situation we first encountered way back in chapter 1. If everything falls within the international system our subject matter is, well, everything. Few of us will be so intellectually arrogant or ambitious as to regard this prospect cheerfully.

An obvious solution is to talk about the international *political* system with all other aspects of world affairs serving as the environment. Sure enough this has been tried, but the system boundries that result are often discouragingly amorphous. It was also in chapter 1 that we noticed how almost anything can be political at one time or another. This problem is particularly acute when it comes to specifying the members of the international political system. As we have seen, some analysts would only include political units, states; others would add intergovernmental organizations or multinational corporations (some of which are larger than most of the world's states). In regime theory there are hints of regimes as possibly independent variables—once they are up and running they bend and shape states' interests and behavior. Would this mean they are also "actors" of some sort?

The difficulty of defining the relevant system for analytical purposes extends still further. According to Gilpin and Luard, even Waltz, we should be looking at systems of autonomous states wherever they have existed in history. Most analysts have been reluctant to treat international politics as just Greek city-state politics writ large, preferring to date the onset of the relevant system from the Treaty of Westphalia in 1648 when modern states seem to have emerged. George Modelski generally agrees with this but adds a special twist. In his view the international politics of Europe must be distinguished from *world* politics—a true global system began to emerge about 1500, and it is this system that most deserves our attention. It really would be nice in constructing a theory about something to have a bit more agreement about what that something is!

As to how the system works, we reviewed the deficiencies in the realist perspective that have led to considerable disenchantment with it. Waltz's spirited defense of the essential features of realism does not fully cope with these difficulties. Waltz strives to avoid "reductionism" by not referring to internal elements or characteristics of states as driving their behavior. But the structure of his system rests on the capabilities of states, and many of those capabilities are readily subject to domestic manipulation. Waltz also cites states being "socialized" by their system and reference to any such learning/perceptual processes certainly sounds suspiciously reductionist. After all, the classic realist objection to American foreign policy in this century has been that the United States has stubbornly refused to learn to adjust to the painful dictates of international politics. If states learn unevenly this is presumably relevant to explaining what happens when they interact.

We discovered there is no consensus about the structure of the system and its effects. There are devotees of unipolar (hegemonic), bipolar, and multipolar systems. Those who see considerable virtue in the dominance of a single state, particularly in the ability of that state to provide a reasonable amount of order, have done so precisely when they saw the dominance of the United States slipping away. Theirs is a recipe for order with little guidance on what happens in the absence of the chief cook. Kenneth Waltz's bipolarity rests on weapons (nuclear) that are not used and may be unusable, blocs that have fragmented, and giant economies now outclassed in growth and beset by very serious structural difficulties. Classic multipolarity gives us an analysis that turns on the behavior of only five or seven actors in a world of over 100 nations (and lots of other possible actors).

The analysis by Deutsch and Singer looks more promising in that it is not necessarily confined to a handful of nations. They stress national attention capabilities—more states means more interactions, reducing the attention any two nations can give to each other. There are two drawbacks here. One is the tendency to treat a government's ability to pay attention as fixed. Actually, governments can alter their ability to manage contacts with others, mainly by expanding their bureaucratic resources. This means more of their business with the world is handled routinely—the point of departure for analysts at another level of analysis. The other difficulty is that the rulers of a state, who certainly do have limited attention span, are unlikely to scatter their attention widely but rather to concentrate on key problems and conflicts.

Maybe, as Oran Young and other have suggested, the system is not unipolar, bipolar, or multipolar, but has elements of all three. Maybe the system is also multilayered, with a variety of subsystems that need investigation. Maybe on some issues/cleavages a realist perspective captures the dynamics involved, but on other issues/cleavages some other approach like regime theory is better suited. I need hardly remind you that thinking like this expands the number of interrelationships and the variations in the relevant processes that we have to explore to ominous proportions. Such staggering complexity will keep hordes of us employed indefinitely, which is comforting, but leaves us singularly unable to demonstrate that we are producing clear-cut results.

As it stands we have no consensus as to the relationship between system structure and war. What that means, in effect, is that we therefore have no explanation for order either. It could be, as Bull and others assert, that all systems of states are apt to devise rules, patterns, laws, and hierarchies that generate order. Regime theory then becomes a more sophisticated way of grasping this. But if Waltz is correct, much of the contemporary order in world affairs is due to a particular situation—bipolarity. And if Modelski is correct, order is fleeting once the first phase of the long cycle has passed.

On balance, there is no overwhelming evidence that the concept of an international "system" is analytically very powerful. Too many versions of the system presently coexist in the field. Simple conceptions of the system seem all too simple to do justice to the world of today. More elaborate schemes begin to stagger under the weight of proliferating categories and layers, or offer a definition of the system that makes it exceedingly difficult to find. It is not surprising that various system approaches have taken their lumps at the hands of critics.[42]

Nor are these the only difficulties, and we can draw this chapter to a close by sampling others. As we saw, for Hans Morgenthau the nature of the international system resulted in states pursuing interests defined in terms of power. What should we conclude if they do not? Morgenthau described statesmen as rational, so if states do not behave as expected they are failing to grasp the rational course of action. Morgenthau often took up his pen in cogent criticism of statesmen for ignoring the national interest. Yet the central justification of his theory was that it fit well with the behavior of states. This would put us in danger of asserting that what governments do is rational and that when they do it they are often irrational.

Morgenthau insisted he was abstracting an ideal (rational) model from the (inevitably messier) real world. Kaplan also constructs ideal models. Waltz lays special emphasis on theory as abstracting (i.e., standing apart from reality) in this way. But what if the *actual* behavior of states departs from the theory in significant ways? Should we then discard the model or decide that the world is not in the situation the model was intended to describe? All too often the question is unanswerable—the evidence will often lend itself to either conclusion.

The notion of the international system as a "society" of states, with its rules, conventions, and "regimes," is attractive in many ways. However, the central analogy—a domestic society—seems inappropriate. All societies have really quite elaborate control mechanisms including government, an extensive culture, legal and punishment sytems, elaborate socialization processes, and the like. In no society are all these things markedly different for different parts of it. Yet we are asked to apply the term "society" to a world of many different governments, cultures, normative structures, etc. A more appropriate analogy would appear to be something like the Mafia—elements of a society but shot through with brutal competition for high stakes that can sweep away the rules.

Susan Strange has attacked regime theory in particular as yet another in a seemingly endless series of fads in American thinking, one that reflects the narrow American perspective on the shocks and disruptions (OPEC, for instance) of recent years.[43] She emphasizes how imprecise the concept of a regime appears to be. Perhaps most important is her charge that regime theory treats order as the preeminent product of international politics and thus reflects the bias toward the status quo of the "haves" in international politics.

An interest in order also shows up in the analysis of Modelski and Gilpin. Recall that in their view "global" or "hegemonic" war has always provided an important function in the international system, namely a rearrangement so that a greater degree of order results. Such functionalist conceptions must bear the burden of all functional approaches (the literature on which in the social sciences is mountainous), explaining why we must assume one function is important but not another. The answer cannot come from human experience, for human beings have sought though international politics much more than order. They have sought justice. They have also, unfortunately, sought unlimited power, glory, the gratifications of adulation, even a kind of death. This means the choice of a function to serve as the basis for evaluation is crucial, but it ends up being made by assumption.

Now that is all right if it leads to productive theory in the sense that we are then able to describe reality more satisfactorily, to predict the shape of things to come, and to prescribe policies accordingly. However, serious challenges to functionalism have been mounted in political science and other disciplines on the grounds that it is theoretically unrewarding, that the theory that results does not justify the starting assumptions as to which function (or functions) matters most.

Our topic in this chapter has been Hobbesian and Grotian types of approaches. Stimulating as they may be, they are sufficiently diverse and diffuse to induce a certain pessimism about the progress of our theoretical understanding. Worse than this, they sometimes invite dismay as to the prospects for our survival in a decent world. As Keohane says, with just this in mind, economics was once seen as the "dismal science," but now that "economics has become more cheerful, politics has become gloomier."[44] In search of good cheer, let us take up Hedley Bull's third category, approaches of the Kantian sort.

Notes

1. Oran Young, "Professor Russett: Industrious Tailor to a Naked Emperor," *World Politics* (April 1969), pp. 509-10.
2. Stanley Hoffman, "Theory and International Relations" in Hoffmann, *The State of War* (New York: Praeger, 1965), p. 16.

3. Hedley Bull, *The Anarchical Society* (New York: Macmillan, 1977), pp. 24-46.
4. Robert Jervis, *Perception and Misperception in International Politics* (Princeton, N.J.: Princeton University Press, 1976), pp. 58-113.
5. I am drawing here on Hans Morgenthau, *Politics Among Nations,* 5th rev. ed. (New York: Knopf, 1978), especially pp. 173-228, 337-87.
6. Classic critiques: Inis Claude, *Power and International Relations* (New York: Random House, 1962), pp. 11-39; Ernst Haas, "The Balance of Power: Presumption, Concept or Propaganda," *World Politics* (July 1953), pp. 446-47.
7. Kenneth Waltz, *Theory of International Politics* (Reading, Mass.: Addison-Wesley, 1979), p. 78.
8. Ibid., p. 113.
9. Ibid., p. 128.
10. Morton Kaplan, "Traditionalism vs. Science in International Relations," in Morton Kaplan, ed., *New Approaches to International Politics* (New York: St. Martin's, 1968), p. 7.
11. Morton Kaplan, *System and Process in International Politics* (New York: Wiley, 1957), pp. 21-53.
12. Ibid., p. 23.
13. Waltz, pp. 50-58.
14. Morton Kaplan, *Towards Professionalism in International Theory: Macrosystem Analysis* (New York: Free Press, 1979), pp. 7-13.
15. Morton Kaplan, "Some Problems of International Systems Research," in *International Political Communities* (New York: Doubleday, 1966), pp. 486-94. See also Kaplan, *Towards Professionalism* pp. 147-53.
16. Roger Masters, "A Multi-Bloc Model of the International System," *American Political Science Review* (December 1961); pp. 780-98; and see Donald Reinken, "Computer Explorations of the 'Balance of Power': A Project Report"; Hsi-Sheng Chi, "The Chinese Warlord System as an International System"; and Winfried Franke, "The Italian City-State System as an International System," all in Kaplan, ed., *New Approaches* (note 10).
17. Kenneth Waltz, "The Stability of a Bipolar World," in David Edwards, ed., *International Political Analysis* (New York: Holt, Rinehart & Winston, 1970), p. 340.
18. Waltz, *Theory,* pp. 134-38, 146-93.
19. Karl Deutsch and J. David Singer, "Multipolar Power Systems and International Stability," in Edwards.
20. The quotation is from Steve Chan, *International Relations in Perspective* (New York: Macmillan, 1984), p. 140. The argument in the next paragraph is offered in Bruce Bueno de Mesquita "Systemic Polarization and the Occurrence and Duration of War," *Journal of Conflict Resolution* (June 1978), pp. 241-67.
21. Evan Luard, *Types of International Society* (New York: Free Press, 1976), p. vii.
22. Maurice East, "Status Discrepancy and Violence in the International System: An Empirical Analysis," in East, James Rosenau, and Vincent Davis, *The Analysis of International Politics* (New York: Free Press, 1972), p. 303.

23. Michael Wallace, *War and Rank Among Nations* (Lexington, Mass.: Lexington, 1973), pp. 24, 27.

24. Frederick Kratochwil, *International Order and Foreign Policy: A Theoretical Sketch of Post-War International Politics* (Racine, Wisc.: Western Press, 1978).

25. Gilbert Winham, "Negotiation As a Management Process," *World Politics,* no. 1 (1977), pp. 87-114.

26. Raymond Cohen, *International Politics: The Rules of the Game* (New York: Longman, 1981), p. v.

27. Stephen Krasner, "Structural Causes and Regime Consequences: Regimes as Intervening Variables," *International Organization* (Spring 1982), p. 186.

28. Robert Keohane and Joseph Nye, *Power and Interdependence: World Politics in Transition* (Boston: Little, Brown, 1977).

29. Donald Puchala and Raymond Hopkins, "International Regimes: Lessons From Inductive Analysis," *International Organization* (Spring 1982), p. 247.

30. Ibid., pp. 251-59.

31. Krasner, pp. 194-204.

32. Oran Young, "Regime Dynamics: The Rise and Fall of ·International Regimes," *International Organization* (Spring 1982), pp. 277-97.

33. Arthur Stein, "Coordination and Collaboration: Regimes in an Anarchic World," *International Organization* (Spring 1982), p. 321.

34. Robert Keohane, *After Hegemony: Cooperation and Discord in the World Political Economy* (Princeton, N.J.: Princeton University Press, 1984).

35. Robert Gilpin, *War and Change in World Politics* (Cambridge University Press, 1981), p. 7.

36. Ibid., p. 28.

37. Ibid., p. 187

38. Ibid., p. 198.

39. George Modelski, "Long Cycles of World Leadership" in William Thompson, ed., *Contending Approaches to World System Analysis* (Beverly Hills, Calif.: Sage, 1983), pp. 115-39.

40. Kaplan, *System and Process,* p. 4.

41. Fred Riggs, "International Relations as a Prismatic System" in Klaus Knorr and Sidney Verba, eds., *The International System* (Princeton, N.J.: Princeton University Press, 1961), p. 151.

42. Examples: John Weltman, *System Theory in International Relations* (Lexington, Mass.: D.C. Heath, 1973); Jerone Stephens, "An Appraisal of Some System Approaches in the Study of International Systems," *International Studies Quarterly* (September 1972), pp. 321-49; and Waltz, *Theory,* pp. 38-59.

43. Susan Strange, "Cave! hic dragones: A Critique of Regime Analysis," *International Organization* (Spring 1982), pp. 479-96.

44. Keohane, p. 5.

Bibliographical Remarks

Works on international systems analysis can be divided into general systems theory (as it bears on international and other spheres) and more specifically international systems approaches. The former would include works such as

Ludwig von Bertalanffy, "General Systems Theory," in J. David Singer, ed., *Human Behavior and International Politics* (Skokie, Ill.: Rand McNally, 1965), pp. 20-31; Ervin Lazlo, *Systems Science and World Order: Selected Studies* (Elmsford, N.Y.: Pergamon, 1983); J. David Singer, *A General Systems Taxonomy for Political Science* (General Learning Press, 1971); and Oran Young, Systems of Political Science (Englewood Cliffs, N.J.: Prentice Hall, 1968).

International systems approaches are either presented or reviewed in J. W. Burton, *Systems, States, Diplomacy and Rules* (Cambridge University Press, 1968); Andrew Scott, *The Functioning of the International Political System* (New York: Macmillan 1967); Charles McClelland, "On the Fourth Wave: Past and Future in the Study of International Systems," in James Rosenau, et al., eds., *The Analysis of International Politics* (New York: Free Press, 1972); and Jerone Stephens, "An Appraisal of Some System Approaches in the Study of International Systems," *International Studies Quarterly* (September 1972, pp. 321-49). Also relevant here might be Ronald Rogowski, "Structure, Growth, and Power: Three Rationalist Accounts," *International Organization* (Autumn 1983), pp. 713-38, which contains a review of Robert Gilpin's conception of the workings of the international system.

One persistent complaint about systems approaches is that they do not cope well with change in international politics. On this see Barry Buzan and R. J. Barry Jones, eds., *Change and the Study of International Relations: The Evaded Dimension* (New York: St. Martin's Press, 1981); and some of the articles in Ole Holsti et al., eds., *Change in the International System* (Boulder, Colo.: Westview Press, 1980).

It is not surprising that Kenneth Waltz's forthright attack on a good deal of the work that has been done in international systems theory has provoked a large number of responses. Here are some of the review articles or critiques that are available: Ronald Yalem, "International Politics: The Continuing Search for Theory," *International Interactions* 9, no. 3 (1982), pp. 235-57; John Ruggie, "Continuity and Transformation in the World Polity: Towards a Neorealist Synthesis," *World Politics* (January 1983), pp. 261-85; Richard Rosecrance, "International Theory Revisited," *International Organization* (Autumn 1981), pp. 691-713; and Chris Brown, "International Theory: New Directions?" *Review of International Studies* (July 1981), pp. 173-85. A much broader attack on "neorealism" that covers not only Waltz but many others as well is Richard Ashley, "The Poverty of Neorealism," *International Organization* (Spring 1984), pp. 225-86, an attack which provoked responses by Robert Gilpin, Friedrich Kratochwil, and Bruce Andrews on pp. 287-327 of the same issue.

The debate over the relative virtues of bipolarity and multipolarity has been muted in recent years. Sources I would suggest apart from ones cited in the footnotes are all older: Kjell Goldman, "Bipolarization and Tension in International Systems: A Theoretical Discussion," *Cooperation and Conflict,* (no. 1 (1972), pp. 37-63; Brian Healy and Arthur Stein, "The Balance of Power in International History," *Journal of Conflict Resolution* (March 1973), pp. 33-61; and Richard Rosecrance, "Bipolarity, Multipolarity and the Future" in David Edwards, ed., *International Political Analysis* (New York: Holt, Rinehart and Winston, 1970), pp. 319-42.

The idea that international politics should be studied along sociological lines is developed in Ralph Pettman, *State and Class: A Sociology of International*

Affairs (New York: St. Martin's Press, 1979). A work that adopts Hedley Bull's notion of a society of states is Terry Nardin, *Law, Morality and the Relations of States* (Princeton, N.J.: Princeton University Press, 1983).

There is a growing literature on regimes in theory and practice, much of which is cited in the sources listed in the footnotes. Two additional works of value as introductions to the subject are Oran Young, "International Regimes: Problems of Concept Formation," and Ernst Haas, "Why Collaborate? Issue-Linkage and International Regimes," both in *World Politics* (April 1980) on pp. 331-56 and 357-405, respectively.

The somewhat related topic of hegemonic stability is discussed in Robert Keohane, "The Theory of Hegemonic Stability and Changes in International Economic Regimes, 1967-1977" in Ole Holsti et al., eds., *Change in the International* System (Boulder, Colo.: Westview Press, 1980), pp. 131-62. Quite a different perspective is offered by Arthur Stein, who rejects the theory of hegemonic stability. See Arthur Stein, "The Hegemon's Dilemma: Great Britain, The United States, and the International Economic Order," *International Organization* (Spring 1984), pp. 355-86.

The Modelski theory of long-cycles literature is collected and briefly described in George Modelski, "Long Cycles of World Leadership: An Annotated Bibliography," *International Studies Notes,* published by the International Studies Association (fall 1983), pp. 1-5. Applications of this perspective are illustrated in Karen Rasler and William Thompson, "Global Wars, Public Debts, and the Long Cycle," *World Politics* (July 1983), pp. 489-516; William Thompson, "The World Economy, the Long-Cycle, and the Question of World-Systems Time," in Pat McGowan and Charles Kegley, Jr., eds., *Foreign Policy and the Modern World-System* (Beverly Hills, Calif.: Sage 1983), pp. 35-62; and George Modelski and Patrick Morgan, "Understanding Global War," *Journal of Conflict Resolution* (September 1985), pp. 391-417.

Finally, a brief reference is made in the chapter to the "ecological perspective." Someone interested in pursuing this could begin with the world of Harold and Margaret Sprout, including their *The Ecological Perspective on Human Affairs* (Princeton, N.J.: Princeton University Press, 1965) and *Toward a Politics of the Planet Earth* (New York: Van Nostrand Reinhold, 1971). A major statement of this view is Dennis Pirages, *The New Context For International Relations: Global Ecopolitics* (North Scituate, Mass.: Duxbury Press, 1978). The ecological perspective is further discussed in the articles in a symposium organized as a tribute to the Sprouts in *International Studies Quarterly* (September 1983), pp. 241-69.

9

Kant—Or Cant—Or Can't?

As I write, a massive effort is underway to ship and distribute food to starving millions in Africa. The campaign in the Western world was sparked by a British television documentary, then propelled by further international media attention. I live in an agricultural area where for some years farmers have experienced hard times, yet many joined together to donate grain plus the trucks and labor to move it. Large sums for the campaign have been raised through an unprecedented global rock music concert plus sales of albums by rock stars who donated their talents, all managed by new organizations that have sprung up. Private international aid agencies and international organizations have mobilized vast human and material resources. Governments have joined in, of course, but not without friction and attempts to direct aspects of the campaign for their own political purposes, purposes that private efforts have sometimes overridden or circumvented.

What does this tell us about the nature of the world? What analytical tools would we pull out of our kit bag to explain this phenomenon? Or is it the case that our usual tools are entirely inadequate? These are the questions to keep in mind as we move into this second chapter on the international system level of analysis, the chapter that concludes this book. Our subject is analyses that fall within the Kantian perspective.

In the Kantian perspective there is a global community or world society, a conception that should shape our analytical undertakings. In an era fond of "spaceship Earth" terminology, this image is also not unlike that of the most profound human association as it is reflected in the graceful words of the traditional marriage ceremony. We must live together "for better or for worse" on this crowded planet. How we do determines whether it is "for richer or poorer"—till now too many of us were on the poorer side, too many living "in sickness" rather than "in health." One sign of our mismanagement is that in the nuclear age we are forced to live at constant risk, for "till death us do part" must be our constant fear.

Like any community the global one needs a certain amount of governing, that is, it needs and has a political system. The study of international politics then becomes the study of how the world governs itself, not just how a set of states interact. Most interesting about a shift to this perspective is the fact that it virtually forces us to ask some new and different questions.

For one thing there is the question of *why* the world's political system developed into what it is. Preliminary answers can be derived by using historical analysis to trace the emergences of independent nation-states and to see how their struggles to survive and prosper led to unruly, often violent, competition for power and influence. And we can use approaches such as those reviewed in the previous chapter to uncover the structural patterns which that competition creates and by which in turn it is shaped. But what if that competition masks the underlying growth and development of a global community in economic, social, and cultural terms? The global political system may appear unchanged while beneath it there is a ferment that will soon wash it away as obsolete. Or maybe that political system has already changed a good deal but we have been slow to detect this. The real political system is not fixed or obsolete, just our view of it. These sorts of questions are now the subject of much debate in the field.

To say that the world community needs a political system is to imply that there are certain services the system provides (for better for worse), services the community cannot readily do without. So if we assume there is a world community, another question that arises is: What important *functions* does the global political system perform? If we need a world political system, what do we need it for? This also invites us to compare that system against some ideal conception of how those functions could be performed.

Having come this far we find, lurking in the corners of our mind, another tantalizing question. In view of the functions a political system performs, how might world governance be improved? What kind of world political system would better, or best, perform those functions? This, in turn, opens the door to what is ultimately a *normative* question—that is, a question that calls on us to decide what is "good" or "bad" in terms of our values (a subject annoying to some students of politics but the essence of the field to others). What functions *should* a world political system perform if we are to live in the "right" kind of world? In the end, this would require probing more deeply for answers to the first question on why the world is governed as it is. It would not be enough simply to show how we got where we are today—once normative considerations arise, we want to know what is so as to figure out how to do better. Thus, Hedley Bull suggests the ultimate Kantian view is that conflicts of interest and strife among states are only a superficial aspect of reality, and that the full realization of a world community will sweep them away in favor of a far more suitable political system.[1]

These remarks are an introduction to approaches which take as their starting point the assumption that there is a global community, set out some conception of the chief purposes of its political system, and then analyze historical or hypothetical systems accordingly. There is nothing really new in studying international politics in this way; it has a history stretching back to the post–World War I era or before. However, its academic ancestors fought and lost a great battle in the field with the Hobbesian "realists," whose prime point of reference was the nation-state and the national interest, not global society and what is good for the world. Now, however, there has been a strong revival of interest in the losers' cause.

Has the World Changed?

We must begin our discussion by setting forth the main elements of a new orientation that has spread in the field in recent years. It goes by various names including the "globalist" perspective, and that is a convenient term to use here.[2] The following summary highlights its main features and, like any summary, may not exactly fit the views of any one of its proponents.[3] We must also try to see, as we move through it, not only how this perspective clashes with others we have discussed but also what it borrows from some of them. Like a child, it has been developing its own view of the world but is not unaffected by the view of its parents.

A good place to begin is with the nation-state. Throughout this book we have noted that the term *international politics* implies that nations (i.e., national governments) are at the heart of the subject, that our concern is with politics among *nations*. Accompanying this view is the tendency to see states as territorial, social, and political lumps, hard and unyielding things for the most part. The usual analogy is the world as a collection of billiard balls, bouncing off each other. To the globalist this is no longer appropriate. New kinds of actors, nonstate actors, have become too important to ignore—multinational corporations, intergovernmental organizations, cross-national groups like Amnesty International, terrorist groups, etc. At the same time, the globalist emphasizes, the nation-state has become steadily more porous, readily penetrated by economic forces or ideological and cultural elements, increasingly unable to maintain a meaningful sovereignty. (More like a wiffle ball than a billiard ball.)

Closely related is the assertion that military force has become steadily less relevant and useful. In part, this is simply an extension of the previous point, for one way states can be more readily penetrated these days is by military force—their defenses are leaky. However, it also derives from the concept and practice of deterrence; to the extent that deterrence operates, the most powerful states find their military might balanced and nullified by that of their rivals. It also reflects the view that a good deal of military power is in an unusable form; nuclear weapons are so ghastly that under all but the most extreme circumstances they cannot be used. For the United States in Vietnam, the Soviet Union in Afghanistan, the United Kingdom in the Falkland Islands, the massive power of their nuclear forces had to remain sheathed. Finally, this depreciation of military power often descends from the observation that even nonnuclear forces are frequently unable to achieve the nation's objectives at reasonable cost. Vietnam is one example, the Israeli invasion of Lebanon another, the Iran-Iraq war a third. What this ultimately leads to is the assertion that our conception of national power is deficient, that a capacity to coerce is of declining relevance, and so, therefore, is continuing to talk about international politics in terms of the distribution of military power. In turn, these considerations feed into the concept of *interdependence* and the belief that it is spreading, deepening, and thereby markedly altering our world. From the globalist perspective nations have become porous because they are increasingly interdependent, not in charge of what happens to them, and more and more subject to penetration and manipulation by external forces. If true, this means something like a global community has emerged or is emerging, to replace the old collection of hard-shell nuts run by hard-nosed governments.

Interdependence is partly responsible for the development of a new set of issues and problems which, to the globalist, are symptoms of how the world has changed. These problems are new in at least two senses—they arise only when people are being forced to think in transnational and even global terms, and they will not yield to national solutions but require broader cooperation. A good example might be pollution of the oceans and the atmosphere (acid rain, the "greenhouse effect," etc.). There are the periodic world food crises (the famine in Africa being the latest), which reflect the world population problem. Actual or potential global shortages of raw materials or the safe management of peaceful nuclear technology also fall in this category. When new sorts of problems arise and old methods seem unable to cope, there is a tendency to assert that the system has outgrown both its management capabilities and the intellectual frameworks based on them—precisely what globalists conclude.

Finally, the globalist view has been influenced by a mounting insistence on raising normative concerns in analysis—on getting more attention paid to making a better world. An excellent example is the presidential address of Harold Jacobson when he served as the head of the International Studies Association, the single most important organization in the field. Herewith a sample of his remarks:[4]

> The time has come to expand our conception of international studies so that it self-consciously includes the status of individuals and the extent to which they are accorded human dignity and justice. . . . [O]ne of our important tasks as scholars should be the devising of international strategies that promote the realization of human dignity and justice.
>
> In judging a global system, the ultimate issue should be how it affects the status of individuals.
>
> A historic consensus has been formed in the years since World War II on the meaning of human dignity and justice, and thus on the overarching goals of international and national public policy and on the broad outline of world order.
>
> If the ultimate object of our concern is the status of individuals [in terms of] . . . human dignity and justice, then we cannot treat states as if they were black boxes. We must remove the protective shell of sovereignty.

This is a sober, humane, and generous call for implementing the essence of a Kantian perspective. Notice the emphasis on *individuals,* not states, and the reference to "judging" the international system as to how it is developing when set against a "consensus" on the key values of the human community. I need not tell you that human dignity and justice are incompatible with nuclear war, famine and poverty, destruction of the environment, or the denial of human rights. Achieving dignity and justice would mean changing the world.

Functionalist Approaches

Now we have to look at some illustrative approaches embedded in this globalist perspective. We may start with functionalist analyses. As mentioned above, thinking in terms of a global community with its own political system invites us to pick out functions that the political system in question (or any political system) should perform. Here are approaches that do just this, starting with someone who chose to compare international systems in terms of their ability to perform one overriding function. I refer to Inis Claude and particularly his book *Power and International Relations*. Claude's position can hardly be called a globalist one, but as his analysis foreshadows many of the points we will be making further on it is a very useful point of departure.

Claude was preoccupied with the idea that the central purpose, and problem, of an international system is the *management of power* in order to maintain peace. The seminal fact of the twentieth century seemed to be that power had not been successfully managed. What are the alternative systems for managing power? Claude identified three: balance of power, collective security, and world government. His comparative analysis employed two different strategies. One was to set forth the conditions that had to prevail if the system was to work. The other was to refer to relevant historical examples to see if the system had ever worked as it was supposed to.

Claude's analysis of balance of power as concept and system is still widely cited. He listed the following as preconditions for it to success-fully manage power: a diffusion of power—multipolarity; skilled pro-fessionals in charge of foreign policy; governments free to shift align-ments readily; power as readily measurable; wars as "imaginable, controllable, usable"; a consensus that wars should be limited and states' autonomy preserved. Finally, a desirable if not necessary condition is the existence of a balancer.

Claude assessed the historical effectiveness of balance of power and concluded that "a case can be made for the judgment that the system functioned reasonably well as a provider of order in international relations." On the other hand the preconditions for it no longer existed so that "it is clear that the suitability of the world for the operation of the balance of power system has been steadily diminishing for well over a century"[5] (something Morgenthau detected as well).

This led him to collective security. The term "collective security" crops up frequently as another name for alliances. It is important that you realize how different this is from Claude's use of the term. He applies it to the system Woodrow Wilson envisioned in this plans for a League of Nations. In such a system *all* states agree to halt, by force if necessary, aggression by *any* state. Thus, it is an alliance of all against anyone who would break the peace, not just an alliance among some states for their own protection.

Claude did not state the conditions for a true collective-security system precisely, but we can derive them from his discussion: a "war for peace" must be imaginable, controllable, and usable; power must be dispersed, so an alliance of all can defeat any one state; the aggressor must be one state or a small minority; it must be easy to spot aggression and aggressors; people everywhere must see aggression anywhere as threatening them.

Once again the system seemed inappropriate. Claude thought that it might have had a chance if adopted back in 1919, but not in our time. Some nations and blocs were too powerful, war had become too terrible, and aggression too difficult to define. Nor were people ready to treat peace as indivisible; we would deplore far-off wars but were not ready to fight to stop them.

This left world government. Claude reviewed the idea of creating powerful world political institutions that would enjoy a "monopoly of force." He dismissed the immediate prospects for such a development and so he analyzes a hypothetical world government instead. He found two central themes in the literature; one is that any system short of world government would fail to secure peace, the other that world government would ensure it. Looking at the history of international politics and of national governments, he concluded that neither proposition was self-evident: "Peace without government is, despite dogmatic denials, sometimes possible; war with government is, despite doctrinal assurances, always possible. Wars sometimes occur in the absence of government. . . . Wars also occur in the presence of government, in protest against and defiance of the central control which is attempted."[6]

What, then, can we say about a theory of managing power to achieve peace? Claude suggested that any such theory would most likely be built in piecemeal fashion, and that each of the three systems offered something of value. Balance of power has the virtue of concentrating on the nation-state as the source of the problem, not offering solutions that simply wish it out of existence. It also emphasizes the pluralistic pulling and hauling of politics as the controlling mechanism, rather than the abstract appeal to world law or a supposed monopoly of force. Collective security and world-government views, on the other hand, force us to recognize that power in international politics must be consciously managed, not left to some "unseen hand" of a balance of power. They instruct us on the indivisibility of peace, the dangers of unchecked national sovereignty, and the increasing interdependence of nations. In the end it is by welding these insights together, and grafting on some new ideas, that Claude felt we might advance our understanding of the slowly developing world community. Claude insisted that the world was still experiencing a "rising tide of statehood" and that international institutions had to be seen not as replacing the nation-state system but as adjuncts to it, as facilitating it rather than as harbingers of a new world political system.[7]

Anticipating some comments to come, Claude's perspective is worth our attention as a road not taken. As we shall see, analysts have chosen to see the nation-state as passing away, the management of power as something quite different because power itself was slipping out of the picture, and international or transnational organizations as far more than adjuncts to nations, more like rivals that are displacing nations. In some cases even the central importance of politics is rejected. In short, Claude offered something like a modified realist way to trace the development of a global community; instead, we will be examining approaches that seek to discard much of that view.

There are other functionalist approaches that could be reviewed at this point, and in fact this is how the preceding edition of this book carried on the discussion. Two other analysts, Werner Levi and George Modelski, were cited to illustrate how one might see the international system as deficient because it fails to perform a key function—the maintenance of order for Levi, and justice, as well as order, for Modelski. In each case the analyst suggested that what was needed was an undermining of national governments via the emergence of new groups and communities which provide psychic satisfactions and meet human needs. Some of these groups would cut across national boundaries, while in other cases the result would be the reinvigoration of local communities and subnational political institutions. As a result, individuals would find themselves immersed in a web of communities—with varying degrees of attachment and loyalty—at many levels simultaneously in a new pluralism that resulted in multiple, cross-cutting loyalties amidst a spreading interdependence. This general idea has been taken up by a number of theorists.[8]

Interdependence

We have reviewed the depiction of nations as relatively self-contained units, so that the world becomes a collection of territorial, social, and political lumps. An initial point of attack for those of a Kantian disposition is right here. They assert that, in fact, nations are increasingly interdependent, not in charge of what happens to them, more and more subject to penetration from outside by ideas, economic forces, cultural pressures, and the like. This need not be carried too far; many analysts interested in regimes or other limited forms of international cooperation, but not in a Kantian perspective, have been impressed by the effects of interdependence. But one way to make use of the concept is to see it as inexorably leading to the emergence of a global community.

We need to take a brief look, at this point, as to how interdependence might be defined and analyzed.[9] For the umpteenth time we have arrived at a major subject in the field that is in dispute. Analysts do not fully agree on how to define interdependence. They do not agree on how to detect and measure it. Therefore they do not agree as to whether it is increasing or, if it is, just what that means.

A simple conception of interdependence would refer to contacts and exchanges among nations: the more they have (in phone calls, mail, trade, tourism, television shows, arms sales, etc.) the more interrelated they are. The trouble with this is that everything is relative. For example, you undoubtedly have vastly more contacts with many more people than you did when you were age ten, but your degree of dependence on others has almost certainly declined. Thus, we want to know the larger context for international transactions; if international phone calls are up but domestic phone calls are up even more, what would this tell us about interdependence?

Another notion is that interdependence exists when changes in one nation produce significant changes in one or more others, or when the effects of one government's actions are significantly determined by what other governments do.[10] The most important implication of this is that it exists among enemies as well as friends. An arms race is a good example of such interdependence. Thus, a distinction must generally be made between *negative* and *positive* interdependence, the latter referring to a relationship that improves cooperation among nations. It is positive interdependence that is of interest to us here.[11]

Once we get to the reactions by a state to events or pressures elsewhere, further refinements are possible. For instance, some analysts insist we link interdependence to elements like "sensitivity" and "vulnerability."[12] A nation can be *sensitive* to outside events, in that it will face various costs and difficulties if it fails to do something. It is *vulnerable* to outside events when it will face those costs and difficulties because it cannot do anything about them. The United States is sensitive to world oil-price hikes. A poor non–oil producing nation will be vulnerable to the same events. An extreme form of vulnerability would be dependence. This implies that interdependence must involve a degree of *mutual* sensitivity and/or vulnerability; otherwise there is nothing "inter" about it.

Which brings us to the argument that with interdependence governments find an increasing part of their domestic affairs conditioned by external forces and must act accordingly. Some people feel this compels governments to negotiate and compromise more, making for a more peaceful world, but others think governments will not necessarily respond this way. Earlier in this century, Japan discovered its rising dependence on imports for food and energy, but the response was to attack, conquer, and seize the necessary resources and markets—not exactly a policy of negotiation and compromise! Governments can also take steps at home to try to reduce an uncomfortable degree of interdependence, such as setting up barriers to imports. Some analysts now believe this is how global interdependence proceeds; it rises to a certain point, then governments deliberately move to reduce it. Others insist that it must be deliberately controlled in this fashion.[13]

Is the world getting more interdependent? It is hard to say for sure, though it is not hard to find opinions expressed in no uncertain terms. We will shortly look at approaches which conclude that interdependence is growing, so at this point we will just consider the alternative view. Karl Deutsch and Kenneth Waltz have been identified with a negative answer to the question. Earlier we noted Deutsch's view that a nation is a set of intense communication patterns. This suggests that due to the rising nationalisms in this century, each nation's people would be having much more to do with each other than outsiders, so that interdependence has declined. When Deutsch compared transaction figures (at home and abroad) for the later nineteenth/early twentieth centuries with more recent ones, that is what he found.[14] After all, prior to World War I there was free trade, many states had no passport requirements, there were millions of immigrants to the United States and other places, and so on.

Waltz has pointed to other factors. In the nineteenth century, Britain and other great powers depended heavily on trade, but today's superpowers rely on trade for a relatively small portion of their economies. The developing countries are less closely linked to the rich countries than when they were colonies. True, lots of countries import a good many foodstuffs and raw materials, but often they do so because it is cheap and easy, not because they must. Also, interdependence to Waltz would mean a good deal of specialization—but most governments do basically the same things; they do not specialize, so how can they be all that interdependent? Waltz concedes there is more sensitivity about, but not necessarily more vulnerability, at least where the really major states are concerned.[15]

Now that you are in the picture on interdependence, we are ready to see how it can be used theoretically. James Rosenau has recently set forth a major new view of the international system in which it is said to have entered an era of "cascading interdependence." By this he means that what Modelski and Levi were talking about in the way of a more diversified, multilayered world has already begun to come about. The rapid transformations that he sees occurring have been bothering analysts for some time now, leading to a proliferation of new terms. Rosenau is one of the best at generating new terms.

He feels we are experiencing a "world crises of authority," so much so that in order to understand it we have to "presume that any and every system comprising global life is always on the verge of collapse."[16] One facet of this is *subgroupism* in which people everywhere are developing stronger attachments to collectives smaller and closer at hand than the nation-state. This weakens the authority of national governments at home. At the same time, ties among those governments are breaking down in the face of the emergence of new global issues, the tensions associated with interdependence, and the impact of technological change (especially in communications). To this he adds another, rather interesting, idea which is that the "analytic aptitudes" of people everywhere have grown—they have a richer, more sophisticated picture of how interrelated the world is and how flexible their loyalties and activities have to be to cope with that world.

From this he concludes that "it becomes increasingly difficult to perceive power as distributed primarily among states" and "it no longer seems compelling to refer to the world as a State system."[17] What do we put in place of this view? Well, we could go back to individuals as the crucial unit of analysis but Rosenau rejects any simple form of this. Individuals are caught up in myriads of groups and systems, however flexible and amorphous those may be. Hence we need to look at individuals all right, but not as persons so much as collections of *roles*. Each individual—policymaker, citizen, scholar— has a collection of roles in the various groups and systems of which he or she is a part, and action results from the interplay of these roles, or more particularly of the expectations as to what one ought to be doing associated with each of those roles.

This leads him to yet other terms: *role scenarios* or *action scripts*. These are the expectations we carry around as to how we, and others, will behave in various roles under various circumstances. Any group or system then derives its cohesion from the interlocking, congruent role scenarios of its members. But in an age of flux and breakdowns in authority the only way to get a handle on this is to see how role scenarios are constantly being shuffled into new and different combinations. We need to study the dynamics whereby roles and their scenarios get aggregated into collectivities and the processes whereby the collectivities then adapt to threats and challenges. The more crisis of authority cascade sub-groupism across the global landscape, the more extensive is the disaggregation of wholes into parts that, in turn, either get aggregated or incorporated into new wholes. That is, cascading interdependence can readily be viewed as continuous processes of systemic formation and reformation.[18]

Any collective system, in order to survive, must therefore constantly adapt, and it is this adaptation that should be our major subject of investigation. In turn, Rosenau has for some time been developing an analysis of adaptation in the foreign policies of governments, as we saw back in chapter 6.

Quite a different approach is offered by Richard Mansbach and John Vasquez. Professor Mansbach has earlier contributed research in support of the argument that nonstate actors are quite significant and must not be neglected.[19] Professor Vasquez is well known for his criticisms of Morgenthau-like realism as no longer useful as a guide to international politics.[20] Recently they have designed a new "issue paradigm" as a guide to theory and research.[21] They start by rejecting the usual way of thinking about international politics for reasons that are now familiar to us: national states are no longer the only significant actors (in fact, they cite five other types of actors), they are so interdependent and penetrated that the old distinction between foreign policy and domestic politics no longer applies, and there are so many new problems and issues that there is a lot more to international politics than the struggle for power. There is also something much more like a global community emerging.

Of these, the critical argument is, in many ways, that international and domestic politics are no longer separate. If so, then we can draw on domestic politics for concepts and ideas. Mansback and Vasquez proceed to do just this. For instance they adopt David Easton's definition of politics (which has been the most influential definition of the past three decades) as the authoritative allocation of values and they apply it to international affairs. They conclude that world politics is really a collection of struggles over issues—hence term the "issue paradigm."

We can only outline some of the elements of this approach here. An issue always concerns the allocation of stakes, of the thing or things desired. Actors put forward proposals as to how the stakes should be distributed and contend with each other accordingly. There are lots of issues, hence lots of political games at any one time—for different stakes, among different actors, with different levels of contention. Of importance is whether and how the stakes in various issues are linked. If the stakes are relatively tangible and actors see the same values involved for each other (say, in trade issues where the stake is money and everyone involved wants a piece of the action), it is often possible to cut a deal and reach a compromise. But where the stakes are symbolic or about ultimate, and differing, values and where the outcome is seen as helping friends or hurting enemies, then compromise becomes much more difficult and many issues may get tangled into a huge knot that is hard to unravel. This is what happened to U.S.-Soviet relations many years ago. For instance, in the U.S.-Soviet rivalry a simple trade agreement becomes a symbol of giving into or benefiting those nasties on the other side, people who are nasties because their basic values are incompatible with ours.

With this in mind Mansbach and Vasquez offer an agenda for research and some theoretical ideas they think should guide the research. For instance, we should be studying how global issues are formed or arise, and how they become part of the global political agenda. They think there is at least a rudimentary cycle in the way issues emerge and are treated. We also need to look at how actors appear—how do local governments, multinational corporations, or national governments get drawn into the political process on a particular issue. Then we need to know what shapes actor attitudes toward issues—they list three different attitudes and suggest the factors that determine which attitude will be adopted. Next we must uncover how links among issues sometimes promote cooperation, like the spillover thesis in integration theory, and sometimes heighten conflict—as when U.S.-Soviet disagreements on one issue after another soon developed into the Cold War. Finally, we want to know how issues are resolved. Sometimes stable and compatible expectations develop, but sometimes issues culminate in war. What determines which outcome prevails? They offer an extended analysis on this point, which turns on the idea which we discussed in the previous chapter that status inequality among nations give rise to war under certain conditions.

Our concern here is less with the detailed application than with the overall perspective. Notice that while the concern is for the global system, there is plenty of room for integrating work at other levels of analysis. There is also, in a fundamental sense, a rejection of the view that there really is a single system in other than the most general way. Gone is the expectation that one can describe the system in terms of its major members and the distribution of power among them. Finally, I should point out that these two analysts see their work as strongly supporting detente, i.e., as having important policy implications. The U.S.-Soviet rivalry can only be eased or resolved if the two sides move away from emphasizing symbolic stakes or ultimate values and learn to live with each other. Then the issues between them would turn on more concrete, tangible stakes and compromises would be possible.

Now let us look at quite a different approach to the global community, one that has stirred up a good deal of attention and controversy in recent years. Up to this point we have been using the concept of global community as something just recently or just now emerging, with all sorts of implications for how we are to think. And we have been focusing on politics—political actors, issues, structures, etc. Immanuel Wallerstein asserts that there has been a global community around for quite some time, right under our analytical noses, but we have not seen it because we were excessively preoccupied with its political features.[22]

Some pages back we briefly summarized George Modelski's theory of long cycles, which attempts to denote and analyze a world or global political system as it has existed and developed since roughly 1500. Wallerstein offers a competing conception of the "world-system." In his view (and that of several others), sometime around 1450 a series of developments—political, technical, demographic, even environmental, led to the rise of a set of "core" societies in northwestern Europe amidst the emergence of capitalism. This capitalism as a system spread outward to eventually encompass the globe. In the process, a massive division of labor emerged as the peripheral and semiperipheral societies were subjected to the domination and exploitation of the core societies. Sometime around 1600-1650 this first stage was replaced by a long era of stagnation and consolidation. By 1750 a third phase was under way, in which industrial production and the resulting need for raw materials and markets led to a new surge of development and a new wave of colonial expansion and core exploitation. The end of World War I ushered in the latest phase of consolidation in the world capitalist system. Thus, the world community has been fashioned primarily by economic processes, driven by the cyclical patterns of capitalism's development.

To this is added a recognition that these developments have taken place within a system of politically autonomous states immersed in rivalry and competition, a system ultimately extended to all corners of the world. Providing some structure to this system has been the periodic dominance of certain hegemonic states: the Netherlands (1625-1675), Great Britain (1763-1815 and 1850-1873), and the United States (1945-1967). Being top dog is an onerous task with high costs, so there are cyclical features to the rise and decline of hegemonic states, a decline that has often led to heightened rivalry, competition, and war. But that should not obscure the fact that the underlying system has been anything but fragmented and diffuse—it has steadily integrated the world, drawing societies into its orbit. Some analysts would emphasize that the power of capitalist development has gradually undermined even the socialist states' efforts to stand apart from it— today the socialist states are borrowing money, technology, and techniques from the core states, paying in cheap raw materials and simple industrial goods like other periphery states.[23]

Thus, for hundreds of years the world has been steadily more tightly knit via an economic system that brings with it profound social and cultural changes, trapping whole societies in relationships and patterns of development they cannot control. All this had been hidden by our preoccupation with the political rivalries of seemingly autonomous states. One implication is that our whole conception of development is wrong. Development is not a matter of passing through the same phases that the core societies went through earlier, or of devising one's own independent path. It is deeply shaped by where one's society is in the international division of labor and how that division changes over time.

This sort of analysis has a distinctly Marxist flavor, with a kind of international class structure among societies, oppressors and oppressed, all based on a capitalism driven by fundamental processes operating over a long stretch of time. While this is readily apparent, some other features are at least as important for our purposes and are far less obvious. For one thing, Wallerstein defines away the existence of international politics as a field of study—there is no such field! All the standard "disciplines" in the social sciences are arbitrary and handicap analysis. To repeat a quotation we saw back in chapter 1: "There is no such thing as sociology; there is no such thing as history; there is no such thing as economics, political science, anthropology, or geography."[24] The world community is about all these things, and more, all at once—and it is the community as a whole we want to understand.

Next, you can readily see why Wallerstein and his supporters naturally discard the nation-state as the primary focus of attention. Discussing international *politics* based on *states* is silly. States are just one kind of actor, their relations only a small part of the global system. Another crucial point is that if there is only the one global system, which emerged at a specific time and has been developing ever since, we can not expect an inductive analysis of numerous cases to tell us very much—we can not be looking for many systems about which to generalize. Thus lots of what we typically refer to as theoretical analysis is pretty much useless.

A final comment on Wallerstein's approach is that he sees the ultimate objective as one of "describing complex reality in politically useful ways." What he means by this is that the ultimate test of our theorizing lies in our ability to manipulate reality (because we understand it). "As we become more political we become more scientific; as we become more scientific we become more political."[25]

Lets Build a Better System

I suggested early on in this chapter that a Kantian disposition tends to push analysts toward normative concerns, going beyond description of the world as it is to offering advice on how to make it better. We saw Professor Jacobson calling for more scholarly attention to how the international system is doing when it comes to the satisfaction of important human values. We have just found Wallerstein asserting that the point of our endeavors must be to find ways to change the world.

They are certainly not alone. Signs of a surge of interest in normative analysis abound, perhaps because it is hard to take comfort from the current state of the world and because we have good reason to fear that things might get worse.[26] One illustration is the revival of moral critiques of nuclear deterrence, sustained arguments that to rely for our security on the threat to obliterate whole nations violates every "law" of war and is morally indefensible. Another can be found in the tenor of the textbooks now being offered.

Not the least of the burdens of being a professor in this field is the necessity to wade through the texts that annually pile up on one's shelves. But in doing so I find there is a discernible shift toward giving more attention to normative considerations. An early example was Richard Sterling's eloquent plea that we adopt a "macropolitical" approach. He asserts that those approaches that concentrate on nations and the national interest are inadequate. In an increasingly interdependent world we must start by asking, "What is the *international* interest?" What needs do we all share? What would benefit all mankind? Such questions call for thinking in terms of macropolitics, not micropolitical attention to the exclusive authority and sovereign prerogatives of nation-states (The analogy is with economics: macroeconomics is the analyses of an entire econony, whereas microeconomics starts with the individual firm.)

Sterling subsumes the various services the world's political system ought to provide under the rubric of *justice*. Historically, extending the sway of justice has required enlarging the human sense of community and trust, so that fear—the enemy of justice—can be quelled and security sustained. Only an expanding sense of global community can provide the proper setting. Within it, justice requires "a far-reaching, global redistribution of power, wealth, education, and status and of the psychological satisfactions that go with the enjoyment of these values."[27] As you can see, this is designed to point out how the contemporary international system fails to provide justice; its inequities leave us ill-equipped to deal with worldwide problems—peace, population, pollution, poverty—on a worldwide scale. We must reject the perspectives and values of micropolitics: "The sovereign state . . . has reached the terminal point of its development. It follows that it must begin to divest itself of the ancient sovereign claim to the exclusive loyalties of its inhabitants. It must be willing instead to foster a sharing of loyalties between the states and transnational institutions.[28]

Another example is the recent and quite effective text by Steve Chan that combines a careful review of the empirical evidence on many questions with a concluding section that is normatively focused. (Hence the subtitle of his book: *The Pursuit of Security, Welfare and Justice*). As he says in introducing that section:

> Much of the discussion . . . is written from a perspective that treats all of us as "world citizens." Many of the issues dealt with [earlier] . . . have worldwide implications. Problems such as nuclear war, population explosion, and ecological degradation concern all people as inhabitants of the global village, and they call for judgments and policy positions that take into account the well-being of humankind as a whole.[29]

It is not too difficult to see the final resting point of this way of thinking. Thus, our last group of theorists consists of those who do not simply offer an analysis of the international system and suggestions as to what a better one might look like. They want us to get out there and create a better system. Their analyses set out certain values as important and then encourage specific steps to change the world so as to achieve those values.

I refer here, as one illustration, to the scholars associated with the World Order Models Project (WOMP). This project was initiated in 1968 and has now produced a long series of studies.[30] It is an effort undertaken by a network of scholars around the world to promote reform of the international system by the turn of the century. To illustrate it, we may briefly review one of the latest of these studies, Samuel Kim's *The Quest for a Just World Order*.

Kim begins in the familiar vein. We need a "normative-empirical" approach that synthesizes and integrates factual observations with our values. This is a departure from the ways international politics has usually been studied but the old ways do not work any more because the world has changed. And he echoes Wallerstein in asserting that we have to break out of the standard academic disciplines—an interdisciplinary approach is vital. He then adds an extended review of the deplorable state of the world in terms of the presence of violence and military capacities, the unequal distribution of goods and services, the pressures against human rights, and the damage being done to the world's environment. This is linked to an exploration of the evidence as to the trends that can or will shape the future state of the world.

These are the first three steps in the world-order models approach as Kim has outlined it in Figure 9.1.[31] Notice that an integral element

FIGURE 9-1
World Order Approach to Designing a Better World System

		WORLD ORDER VALUES			
STEPS	TASKS	*WOV_1	WOV_2	WOV_3	WOV_4
1	Clarification of Assumptions				
2	Diagnosis of the State of the World				
3	Exploratory Forecasting of Trends				
4	Normative Forecasting of Preferred Futures				
5	Mapping Transition Strategies				
6	Review and Evaluation				

*WOV_1=Maximization of Nonviolence
WOV_2=Maximization of Economic Well-Being
WOV_3=Maximization of Social Justice
WOV_4=Maximization of Ecological Balance

throughout is the four overarching "world-order values" that are listed at the bottom and which figure prominently in WOMP studies. In outlining the WOMP objectives, Professor Kim offers (see Table 9.1)[32] three alternative scenarios, in which the future state of the world by the year 2000 on various measures is compared with 1980. Scenario C is a rough projection of present trends. Scenario B lists the minimum WOMP goals and Scenario A contains its maximum objectives—the ambitious nature of which is quite clear.

Kim's discussion of the process by which the world is to be moved in the right direction is relatively brief. The central feature is nonviolent, yet revolutionary, change via a struggle by the disadvantaged that raises the global consciousness about the necessity for change. The result will be a "power-sharing and coalition-building process first starting outside the governmental process and then working its way into all key decision-making points."[33] He expects the path to be long and tortuous. In another article, Kim and Richard Falk note that in view of the difficulties to be overcome, a WOMP approach is "not necessarily optimistic about the future," which certainly seems realistic.[34]

Difficulties and Drawbacks

It is entirely possible that international politics is in the midst of a great transformation, one that will in the end lead to its disappearance, as the politics of the world as a global community takes its place. It is also possible that such a transformation is absolutely necessary if we are to avoid catastrophic convulsions that end civilization. It is certainly a good thing that able analysts are alert to the possibility this is happening and are trying to understand and cope with it. Engaging in work of this sort is the highest calling of the scholar. We can be proud that the field has not lost touch with its roots, its origins in the realization after World War I that international politics had become terribly dangerous and needed either better management or a fundamental refashioning.

However, we are entitled to be at least a wee bit skeptical. We can begin by asking why the times are now right for transcending international politics, for ideas and analyses that, albeit in other forms, in the 1920s and 1930s turned out to be inadequate? The "utopians" or "idealists" of that day had a similar understanding of the inadequacies of the international system, and could build on decades of rising interdependence that, it seemed, the Great War had interrupted. What was missing was a set of remedies that would take hold. International politics, it came to be understood, was more unyielding, more resistant

TABLE 9-1
Alternative Scenarios for the Year 2000

CATEGORY	1980	Scenario C	Scenario B	Scenario A
World Military Expenditure (1980 prices in million dollars)	500,000	940,000[a]	1,000	Neglible[b]
Number of Soviet-American Strategic Nuclear Weapons	15,200	104,338[c]	400[d]	None
Global Arms Exports (1980 prices)	26.1	283.8[a]	0.5	Neglible[b]
Armed Forces (thousands)	24,642	32,527[a]	10,000	5,000[b]
Per Capita Income Gap Between Rich and Poor Countries	12:1	11-12:1[a]	5:1	1:1
Foreign Economic Aid (ODA As Percentage of GNP)	0.37	0.23[a]	1.5	3.0
Developing Countries' Outstanding Debt (billions of current dollars)	438.7	2,843[c]	20.0	10.0
Number of Absolute Poor (Per Capita Annual Income of Less Than $150 in 1975 prices; in millions)	825	975[c]	50	None
Number of World's Refugees (in millions)	12.6 (1981)	14.0[e]	1.0	None
Number of Repressive Regimes in the Third World	41	40-50?[f]	Neglible	None
Rate of World Population Growth (percentage)	1.72	1.5[g]	1.0	0.5
CO_2 Concentration in the Atmosphere (parts per million by volume)	338 ppm	363 ppm[c]	300 ppm	280 ppm
Desertification (thousand square kilometers)	7,992 (1977)	23,976[h]	10,000	8,000
Deforestation (World's Closed Forest in millions of hectares)	2,563 (1978)	2,117[h]	2,500	3,000

(Explanatory notes to 9-1 continued)

EXPLANATORY NOTES:

Scenario A=The maximum desirable goals and targets for 2000 set by a normative forecasting.

Scenario B=The minimum desirable goals and targets for 2000 set by a normative forecasting.

Scenario C=The medium-growth exploratory forecasting based on the historical trends of 1960-1980 or 1970-1980 depending on the availability of data.

a=Exploratory forecasting based on the historical trend of 1960-1980.

b=Assuming the existence of some transnational security system and making some allowance for domestic police functions.

c=Exploratory forecasting based on the historical trend of 1970-1980.

d=Based on the assumption of finite mutual deterrence, which is believed to require only 200 nuclear warheads by each side sufficient to destroy about 100 of the opponent's cities.

e=This merely represents the annual average during the period 1961-1982, based on the annual survey of U.S. Committee on Refugees.

f=Based on Ruth Leger Sivard's estimations of the number of repressive regimes in the Third World in the 1980-1982 period.

g=The latest UN projection.

h=Based on the projections of *The Global 2000 Report to the President*.

to change, than people hoped or believed. Why is it any better now? There are more national governments than ever, no letup in the U.S.-Soviet rivalry, rising neomercantilist pressures that have slowed or stopped the growth of world trade, etc. If the millenium is at hand, God does indeed work in mysterious ways.

Along the same lines, we should be suspicious when we find many of the themes in the globalist school to be strikingly similar to ones we encountered in integration theory. We know what happened there—integration proceeded to a point and then stalled, frustrating the theorists. As a number of people have noticed, "more recently—and somewhat ironically—the study of regional integration has tended to be swallowed up by the study of international interdependence and system change."[35] In effect, the concerns and analytical perspectives of regional integration theory have simply been shifted to a higher level of analysis. No one has yet explained why we should expect the ultimate results to be any different.

These reservations are not eased by the way in which much of the globalist literature lifts off from a critique of the realist perspective. It is true that the dominant paradigm in the field has stressed the central role of states, their preoccupation with security, and their struggles for power. However, the essence of the realist perspective was not that this was desirable or that operating international politics along classic balance of power lines was suitable. Rather it was that anarchy plus human nature made it extremely difficult for international politics to operate any other way.

If we are skeptical, how would we respond to the globalists' arguments? Well, we could return to some of the analyses explored in chapter 8. If the world seems more interdependent, as international organizations abound and security issues become prominent, how much of this has been due to the dominance of a hegemonic state for a long period after World War II? Perhaps the flourishing of the things cited as signs of an emerging global community will not survive the decline of American management of international politics. Maybe the growing disorder Rosenau points to will not be creative but ultimately destructive. A nasty thought. It would mean that our scholars are lagging *behind* rather than anticipating developments, spotting high levels of interdependence and transnational activity just when the underlying conditions that made those things possible are passing away.

Also worth questioning is the degree of interdependence and its implications. K.J. Holsti finds numerous indications of fragmentation alongside those of interdependence. In fact, he asserts, interdependence provokes steps by government to reduce its effects: "Little attention has been directed to the efforts by many governments to control, reduce, and sometimes even eliminate the influence of transnational groups and processes on their societies and politics."[36] Now it could be that those efforts will fail, that national governments will continue to lose ground. A favorite illustration of the way they are being eclipsed is the rise of the multinational corporation. But Robert Gilpin finds "little evidence to support the view that they have been very successful in replacing the nation-state as the primary actor in international politics." Instead, increased economic interaction through MNCs and in other ways breeds ever more government intervention to manage its effects, so that "the role of the nation-state in economic as well as political life is increasing."[37]

What about all those new issues on the international agenda and the suggestion that an "issue paradigm" is now necessary? Michael Sullivan, among others, has argued that new issues are not in themselves sufficient evidence that things have changed. It has to be shown that the ways issues are handled and resolved have also changed, that—as an example—power does not still play an important role.[38] Otherwise, issues come and go but beneath them it is business as usual, with international politics still essentially about the interactions of states. Enough analysts have been persuaded by this view that Rosenau is moved to complain about the fact that "reliance on the State appears to have had a renaissance in recent years, with an increasing number of scholars of various theoretical persuasions . . . relying on the State as the prime analytic unit."[39]

One reason perhaps is that analysts reviewed in this chapter are often a bit vague when it comes to describing the world here and now or laying out the specific processes that will bring about the world they anticipate. Inis Claude found that a balance-of-power system could not operate today, nor could collective security, and described world government as remote. This means we are currently living in what system? His is an analysis of what we have not. James Rosenau sees systems and authority everywhere collapsing so that adaptation is essential. But this makes it very difficult to describe just what it is that everyone should be adapting to. It may be that "subgroupism" is on the rise but nation-states have fought endless battles with lower level claimants for authority and popular support in the past, and have won nearly all of them—except where the subgroups were striving to create their own nation-states! The historical record strongly suggests we should bet that they will win the latest round, too.

The world-system analysis offered by the Wallerstein camp is only the latest in a long series of attempts to describe what happens in politics, in this case international politics, by putting primary emphasis on nonpolitical phenomena. To Wallerstein the whole field of international politics is artificial, and tends to distract attention from the essential features of the world system. Now it may be that politics is always derivative; it is certainly a possibility to be kept in mind. But it is surely just as plausible that politics is an intrinsic feature of the organization and management of human communities, something human beings always and everywhere engage in, that stands somewhere apart from other social and economic processes, and must be studied that way.

And what shall we make of WOMP analysts? First, their critique of the existing system is not unique and does not have any special theoretical foundation. Next, the values put forth as the basis for analysis are admirable but also have no theoretical foundation. In reading WOMP studies, one often finds the same ground being plowed again and again, in a continuous refinement of the same normative critique. Nor is this approach very rewarding in terms of explicit guidelines for constructing a better world. Kim's discussion on this point is notably brief. In an earlier world Professor Falk reported that he could not "further characterize the central guidance system [of a better world order], except to emphasize that no single, fully articulated model of a preferred world can be offered as prescriptive before we have had much greater experience with the early stages of transition."[40] We are therefore invited to embark on a momentous journey toward an uncertain end with not much in the way of a map.

Difficulties such as these encourage eclectic aggregation, the suggestion that no one approach quite covers reality sufficiently so what we need to do is pull a number of them together. We saw Claude suggesting that we borrow insights from balance-of-power, collective-security, and world-government conceptions because no one approach was satisfactory. Ray Maghroori and Bennett Ramberg conclude their survey of globalist versus realist approaches by arguing that some aspects of the international system fit one, some the other, while some fall somewhere in between.[41] This may, indeed, be the best we can do, but it leaves us with rather complicated answers to many simple questions. And maybe "answers" is too strong a world for what, to an observer, are more likely to appear approximations by compromise.

Conclusion

Let us hope that all these problems can be overcome in some fashion and that just ahead is a clearer understanding of our subject. One aspect of the Kantian perspective I have yet to review is that it places considerable emphasis on the dignity and autonomy of individual human beings. Kim cites with approval the title of an article someone else once wrote: "Can We Study International Relations as If People Mattered?" James Rosenau cites individual policymakers as the focal point of many relevant variables, while individuals everywhere "have become a major battleground on which States, governments, subnational groups, international organizations, regimes, and transnational associations compete for their loyalties, thereby posing for them choices that cannot be easily ignored and that, for us as analysts, can serve as both a measure of global change and a challenge to global stability."[42] This would seem to call for some vigorous research at a lower level of analysis. Having climbed to the top of our level-of-analysis ladder, we now face the possibility of having to go back down! No wonder our theorizing in international politics so often goes in cycles, or circles.

On this note it is time to see about ending this book. I hope you feel that a lot of ground has been covered, but I must emphasize once again that the book is not comprehensive. There are details missing, approaches not considered, and any number of studies that could have (and critics will feel should have) been cited.

It should at least be clear that thinking about international politics can be a strenuous business. In the evening I often retreat from it to the serenity of works like Ralph Vaughan Williams' *Pastoral Symphony*. In that quiet and peaceful mood it is hard to believe that somewhere out there the violent and precarious world of international politics is throbbing away. Wars are progressing, talks are going on, and cables are flooding into Washington, Moscow, London, and Beijing. A number of people are just now being killed. Some hands are within reach of buttons that could kill us all. Yet even on a quiet evening I can conjure up in my mind's eye a vision of that seemingly distant world, just as, in reverse, Vaughan Williams sketched his peaceful symphony during evenings spent near the front lines in World War I.

Theory is a handmaiden of mind's eye, a way of seeing when one is not there. You should by now have a sense of the challenges and frustrations of theory in international politics. Statesmen, diplomats, military leaders and ordinary citizens make international politics in the intricate interplay of their lives. But all of them often feel caught up in the rush of events, driven and determined by institutions and forces beyond their control. Theory is an intellectual device for reasserting control, for mastering the world by understanding it. The reasons we lack satisfactory theory are many. There is the question of which level or levels of analysis to examine. There is debate over which methods are appropriate. There are serious problems of information and measurement. International politics resists intellectual understanding as much as it does practical political management.

Thus, in both theory and practice international politics can bring on despair. This is an occupational hazard in the field for which there is no ready remedy. Those who would study it can surmount despair only by bringing to it a certain sensitivity to and appreciation for the human elements, something this book has attempted to display. It also helps to cling to the inspiring thought, the note on which I end my classes, that William McNeill offers at the conclusion of his history of civilization:

> Great dangers alone produce great victories; and without the possibility of failure, all human achievement would be savorless. Our world assuredly lacks neither dangers nor the possibility of failure. It also offers a theater for heroism such as has seldom or never been seen before in all history.
>
> Men some centuries from now will surely look back upon our time as a golden age of unparalleled technical, intellectual, institutional, and perhaps even of artistic creativity. Life in Demosthenes' Athens, in Confu-

cius' China, and in Mohammed's Arabia was violent, risky, and uncertain; hopes struggled with fears; greatness teetered perilously on the brim of disaster. We belong in this high company and should count ourselves fortunate to live in one of the great ages of the world.[43]

Notes

1. Hedley Bull, *The Anarchical Society* (Columbia University Press, 1977), pp. 26, 38.
2. "Globalism" is used in Ray Maghroori and Bennett Ramberg, eds., *Globalism Versus Realism: International Relations' Third Debate* (Boulder, Colo.: Westview, 1982)
3. There are several summaries to be found in Maghroori and Ramberg.
4. Harold Jacobson, "The Global System and the Realization of Human Dignity and Justice," *International Studies Quarterly* (September 1982), pp. 315-32. The passages cited can be found on pp. 315, 316, 319, 320, 329.
5. Inis Claude, Jr., *Power and International Relations* (New York: Random House, 1962), p. 92.
6. Ibid., p. 223. See also his *Swords Into Plowshares,* 3rd ed. (New York: Random House, 1964), pp. 371-92.
7. Inis Claude, Jr., "The Growth of International Institutions," in Brian Porter, ed., *International Politics, 1919-1969* (Cambridge: Oxford University Press, 1972), pp. 281-300.
8. Werner Levi, *International Politics, Foundations of the System* (University of Minnesota Press, 1974); and George Modelski, *Principles of World Politics* (New York: Free Press, 1972) An earlier presentation of Modelski's ideas appears in "Agraria and Industria: Two Models of the International System" in Klaus Knorr and Sidney Verba, eds., *The International System* (Princeton, N.J.: Princeton University Press, 1961), pp. 118-43.
9. A careful and thoughtful analysis is provided in Andrew Scott, *The Dynamics of Interdependence* (University of North Carolina Press, 1982)
10. This is roughly the view offered by Edward Morse in "Interdependence in World Affairs" in James Rosenau, et al., eds., *World Politics: An Introduction* (New York: Free Press, 1976), pp. 660-81. See also his *Modernization and the Transformation of International Relations* (New York: Free Press, 1976)
11. This is discussed in Richard Rosecrance, "International Interdependence" in Geoffrey Goodwin and Andrew Linklater, eds., *New Dimensions of World Politics* (New York: Wiley, 1975), pp. 20-35: Rosecrance, et al., "Whither Interdependence?" *International Organization* (Summer 1977), pp. 425-71; and Robert Keohane and Joseph Nye, *Power and Interdependence: World Politics in Transition* (Boston: Little, Brown, 1977), pp. 8-10.
12. Keohane and Nye, pp. 11-19.
13. Rosecrance, et al.; and Andrew Scott, "The Logic of International Interaction," *International Studies Quarterly* (September 1977), pp. 429-60.
14. Deutsch's work is reviewed and somewhat contrary findings are presented in Peter Katzenstein, "International Interdependence: Some Long-Term Trends and Recent Changes," *International Organization* (Autumn 1975), pp. 1021-34.

15. See Kenneth Waltz, "The Myth of National Interdependence" in Charles Kindleberger, ed., *The International Corporation* (Cambridge, Mass.: MIT Press, 1970), pp. 205-23; and his *Theory of International Politics* (Reading, Mass.: Addison-Wesley, 1979), pp. 138-60.
16. James Rosenau, "A Pre-Theory Revisited: World Politics in an Era of Cascading Interdependence," *International Studies Quarterly* (September 1984), pp. 245-305. The quotation is on p. 246.
17. Ibid., pp. 263-64.
18. Ibid., p. 281.
19. Richard Mansbach, et al., *The Web of World Politics* (New York: Prentice-Hall, 1976) Other views on this point are in Judy Bertelson, ed., *Nonstate Nations In International Politics, Comparative System Analysis* (New York: Praeger, 1977)
20. John Vasquez, *The Power of Power Politics: A Critique* (New Brunswick, N.J.: Rutgers University Press, 1983), which pulls together some of his earlier work.
21. Richard Mansbach and John Vasquez, *In Search of Theory: A New Paradigm For Global Politics* (New York: Columbia University Press, 1981)
22. Core Wallerstein's works include *The Modern World-System* (New York: Academic Press, 1974); *The Capitalist World Economy* (Cambridge University Press, 1979); and *The Modern World-System II* (New York: Academic Press, 1980) A large number of works in this vein are cited in various articles in William Thompson, ed., *Contending Approaches to World System Analysis* (Beverly Hills, Calif.: Sage, 1983)
23. An example is Andre Gunder Frank, "World System in Crisis" in Thompson, pp. 27-42.
24. Immanuel Wallerstein, "An Agenda for World-Systems Analysis" in Thompson, p. 300.
25. Ibid., p. 307.
26. A list of recent works raising normative concerns would include: Charles Beitz, *Political Theory and International Relations* (Princeton, N.J.: Princeton University Press, 1979); Kenneth Thompson, *Morality and Foreign Policy* (Baton Rouge: Louisiana State University Press, 1980); Kenneth Thompson, *Ethics, Functionalism and Power in International Politics* (Baton Rouge: Louisiana State University Press, 1979); Robert Johansen, *The National Interest and the Human Interest: An Analysis of U.S. Foreign Policy* (Princeton, N.J.: Princeton University Press, 1980)
27. Richard Sterling, *Macropolitics* (New York: Knopf, 1974), p. 21.
28. Ibid., pp. 566-67. A similar perspective is offered in Charlotte Waterlow, *Superpowers and Victims: The Outlook for World Community* (Englewood Cliffs, N.J.: Prentice-Hall, 1974)
29. Steve Chan, *International Relations in Perspective: The Pursuit of Security, Wealth and Justice* (New York: Macmillan, 1984), p. 309.
30. Many of these are cited in Richard Falk and Samuel S. Kim, "World Order Studies and the World System" in Thompson, pp. 203-37.
31. Samuel Kim, *The Quest For a Just World Order* (Boulder, Colo.: Westview, 1984), p. 309.
32. Ibid., pp. 332-33.
33. Ibid., p. 338.
34. Falk and Kim, p. 210.

35. Stephen Genco, "Integration Theory and System Change in Western Europe: The Neglected Role of Systems Transformation Episodes" in Ole Holsti, et al., eds., *Change in the International System* (Boulder, Colo.: Westview, 1980), p. 56.
36. K. J. Holsti, "Change in the International System: Interdependence, Integration, and Fragmentation" in Holsti, p. 26.
37. Robert Gilpin, "The Politics of Transnational Economic Relations" in Maghroori and Ramberg, pp. 191-92.
38. Michael Sullivan, "Transnationalism, Power Politics, and the Realities of the Present System" in Maghroori and Ramberg, pp. 195-221.
39. Rosenau, p. 264.
40. Richard Falk, *A Study of Future Worlds* (New York: Free Press, 1975), p. 52.
41. "Globalism Versus Realism: A Reconciliation" in Maghroori and Ramberg, pp. 223-32.
42. Rosenau, p. 271.
43. William McNeill, *The Rise of the West* (Chicago: University of Chicago Press, 1963)

Bibliographical Remarks

I will include just a brief list of additional works on the concept of interdependence: James Rosenau, *The Study of Global Interdependence: Essays on the Transnationalisation of World Affairs* (Frances Pinter, 1980; David Baldwin, "Interdependence and Power: A Conceptual Analysis," *International Organization* (Autumn 1980), pp. 471-506, which is a useful examination of the concept; Philip Reynolds and Robert McKinlay, "The Concept of Interdependence: Its Uses and Misuses," in Kjell Goldman and Gunnar Sjöstedt, eds., *Power, Capabilities, Interdependence* (Beverly Hills, Calif.: Sage, 1979), pp. 141-66.

The emphasis in the work of Richard Mansbach and John Vasquez on nonstate actors is supported by Phillip Taylor, *Nonstate Actors in International Politics: From Transregional to Substate Organizations* (Boulder, Colo.: Westview, 1984), which contains a brief description and history of numerous such actors ranging from intergovernmental organizations to subnational ethnic groups. The Mansbach and Vasquez conception of how issues change in the international system is laid out not only in their book (cited in the chapter) but in their "The Issue Cycle: Conceptualizing Long-Term Global Political Change," *International Organization* (Spring 1983), pp. 257-79.

The Wallerstein world-system analysis, and related approaches, are covered in Albert Bergesen, ed., *Crises in the World System* (Beverly Hills, Calif.: Sage, 1983); Terence Hopkins and Immanuel Wallerstein, eds., *Processes of the World System* (Beverly Hills, Calif.: Sage, 1980); Edward Friedman, *Ascent and Decline in the World-System* (Beverly Hills, Calif.: Sage, 1982); and Terence Hopkins and Immanuel Wallerstein, *World-Systems Analysis: Theory and Methodology* (Beverly Hills, Calif.: Sage, 1982). Two collections also contain articles bearing on this approach: the symposium on World-System debates in *International Studies Quarterly* (March 1981) and Pat McGowan and Charles Kegley, Jr., eds., *Foreign Policy and the Press*, 1982). I should also note that the entire issue of *International Interactions,* nos. 1-2, in 1981 is devoted to normative analyses of foreign policy matters.

Among the many works published within the World Order Models Project framework are Johan Galtung, *The True Worlds: A Transnational Perspective* (New York: Free Press, 1980); Saul Mendlovitz, ed., *On The Creation of a Just World Order* (New York: Free Press, 1975); Richard Falk, et al., eds., *Toward a Just World Order* (Boulder, Colo.: Westview, 1982); and Burns Weston, ed., *Toward Nuclear Disarmament and Global Security* (Boulder, Colo.: Westview, 1984). A discussion of the prospects for the project can be found in Harold Lasswell, "The Promise of the World Order Modelling Movement," *World Politics* (April 1977), pp. 425-37.

Something not discussed in the chapter, but related to some of the approaches considered there, is the attempt by various analysts to predict or model the future of the globe, something that is often called "World Futures" analysis. Examples of this work include: Herman Kahn and Anthony Weiner, *The Year 2000* (New York: Macmillan, 1967); Herman Kahn, "The Alternative World Futures Approach," in Morton Kaplan, ed., *New Approaches to International Relations* (New York: St. Martin's, 1968), pp. 83-136; Donella Meadows et al., *The Limits to Growth* (New York: Universe, 1972); Wassily Leontief et al., *The Future of the World Economy* (Cambridge: Oxford University Press, 1977); Herman Kahn et al., *The Next 200 Years* (New York: William Morrow, 1976). An excellent summary of much of this literature and a critical assessment of its achievements is Barry Hughes, *World Futures: A Critical Analysis of Alternatives* (Baltimore: Johns Hopkins University Press, 1985).

Index of Names